MORE APPLAUSE FOI

"I MARRIED A MUNSTER" is one unusual biographical romance, as a TV Comedy star of yesteryear, raucous unpredictable Al Lewis, mesmerizes a lovely stage actress and leads her into a labyrinth of humor, anger, and ultimate love despite their age differences. Black-belt wearing authoress Karen Lewis kicks Munster butt when she has to, but also takes him into her arms to make this a moving account that reveals the unique personality of the one-time video horror icon. Tears and laughter are blended on every page."

JOHN STANLEY
Film Critic and former TV horror host

"Karen Lewis's I MARRIED A MUNSTER is a marvelous "Funny Valentine." It tells the tale of an odd couple, as outwardly mismatched as can be. Al Lewis is a wisecracking comic actor from Brooklyn; Karen is a classical performer from Berkeley, the birthplace of "The Revolution." Yet they navigate through their differences—crises and professional challenges, distances and even death—to find themselves forever in each other's hearts.

"Lewis's storytelling is compelling, honest, humorous and bittersweet. In the background of her tale are the lively landscapes of the Bay Area and Manhattan, and glimpses into the worlds of theatre, radio and TV—especially shows like The Munsters and Car 54, Where Are You?, which showcased Al Lewis's talents so beautifully.

"Karen Lewis's voice is genuine and insightful; her heart is on the page. I MARRIED A MUNSTER is an inspiration of a read!"

PROFESSOR LESLIE ANN RIVERS
Historical novelist, actress, director, playwright

"I MARRIED A MUNSTER is expertly crafted, mesmerizing, romantic, enriching, and a deeply fulfilling experience—but not for the squeamish! Be sure to take breaks and hydrate as you may experience fits of laughter and a few tears. Historically, socially, politically, culturally, spiritually, and emotionally important journeys are woven together with warm and brilliant humor. I MARRIED A MUNSTER should be required reading for EVERYONE and possibly the basis for a new world religion—GRAMPISM!"

MR. LOBO
Cinema Insomnia

"Karen is so generous to share her life with Al Lewis with us!" I MARRIED A MUNSTER is an incredible and emotional love story from a strong, funny, and passionate woman's perspective. A must read for any fan of the man behind "Grandpa" and any humanitarian or activist who needs a couple of people to look up to!"

DIXIE DELAMORTO LOBO
Editor-in-Chief at Horror Hosts and Creature Features,
Creative Producer at Cinema Insomnia

"I know Al Lewis starred in My Grandpa is a Vampire, but after reading this book you'll know this can't possibly be true. Just wait until you read the garlic story!!"

JONATHAN MORKIN
Producer & Distributor, Apprehensive Films

"I laughed and cried throughout this book and when it was over I wanted more. What an incredible figure. Al Lewis was a combination of John Brown, Mark Twain and Paul Robeson, an elixir that even Grandpa Munster couldn't cook up in his Transylvania laboratory. Thank you Karen Lewis for this epic work of a true original, inimitable figure in American history."

RANDY CREDICO
Political Activist and Stand-up Comedian

"Karen Lewis' book is hilarious, moving and startling, which is exactly right for a hilarious, moving and startling man. Al Lewis was a walking, shouting history of American show business and politics, as daring as he was corny, as outrageous as he was on target. For those of us who struggle to figure him out, and for his fans who many not be aware of the depth of his commitments, his wife, Karen, has pulled back the curtain to reveal the wizard was indeed magical – and profoundly human."

PHILIP GERSON
Awarding-winning writer

"With, I MARRIED A MUNSTER, author Karen Lewis has created much more than a celebrity biography. As Al's loving wife and partner, Karen has created a vivid portrait – not only of the man she love – but of a flesh and blood American Icon. A one-of-a-kind "character" that only Brooklyn could produce. As the lovable, mischievous Grandpa Munster, Al Lewis entered the hearts of youngsters and baby boomers for more than fifty years. But as himself, Al Lewis was a consummate performer – one who turned his very life into a work of art. In addition to creating a portrait of Al as a gifted and versatile actor, Karen Lewis also discusses the man she loved as an activist, basketball scout, loving father, political candidate – and force of nature. Al Lewis was much more than Grandpa Munster, and Karen Lewis' affectionate memoir is more than its title suggests."

KEVIN BURNS
Television Producer

"I MARRIED A MUNSTER is fantastic! And the format is so interesting."

FATHER LAWRENCE E. LUCAS
Acting Assistant Commissioner NYC DOCS (Ret)

I
MARRIED
A MUNSTER!

My Life with "Grandpa" Al Lewis

A MEMOIR BY

KAREN LEWIS

Edited by Ernie Fosselius

Published by Ancient Juvenile Minds Publishing LLC
Copyright © 2015 by Karen Ingenthron Lewis

Manufactured in the United States of America

ISBN 978-0-9905585-1-4

Cover art and layout by Ernie Fosselius.

For my stepson Ted

And for my grandchildren Bryce, Keenan, Julia, Raphael, Ruby and all the other spirited souls of this great world who call Al Lewis "Grandpa".

I MARRIED A MUNSTER!
PROLOGUE

February 12, 2006

My life with Al Lewis was born in a fierce blizzard, and it died in another fierce blizzard which brought New York City to its knees, snowbound and silent. White-out conditions cancelled the funeral. Otherwise it would have meant an Arctic expedition for even the hardiest of the grief stricken.

We all felt that Al foisted that storm upon us on purpose! He hated funerals. Hated funerals with a fury.

So we felt that now, from the other side, he was once again doing things his way. The Master Clown was yanking the rug from beneath our feet, showing us the absurdity of it all.

One

BOXED IN

Al ... Was ... Gone .... That realization dragged me down to the floor, howling at the ceiling. I lay there in our Roosevelt Island apartment amidst another kind of raging blizzard. A snowstorm of books, papers, magazines, clothes, records ... and cigar boxes, the accumulations my husband bequeathed to me.

I tell my friends I can tolerate the clutter and disarray but it's not true. This apartment has been neglected so long. All I'd been able to do for the past three years was to keep up with Al's healthcare needs. The daily emergencies. Have I paid the bills? I must have, but I don't really know. Housekeeping has been pushed to the bottom of my priority list. Chaos has finally caught up with me and overtaken Order.

I can only eat wet stuff like Jello. Only thing that will get past the lump in my throat. I am drawn. And taut. I need sleep. But our bed is psychologically off limits. I think I sense the sweet smell of his skin. That tender memory drives me away to the living room to bed down on a lumpy couch.

It's morning and I start to feel my energy slowly returning. Our apartment has to be cleaned up, and I need confirmation that I am making headway. Here I go. One emptied shelf. Done! One cleared out drawer. Okay! Perhaps I can tidy up the linen closet. Guess not. My grief wells up and paralyzes me. It seems I always start with an inspired plan, but within hours I no longer see the brilliance of it. There are abandoned archaeological digs in every room, surrounded by all the wonderful unusual finds that Curious Al had collected, stacked like artifacts rising to the windows. Like stalagmites growing up from the floor. So what do I do with all that now?

Any one of these shelves, stacks, piles, bags or boxes might contain a treasure! I must go through all of it piece by piece or I might miss the things he wanted most for me to find. I finger the stuff that surrounds me, hot and magical. It turns on me or it salves me. Why? All I want is to be with my Love and I can feel he's still here in these things that he left behind. Oh Al, help me know what to get rid of and what to keep.

1

Al's voice in my head explains. "Well, you got three options, Hon. SAVE. TOSS. GIVE AWAY!" That's it. Save. Toss. Give Away.

"Thank you, Albie!" I sit down alone before one of the many piles. I take a deep breath. Inhale. Exhale. And I begin. I pick up the first item.

A painting. A colorful forest that appears to sway in a breeze. The first birthday present Al ever gave me. 1979. Easy one. SAVE.

Bath mat. Worn to a frazzle. Why do I still have this? TOSS ... Oh, wait. Maybe it still holds meaning for me. Come on, Karen, it's just a bath mat. TOSS!

A script. TOSS. Whoops, hold it! I want that! I met Al doing that play. It's my copy of *California Suite*, our blocking scribbled in the margins, notes from the director. As an actor, I'd held, folded and abused dozens of these scripts. But this one ... this one shelters North Carolina azaleas, fragrant with a young woman's hopes. As I stare at it, my thoughts and emotions pull me back to a crisp February day ... Yes, it was New York City in 1979 ...

Headshot 1979

Two

WORKING MY BUNS OFF

    I raced down icy Second Avenue, grabbed a copy of Backstage from the corner newsstand on the way to the bus, and narrowly made it, skidding through its closing doors, the last person to board. I needed my day job rolling croissants at the bakery, and couldn't afford to be late, but I also needed to read that trade paper. Slipping into an empty seat, I felt New York all around me, the slurry of bus riders slopping into each other as we lurched over yet another pothole in this steamy overheated chicken coop on wheels. Noisy. The stale air vibrated with a grating boom box grind as street repair jackhammers whacked in time to it inside their taped off construction site, so close that the bus nearly flattened them. Breathless, I leaned against the window and wiped the condensation with my gloved palm. I closed my eyes in overwhelm, remembering my early morning thoughts. Suddenly inspired, I yanked a pen from my jacket and feverishly wrote my recollection all over the margins of my trade rag.

DAWN BREAKS OVER PARK AVENUE SOUTH

Six a.m.

A whispering click eats through the double-paned

glass by my bedded head, insistent,

steely heels strident and commanding,,

flat smacks strike the cement as New Yorkers' soles

slap the sidewalk below our sublet

A rankling, cacophonous delivery

    progresses at the Smiler's

The ring ring ringing declaration

of a delivery truck in reverse

The grating of metal. The sound, a drill in my ear, aurally

describes a rigid bar, brassy and clamorous,

thrust into the basement door to prop it up

its rusted bulkhead hinges screeching,

its pedestrians alarm ding ding dinging,

a flagrant violation of my dreams,

an encroaching, fractious, rasping alarm clock

The misty hum of cabs in motion, predictably increases

in ... approximately... no, exactly, seven minutes ... to

a full Niagara roar

The jarring groans of buses, their air brakes farting

as they heave into stops along Park Avenue South:

33rd... fart, 28th... fart, 23rd... fart ... stop! sucking up

at each corner the gaggle of morning-irritable

passengers

Insomniac workers buzz below –

swarming into their daily tasks: pollinating

Bringing home the honey and the bacon

Getting things done

I was trying to establish myself as an actor in The Big Apple. Yes, me and 1.5 million others! I loved it and hated it. So why didn't I leave? My answer? Remember the old joke about the circus hand who hated his job shoveling elephant poop? When asked why he didn't just leave, he shot back, "What, and quit show business??"

Halfheartedly, I whipped open my poem-splotched copy of Backstage and flipped to the job section. Holy smokes! Jack Hallett was set to direct a dinner theater production of Neil Simon's *California Suite.* Just last year in San Francisco, Jack and I had acted together in Pfeiffer's *Hold Me!* He was such a nice guy and had so much going for him. A veteran of so many hilarious TV commercials, now he was directing. I had to audition for that play!

Two days later, I made it to the try-out where a surprised Jack greeted me with a hug. He assumed that I was just visiting from the Coast. So when I said I was there to audition, he stalled. "Well ..." He shook his head and pulled his lip downward, "you're really not old enough for this. You see, you have to play at least two different parts and the most important one, the actress, is in her forties."

"Well, I'm 33," I enthusiastically replied. "I was in Neil Simon's *Last of the Red Hot Lovers* and my pill-popping character was middle-aged." He shrugged his shoulders and said, "Oh, what's the harm in reading for me? You're here!" The union monitor handed me a script and patiently waited for me to pull off my winter gloves to dig into my wallet for my Equity card.

The character that Jack was so worried about was interesting! A British actress nominated for an Academy Award. She's a bundle of nerves as she dresses for the event, provoking her husband into an argument about what she's wearing. I had a good British accent in my arsenal. I figured for this reading I'd use both the style I'd developed performing Noel Coward plays at the Berkeley Repertory Theater and my own audition anxiety to pull it off. I needed Jack Hallett to just forget about my age and give me the damn part.

Inside the studio, Jack ran down the contract for us. It was a 14 week commitment. "Two dinner theaters, one in Raleigh, one in Charlotte. Only one week of rehearsal and three previews before opening! It's tight." We all groaned at this schedule, but still I was up for the challenge. "Our star is Al Lewis!" Jack looked liked he'd won the lottery. Hmm ... Wasn't Al Lewis that guy ...? "You know *The Munsters*," said Jack, his eyes sparkling. "Well, he was Grandpa!" I remembered seeing that show once. I never watched any TV, much to my mother's chagrin. She thought I needed to know more about popular culture. "And ... *Car 54 Where Are You*?" Jack went on, "He was Schnauzer in that one!" If I got cast, apparently I'd be playing with a genuine star - of television, at least. Schnauzer? "We've pre-cast the other male lead, too. Jay Huguely. A local. They love him in North Carolina. What a singer! Sorry, but Al and Jay are just too tightly booked to audition with you."

When my name was called I handed a newly typed resume to Jack, pointing out the numerous character roles I played. After I read with several actresses, Jack thanked me profusely and told me what a joy it was to reconnect, but he seemed to be mumbling under his breath the whole time about my age. After the audition, the part still seemed up for grabs. If only I knew what Jack was thinking.

I trudged home to my shared, cheap, one-bedroom over a brothel, over a Smiler's Deli, over Park Avenue South, right next door to the famous coffee shop that Scorsese immortalized in his violent film *Taxi Driver*. Just six months earlier, my two roommates and I had moved from California to New York City to prove ourselves in the theater. I'd gone to lots of auditions only to be told I hadn't paid my dues, which considering my ten active years in Actors' Equity, was rather insulting. I wondered if this audition was going to be, as Yogi Berra said, déjà vu all over again.

The next morning the phone rang. It was my answering service informing me that I had a callback at noon! I was so excited that I made the operator read the message twice. "Good luck, kid!" he congratulated me. Only in New York. Everybody's in Show Biz.

I was nervous. I'd had my free ride yesterday and now the heat was on. I was annoyed to feel little sweat rivulets drifting downward from my armpits. Glad I'd remembered my deodorant. I noticed that there were more women trying out today than the previous day. Where did they all come from? Oh, a cattle call. Jack kept asking me back into the studio to read again and again. What was going on here? Did he like what I was doing? Then he paired me with Liz Otto, a redhead with small, flashing blue eyes, a winningly wicked smile and deadpan expression. I guessed Liz to be in her mid forties. We sparked each other. Jack became animated, gave us a few notes, and asked us to read the scene again. After we concluded, he nodded his thanks and dismissed us, promising to let us know his decision as soon as possible. "And, oh by the way, if cast, when could you leave town?" When could we leave town?? What did that mean??

All the way to my karate class, the long ride on the A-train to the bus to Fort Lee, New Jersey, I listened to my personal paranoid loop. The Internal Worry Wart Talk Show. How professionally had I handled the audition? Had I read the lines well? Was knowing Jack a liability? Was I too young for the part? Should I have worn something different? What's the difference between 33 and 43 anyway? Did my deodorant hold out? But the killer question: What happens if I *don't* get cast? Why is this play so important to me? I have never gone this long before as an unemployed actor. Acting's my life. And if I'm not acting on the stage, I don't really feel alive. So I need to be in that play. It feels right for me. But always, always there is the dangling

destiny of disappointment and doom - AKA *rejection*! But now I had
to get to my day job.

Acting is all glory and glamour, I reminded myself as I pulled
on my apron to roll my next croissant at the Voila! Bakery. I was the
only woman and the only non-Spanish speaker in the overheated
rolling room. It was hard work, but sometimes I got a chance to
practice my physical comedy turns, even if only by happenstance. If
the conveyor belt moved too fast and threatened to toss all that
whipped dough onto the floor, my fellow bakers would yell, "Para la
machina!" When I bellowed those Spanish words, throwing my arms
in the air in a mock tragic gesture, I unintentionally re-enacted
Lucille Ball in the candy factory episode of *I Love Lucy*. And
probably got more laughs.

Yes! Yes! Yes! Jack Hallet's voice rose through the telephone
wire early the next morning. "I'm happy to tell you, Karen, you were
the best thing comin' down the pike. I gotta have you in my cast."
Whoopee! I'd be playing three roles: the call girl dumped in Al
Lewis's bed in the first act; the Actress in the second act; the bimbo
tennis wife in the third. I had a job, there'd be some money, and I
dodged rejection again. I think I impressed everyone I knew by
dropping Al Lewis's name into conversations, although I didn't know
his work and I'd never really seen his TV show. I wished I knew more
about this guy. A funny man in a comic tuxedo was about it.

I called each of my parents to tell them the news. They'd been
divorced since I was four and I was used to delivering my updates in
duplicate. "Go straight to the top!" my father exclaimed and started
laughing to cover his tears of prideful joy. He choked up. "Jeez –
Grandpa Munster ..." When I reached my mother, she choked up too,
but managed to get out "Al Lewis!? Schnauser! He was in *Car 54,
Where Are you?* I never missed it, it was so funny. You're playing
with *him*!? Grandpa Munster!" Her voice was suffused with awe. Hey,
I'm in the play, too, Mother. "Do you know how *important* he is?"
she asked loudly. Apparently not. Star-struck Mom filled me in.
"He's just one of the biggest comedic personalities on TV, that's all!
You never watch television, Karen. You're missing out," she scolded.
She was right. I never watched television, and I had stuck the one she
gave me in the closet. "Hey Mom, Al Lewis aside, aren't you just a
little proud of me for landing this big job?"

"Proud?! Are you kiddin'? I'm telling everyone at Bingo that
you're acting ... with *Al Lewis*!"

"Thanks for the support, Mom. I'll tell Al that you're his

biggest fan."

Now I had to give notice. I went to the bakery and told my boss, "I'm leaving for North Carolina to do *California Suite* with Al Lewis!" He gasped in awe. "You're acting in a play? With Grandpa Munster?!" I rolled my eyes. Here we go again! Even though he was sad to lose me, I could tell my bakery boss was impressed! How come this Grandpa guy keeps stealing my thunder?

I also had to say goodbye to Master Lee. He had become a huge part of my New York experience. My Berkeley Karate Master referred me to him and I took his Tae Kwon Do classes several times a week. He'd taken a special interest in me and I knew I'd miss him.

When I told Master Lee I was leaving town to be in a play with Al Lewis, he was happy for me and then all the concerns about my new adventure hit me again like a front punch to the chest.

Gratefully, for that hour of karate, I forgot about learning lines and packing. Snuggled in my belly center, there existed only now and now and now, arrival in the moment, with its attendant relief from worry about the past and future. After class, I stood before my teacher and bowed. He took my hand and said very quietly, "I wish you good luck acting ..." As I turned and passed over the threshold of the karate studio, Master Lee added, "... with Grandpa Munster!" I froze, then slowly turned back to look at him. "You know," he said, scrunching his face up into a caricature, "Herman, you big Schnook!" I smiled and shook my head. I don't believe this. Even Korean Karate Masters watch more TV than I do.

I looked up at the clear, cold winter sky. My hopes for the future were glittering stars. No more pounding the icy pavement in New York. I was slamming the freezer door on this chapter. Hurray, I was acting again! Yeh, that's me, the actor standing behind "Grandpa Munster".

Three

THE NICE MAN COMETH

My heart was racing as I danced down the steps of my sublet at the tail end of a white-out blizzard that had stopped New York City cold. So cold that I couldn't walk more than a few feet before pulling into a doorway to catch my breath. Litter and spittle were frozen to the sidewalk like artifacts on a skating rink. There was icy, white precipitation still fluttering into the avenue canyons, walled on both sides by tall buildings. But I skipped onto the Number 6 IRT subway car, heading north to the appointed rehearsal studio at The Manhattan Theatre Club. I had an acting job! At the uptown exit, I spontaneously burst into Gene Kelly's *Singing in the Rain* routine, but quickly quit, realizing that it was just too damn cold to dance.

Heavy snow at Kennedy Airport, where Al Lewis and Jay Huguely were scheduled to debark, delayed their arrival for our first rehearsal. Meantime Liz Otto and I sat on rickety benches outside our rehearsal room practicing our tennis scene, waiting in anticipation for our fellow cast members. Director Jack Hallett paced, checked his watch, and popped coins into the hallway pay phone, a scene right out of a vintage Hollywood backstage B movie. This act-of-God snowstorm, depriving him of his two male leads, left Jack stalled. Biting his nails, he sent us out for coffee for the third time. When we returned, the two men were still absent.

A voice down the hall pulled Jack into full motion. As he moved forward, a tall, shivering, dirty blonde in his 40s, wearing jeans and a sweater, burst in. When Jack grabbed him for a hug and was swung around by this grinning fellow, it dawned on me that they were friends. Lots of shoulder slapping and laughter, then introductions, when we heard that they'd trod the dinner theater boards together numerous times. This romantic cowboy was Jay Huguely. Still immersed in the crisis of travelling during a blizzard, Jay launched into his story of peril, snowy gloom and no taxicabs, his Tennessee drawl filling the space with liquid honey.

There was an unsettling moment of silence, like the calm before a storm ... then the room seemed suddenly to crackle with electricity, as in charged a giant piece of buttery yellow luggage dragged by a large framed figure. He was tall and imposing, with a ten-gallon hat jammed down onto his head and a long wool scarf wrapped loosely around his neck, the fringed ends flapping. His shoulders and hat were dusted with snow, giving the impression of some kind of Southwestern time traveler who had zoomed in from an alternate reality Arizona. As he turned to greet us, snowflakes sprayed from the shoulders of his stylistically incongruous Navy pea coat into the studio's heated air.

"I'm here! God knows how. Is that you, Jay? You made it! Hello! How is everybody?" he said, knocking the snow off his hat. "Hell, I'm Al Lewis. Al. Call me Al. What a day. Geez. What a day."

So *this* was the legendary Al Lewis, and like a legend, bigger than life. He certainly brought a lot of charisma into this room with his fancy luggage. But I am going to act with him. Is this how it will be on stage? Am I going to wind up being wallpaper in the Al Lewis Show?

When things settled down a bit, Jack wanted to assure us that our star was not some unskilled TV actor playing the dinner theater circuit on his incredible international popularity and fame alone. So Jack asked Al about his stage appearances. "What was your favorite role on Broadway, Al?" With that the floodgates opened!

Al's Headshot 1979

"I guess Circle in the Square isn't really Broadway ..." Wait ... New York credits, too? "Circle in the Square!" an awed Liz Otto emoted, egging Al on.

"Yeh. Did *Iceman Cometh* when the theater was in the Village. Directed by Jose Quintero. Jason was in it. Jason Robards. Played Hickey. I started out as Lieutenant McGloin. Then later I played Jason's part." So this guy claims to have some legitimate acting chops. "But on Broadway," Al continued, "I really loved playing a

10

gangster in *Do, Re, Mi* with Phil Silvers. Opened at the St. James Theatre." Now Silvers? Hmm. Can I hold my own on stage with this Lewis character?

This crowd was impressed and eager to know all about Al's career, to ask questions about whom he knew, and to parade their knowledge of his resume and contacts in order to impress him. The Actors' Studio, Broadway shows like *Night Circus* and *One More River*. Films like *They Shoot Horses, Don't They?* with Jane Fonda and Gig Young. Now it's Jane Fonda? Then there was *They Might Be Giants* with Joanne Woodward and George C. Scott and live TV including *Omnibus* and *DuPont Theater* and *The Bilko Show*. The other performers were lapping up Al's resume. Then I thought: Okay, that was quite an impressive list of credits alright. But, could he be lying about all this?

I'm confused. Half an hour ago, I thought I'd be acting with a hack star from a mediocre TV show. Now I hear all these impressive credits. I need to figure out my relationship with this guy. A logic flow chart is forming in my head. In the first box at the top we have Mr. Lewis. Arrows branch to the following: EITHER Lewis is a genuinely experienced and talented legitimate actor, OR, a big fat liar and blowhard. IF he is for real, then EITHER he'll hog the limelight, completely upstaging me, OR, he'll be a helpful mentor-type interested in bringing us lesser actors up to his level. But, IF this is all fabrication and trumped up self promotion by a puffed up con artist THEN, he doesn't know how to act, he'll chew up the scenery, and we'll have to carry him. OR, the show will close the first week. OR, if he's lying maybe he is actually a brilliant actor but just insecure. Maybe he's just a sheep in wolf's clothing. In any case, I'm keeping my eye on this Fibber McLewis.

It was very late in the day when we sat down around a table for our first read-through of *California Suite*. Al seemed to have the mark of a Method Actor. He just read his lines, letting the meaning bubble up without really interpreting them, listening, letting the play speak to him. His Brooklyn accent and working class speech patterns were perfect for his roles, humanizing them. Okay, maybe he's got the stuff. I was already into memorizing my part, tense about the very short one-week rehearsal period. I couldn't keep my energy in check. I plunged forward at performance level nearly script free, and then as my scene concluded, looked around for confirmation of my skill. Not bad, huh? There were big smiles of approval from the director and my scene partner, Jay. I looked at Al Lewis. Dead pan. What does it take to get a reaction from this guy? Then I remembered that many of my friends had worked with Al's brother. Perhaps mentioning that could break the ice. I took a stab at it.

"Isn't your brother, Philip Meister, the Artistic Director of the National Shakespeare Company? Lots of my friends toured with them," I offered. Al nodded as he tucked his finger into his script to mark the page. Instead of looking me in the eye to answer, he turned to everyone else and asked, "Anyone ever work at my brother's theater, The Cubiculo? They call it The Cube. On West 51st Street."

I piped up, "I know it."

"So, you know The Cube?"

"No, the Cubiculo." And raising my volume to operatic heights, becoming the sea captain in *Twelfth Night*, I blasted out, "Let's to the Cubiculo! The Cubiculo away!" Al grinned and stuffed an unlit cigar into his mouth.

"Where's that from, huh?" he challenged me.

"*Twelfth Night!*"

"Right. How do you know that?"

"I was in that play three times."

Al quoted, "'I was adored once too.'" And pointed right at me to respond.

"*Twelfth Night*, Act II Scene iii, spoken by ... uh ... Sir Andrew Aguecheek."

"Not bad! Not bad!" And he turned back to studying his script. I was left standing there like an idiot and still wondering if he was legit or just a con man.

The next day I prepared for rehearsal, imagining myself as Neil Simon's Actress donning formal attire for her Academy Award ceremony. I chose a long black skirt from my closet to practice in. I whirled around pretending to be in an anxious snit, whispering my lines to myself.

When I arrived, Al and Liz were just taking their break. Al was standing in the doorway between the rehearsal room and the waiting area, teasing the stage manager. He looked like he stepped out of a Western: Red flannel shirt, Native American bolo at the collar, black leather belt with a turquoise buckle, silver rings on every finger. Was he in costume for yet another play? *Annie Get Your Gun*? With a somber face, he eyed my long, black skirt, and queried, "Are you a witch?" Huh? Was he talking to me? I'd gotten the notion that he only lectured to groups. But I snapped back, "You've been watching too many Munster shows!" I flashed him a wry smile and marched past him, silently congratulating myself: That incorrigible spritzer ain't gonna get me. Unfortunately, I never saw Al's response. I had to sign in and our director had just thrown his arm over Al's shoulder.

"What was it like working with Phil Silvers, Al?" Jack leaned forward, eyes shining. He loved comedy and couldn't resist asking Al about this icon of entertainment. "Phil? Huh. Oh ... oh boy. The man was a genius sketch comic. I was with him for *The Phil Silvers Show*, then *Sergeant Bilko*. It was like he had eyes in the back of his head. He knew exactly what was happening on stage at any moment. Doin' *Sergeant Bilko*, that's how I got the part, the gangster tough guy, Moe Shtarker, in *Do, Re, Mi*.

"A very funny man, Phil Silvers. God, he'd bet on anything! Cards, cockroaches, anything! There was always someone chasing him to collect on a bad debt! And he was so cheap. Don't believe me. Ask anybody." I think I looked at my watch right then.

"During *Do, Re, Mi*, I got him. I got him good!" Al's visage turned absolutely wicked. "Yeh, his wife just had twins and it was in all the papers. And Phil wanted to hand out cigars during the curtain call. And he decides to give them to the actors to throw into the audience right after the finale. Hey, it's a good publicity stunt, an audience pleaser." I looked at my watch and thought, this story is going to go on for a while, but I had to go to the bathroom. Even with the door closed, I could still hear his voice booming in the rehearsal room continuing his story.

"So Phil comes to me and asks what cigars I smoke and what he should buy to celebrate. I tell him, but he says, 'No, Al, too expensive. Go buy me a bunch of White Owls.' White Owls? Cheap bastard. I walk over to the cigar store and buy a bunch. What do I do? I go to all the musicians playing in the pit and work out a little bit of business with them. Phil doesn't know nuttin' about this. So, now we come to the end of the show and we bow. Phil reaches into his pocket. That's our cue. We throw all those cheap cigars into the audience. But lots of 'em fall short, right into the pit. The orchestra members grab the cigars up, sniff 'em, turn up their noses, playing it up big, and start throwin' 'em back at Phil! Phil looks around at all the cigars landing at his feet, and under his voice, sotto voce, starts cursing. 'Where's that Al? Where is that Al!' The crowd went nuts." I came back into the rehearsal room and our crowd was going nuts, too, doubled up with laughter. "Yeh, they threw them back. Phil was so cheap," Al said.

What is it about a prankster that other people love so much? Al sat back smiling, rocking in his chair, soaking up the reaction to his story.

At home that evening, my roommates wanted to know all about my rehearsals. These were my closest friends, endlessly supportive and kind, who had lived through many of my life's high moments and lots of the lows, including my disappointing love life, and frequent plaintive blues songs about men. When I described Al, I characterized him as a riddle wrapped in a mystery inside an enigma. "But, when he came into the studio, the whole place lit up! I don't get it."

"Did your eyes light up, too, Karen!"

"Yeah, right. No, he has lots of charisma alright. But he can't shut up. Rehearsals are a talk show, or a monologue. I don't know how we're going to get our work done."

"You mean getting busy with Al?"

"Oh, please. I'm not interested."

Ken Grantham chortled at my dilemma, "Stuck on himself, eh? But you never can tell! Grandpa might take you to his dungeon and put love dust in your eyes!"

"If that's a reference to *The Munsters*, you'll have to explain it to me. Anyway, he doesn't even know I'm in the play ..."

"Oh, you can't get his attention, huh?" Jessica Abbe, my other roommate, smiled coyly. "Sounds like you found Mr. Right. So, how old is he?" she teased.

"Come on, Jess, he's an antique. Who knows how old he is? But all he does is talk about himself, so I guess I'll eventually find out," I said.

"You mean he hasn't asked you out yet, Karen? Don't be sad, maybe tomorrow you'll score!"

"Will you stop. This guy's an egotistical gasbag, a showboater. A motor-mouth. Blah, blah, blah, blah, blah."

"Sounds like the perfect match! So then it's love at first sight."

"Give me a break, Jess. I'd rather die than be stuck in a room with Al Lewis. But then, that would probably kill me too."

"Not a contendah??!" Jess teased, doing her best Marlon Brando imitation followed by an encouraging, vampy, "you-never-know" look.

"Contendah? No way!" I shook off that thought like I was shaking off the plague. "If a Justice of the Peace asked Al Lewis, 'Do you take this woman to be your lawfully wedded wife?' Al'd answer, 'That reminds me of a story. I was in a play in Pittsburgh with The Great Robards ...'"

"Does Al have any scenes with The Great Karen?"

14

"Yeh, I'm a call girl that his brother sends up to his room and ..." With that my tormentors exploded with laughter.

"Do ... you ... know ... what ... call ... girls ... wear?!" Jessica managed to utter while gasping for air.

"No," I said, not getting it. "The designer hasn't ..."

"Nothing!" My two hysterical roommates blurted in unison from their positions rolling on the floor. "They wear *nothing!*"

The next day at rehearsal we got down to business right away.

"Okay, Al and Karen," Jack announced, "I've put this off long enough. No lines, but lots of business. Let's start at the top with the Call Girl scene." I was caught off guard with that. I had no idea we were going to do this today. Jack pointed to a small rectangular raised platform. "For now, that's the bed. Karen, you'll be under the covers." I moved onto it like a pro, but felt pretty apprehensive. "Good. Next to Al." Oh, God, I started sweating. I'd been so concerned with the Actress's scenes that I hadn't studied this character very much. Jack went on, "You're drunk, Karen, ah, 'Bunny,' and dead to the world. Al, you wake up and realize that the lump in the bed is not blankets but the call girl your brother sent over."

"Yeah!" Al concurred, and started laughing. "And, my wife's coming!" The immediate conflict in the scene energized Al. He threw back the imaginary covers and went through a series of hilarious takes as it dawned on him that there was a strange female in his hotel bed. "Hey, can I try something here, Jack?" Al actually asked? "My character wants to get rid of this girl so my wife won't see her, right? Let me try something?" Al softly talked me through his moves. "One. I scoop you up from the bed. Two. I bounce you in my arms. You're drunk, right? So just go limp. Trust me. Three. I'll toss you over my shoulder like a roll of carpet!" Al put me back down on the bed and we began to work each move separately until they flowed into one smooth arc. One. Two. Three. It was actually a brilliant bit of business that Al had just improvised. Surprisingly, we worked well together and fell into a comfortable rhythm. I improvised a little too and practiced a sneak assist with my foot as he hoisted me up.

"Okay, that's it for now, Karen. By the way, your costume's gotta be skimpy. Any ideas for the costume shop?" I froze. I didn't know what to say. "Well then, let's move on. We'll deal with that later." I'm definitely not telling my roommates about this. They'd have ammunition for the next six months.

Jay approached me. "I need to get the inside scoop from Al. I've been planning on moving to Hollywood. I'd love to work for Universal. *The Munsters* was a great show."

"Hey, Al," Jay inquired with childlike enthusiasm, "what was it like working for Universal?"

"Huh ..."

"What did it feel like having a top rated show with the best company in the country and such great scripts?"

"Huh ..." Al paused, ordering his thoughts. "Fred and I had had it up to here." Jay's face dropped. "Yeah, up to here!" Al slit the air in front of his throat with his fingers. "Every week the same old crap." He shook his head in artistic disgust. "We'd get a script every weekend, you know, for the next week, read it, then call each other up. I mean, couldn't they write new dialogue?"

"But, Al," Jay said, incredulous. "That show was successful."

"Yeh, sure, it was successful. But was it good?" Now Al had my attention. "Maybe Fred and I were spoiled," he continued. "We'd worked with Nat Hiken, that genius, on *Car 54*. He'd be there on the set when we arrived in the morning and he was there when we left at night. Always trying to improve on his script. But at Universal, they were satisfied with the same old same old. On *The Munsters*? Sometimes it was hard to tell if it was even a new script! I don't know how many times Fred and I stormed the tower at Universal. Please! Please, we'd beg, give us some new punch lines, some new gags. I thought if I had to repeat the same dopey lines ... vampire jokes, I'd go nuts." Everyone else in the room was shocked to find out that all of this had been going on behind the scenes at Universal. And we were even more shocked that Al would confront the studio. "Yeah, the scripts were terrible." Al sarcastically gave us a sample quote: "Don't cry over spilt blood!!" He shook his head and continued, "All they'd ever say was, 'Why mess with success. Our ratings are up!' Drove us crazy."

Jay protested, "But isn't Universal the pinnacle?"

"Yeh, pinnacle. Pinnacle of what?! Of commercial success? Yeh, maybe. But so what? If you don't want to improve what you're doing, and make it better, I ain't interested. Nope. I just lose interest." Jay shot me a wide-eyed expression that said, Did you hear what I just heard? Liz and Jack gave each other the same stunned look which meant this just isn't done. It's hard enough getting an acting job in the first place, but you don't make demands, jeopardize your position for any reason. Especially if you're in a hit. This is

16

something all actors understand. Just make the best of it and put your check in the bank.

But for some reason, I didn't share their reaction. In fact, what Al said struck a chord with me. "I'm like that, too, Al," I quietly stated. He looked at me with his head cocked to the side assessing my comment. And with a blasé grunt said, "Yeah, why not?" Ouch. Then Al charged ahead. He was on a roll and wasn't about to stop for a measly tête-à-tête. "That's what I told them in the tower. Up there at the *Pin-A-Cull* at Universal.

"They had such an opportunity. We were this weird family ..." Al shook his head in disappointment. "Someone sent me a cartoon from England depicting a long street of row houses and a moving van out front. It showed the Munsters moving in, you know, carrying in lamps and boxes, and two old English biddies watching. Know what the caption was? 'Well, there goes the neighborhood!' Universal had such an opportunity to make something significant out of the show. Something important. But the scripts were so thin, I threatened to quit. 'You can't do that!' they'd yell at me. Up there in the tower. 'Oh, no!? The same plane that flew me out here from New York can fly me right back!'" Jay had already pulled away from Al in horror.

"Heh, heh. Do you know how many times Fred and I stormed the Bastille? Dozens of times. They had the money to fix those scripts. They didn't care!" Al's passion filled the room, with varying effects on the rest of us.

Jay turned away to look for his script. Jack tried hard to give Al a supportive look. Liz's jaw was still on the floor. We went back to rehearsing. Everyone struggled to get back into character – everyone except Al Lewis. He was already on top of it, relaxed, ready to roll.

DEAR DIARY:

Al's words still burn my ears. I can't remember ever meeting anyone with this kind of passion. I came to New York to become the very best actress I could be. To, in my dad's words, 'Go right to the top.' But, if I had to climb the tower at Universal to do that, I'd faint. Sure, I feel that it's good to always strive to make things better, to have integrity about my work. But that Al is challenging my courage. Is he saying we're all gutless? Easy for him, the star of a top rated TV show, he's got the producer's ear. I wonder if he'd try that stuff in the first week?! I've got a question for you, Mr. Lewis. Do you have the courage to admit that you were in an ideal position to go up against them, and it wasn't as big a deal as you make it out to be? They needed you! We theatrical lowlifes would get canned if we tried to speak up, Mr. Bigshot.

Four

ELEPHANT IN THE ROOM

"I love circus people," Al said, apparently trying to grab my attention. He had targeted me as his audience as he entered the room where I sat studying my lines. "You can't bullshit 'em, man." Does he always cross a threshold mid-sentence? I inwardly groaned, anticipating either another long story or another angry yet amusing rant. All I wanted was to quietly go over my script because opening night was fast approaching. "They'll work on one feat for ten hours a day until they're convinced they got it right." Does he ever come up for air? "Mistake? Heh heh. One mistake and you're dead. Ever hear an actor exaggerate and say, Wow, I missed a line and 'died' out there? Not really. Not like dropping 50 feet from a tightrope." I had lines to learn. I shook the script on my lap making paper noises. "Ahem!" I cleared my throat hoping he'd get the hint. But no dice.

"Pop Wallenda, God bless him. I met him. Nothing could stop him from challenging himself. The Flying Wallendas. Ever see them?"

"Yeah, sure." I mumbled. Does this Lewis character have an off switch?

"I met him in the circus," Al continued.

Bing! "Wait. Did you just say 'circus'!?" I felt the pull toward the center ring. "What did you do? Perform?"

"Well," Al responded, assuming his I'm-glad-you-asked-me-that position, arms folded across his chest, leaning back on his wooden chair, lifting the front legs off the ground, and chuckling. "I started as a kid. I like to say I ran away to join the circus." I guess I don't really want to study my lines. The show's only a week away ...

"Know what my first job was?" Al asked.

18

"What? Pilot?"

"Pilot?"

"Yeh. Get your shovel, scrape up the poop, and pile it!" Al moaned then laughed into a punishing groan that tried to exile me to Siberia. Got him. He fake-scowled comically.

"You guessed it!" he admitted. "I followed the elephants."

"You did?"

"You know, elephants eat a lot, and leave behind a lot-to-be-desired. I was the kid that followed them, and swept up the lot-to-be-desired!" Al literally howled at the ceiling at his own dumb joke.

"I always wanted to join the circus. You know, be a clown. But I couldn't do it."

"What? Too scared?" I nodded affirmatively. Al shrugged.

"Circus hierarchy is fierce. Never mess with it. You'll get yourself killed. Like I said, no BS. They know which performers are working the hardest, which performances are really dangerous. They respect that. So do I." And he added, his voice very emphatic, "I-wanted-to-be-a-clown."

"A clown, really?"

"Yeah, that's what I said. Every clown has his own character and his own makeup. It's a code of honor. You don't take nobody else's character."

"What was your clown like?"

"You know, I played off my take-charge side. So I taught myself to ride a trick unicycle and I chased a dwarf. Yeah, he became my partner. I'd chase him with a big slapstick and whack him."

"You whacked a dwarf?"

"Yeah, but then we did a reversal. At the end he knocks me off the unicycle, grabs the slapstick and beats me with it. Audience loved it. You know, the little guy gets revenge!"

"Were you a White Clown? The one you played?"

"I guess you could say that. I had the white pointy hat and white face. The costume with the fluffy buttons."

"Oh, so you were the mean, sadistic clown?" Al just pretend glared. I quickly changed the subject. "Where did you perform, Al?"

"All over the place. Cole Brothers. Ringling Brothers. And Clyde Beatty Circus."

"That's an impressive resume."

"But, circus clowns don't talk. Thing was, I wanted to talk. Know what I mean?"

"Oh, yeah. I know!"

19

"Can't muffle me!" He shot back, grinning. "What about you?"

"What do you mean?"

"You said you wanted to be a clown."

"Al, your story brought back some memories for me. But they're all stuffed into a childhood closet on a dingy Massachusetts shelf. You know, the ceiling sloping into the eaves, way in the back, under the Jerry Mahoney ventriloquist dummy, next to my programs from Barnum & Bailey." I fully expected Al to interrupt me, but he was still leaning back in his chair with his eyes closed, a blissful smile on his lips, just ... listening.

"I remember my mother's torn formal that I wore to play dress-up. There was a dented colander I used as headgear. I had the plastic glasses, red rubber nose, wax lips, buck teeth and mustache, all rolled up in old cotton long johns which were good for all kinds of things. Frequently needed for padding out my skinny kid body. I experimented at dressing funny, practicing clown walks and, spatula-wand in hand, making the neighbor girl do everything backwards. My favorite characters? A rhythmically challenged ballerina, a sad sack, and a forlorn sweetheart. That's how it was at Karen's Kid Klown Kollege. Number of students: one."

"That's beautiful, Kid."

And then silence. We were both quiet. Each falling into some dreamy reverie and we both seemed to be a little uncomfortable about that small intimacy. "We need you, Al. Act One!" called a voice from the other room. Saved by the bell. Without another word Al got up and went back to work.

DEAR DIARY:

I know all that circus stuff was probably just another tall tale but it seemed like we shared something then. He talked with me for the first time. And he listened to my story. Hmm. But did he intentionally push a button in me that touched something? Was that manipulation on his part? Or were we really on the same wave length? Am I just a foolish romantic? Or am I the victim of too many black and white sentimental tear jerker movies? Maybe my circus dreams were only an imitation of films seen in my childhood like The Greatest Show on Earth that imprinted this romantic longing on my impressionable child mind. Just remember Karen, you're the one

*experiencing this "feeling". And Al's feeling? Just
another facet of his self-made public persona, or an
expression of the Real Guy in there? Maybe I'll never
know. Maybe I should have a cup of tea and get some
sleep.*

Five

EDGEWISE WORDS

There I sat alone in our shabby rehearsal hall still thinking about the circus, reminiscing and dreaming about colanders, clown tutus and huge ballet slippers. I was early, as usual. This hall seemed magical to me, like my childhood closet circus, this too was a place where you could make something out of nothing. Out of this drab studio, something shiny and exciting might be born. I guess I still wanted magic in my life. I heard a noise and looked up.

"Mind if I sit here?"

"Sure, Al. Be my guest. I was just thinking about our discussion yesterday and how life is really like a circus."

"You're from Frisco, right?"

"Huh? Yeah, well, the Bay Area. But ..."

"That's where it all began. Yup."

"What's that?"

"All those kids. Runaways. Flocked to California in the 60s, like lemmings."

"Lemmings??" Uh ohh, here we go again. So much for being on the same wave length.

"Thousands of them, up north and in Hollywood. Kids. Missing. The faces on the milk cartons. Thought California would be the answer to all their problems. You know, they would become stars. That'd show their parents." Al made a clown face illuminating hope then quickly dispelling it. "In the meantime, they were sleeping out on the streets, in the parks. Ever been to a love-in?"

"What? I'm sorry, Al, where are you going with this?" I asked.

"Naked kids dancing in the park." His face darkened and his mouth slid downward on both ends. "I don't know ... they were so young. Kinda got to me, ya know?" Al looked sad. "Runaways'd hang out on Hollywood Boulevard. I'd line 'em up in front of a McDonald's, go in and tell the manager to feed 'em and I'd give him the money."

"You paid for all those kids to eat at McDonald's? But then you could afford it, right? You were making good money."

Al looked annoyed. "Hell. Yes, in those years *The Munsters* was king, number one, *numero uno*. So, yes, I could afford to feed kids. And I fed hundreds of 'em. Yup. I can't stand to see kids go hungry. Frisco, huh? Same story there."

"No, Al, I was living in Berkeley." Al laughed in a soft, sarcastic flutter of descending notes.

"Berkeley?" he chortled, "What a place that was."

"Huh?" I retorted indignantly. "I went to the University of California and Berkeley was an amazing place!"

"You're not kidding. Know how many rapes there were in Berkeley? Thousands. Hey, don't take it personally, but that place got a reputation and boy, did the nuts show up. Yeh."

The circus clown in me puffed up to three times her size, her nose turned bright red, and she wound up her giant slapstick, ready to whack her foe. In other words, I was pissed. Who the hell does this guy think he is? And who did I think he was? There we were yesterday sharing a perfectly lovely nostalgic circus reverie, and now he is railing against Berkeley. Runaways? Lemmings? Rapes? Nuts? What the hell?!

Al misinterpreted the annoyed look on my face. "Okay. Don't believe me. Go look it up. A police chief told me. *Car 54*, you know? Because of that I meet lots of police officers. They're always inviting me to dinner. Schnauzer ... ya know. Hey, you okay?"

"No, I'm not, Al." I wasn't okay. I was mentally twistillated and almost speechless. "But, let me get this straight. Just because you played a police officer on a TV show in New York," I continued sarcastically, "you know all about the crime statistics in Berkeley." Then I turned and made my exit.

DEAR DIARY:
Throughout the rehearsal I was still so angry that it blocked my progress. Okay, I'm just going to let it all out. This might not be pretty, Diary. I'm not going to try to organize my thoughts all nice and neat. (Neatly!) Well, here goes. Al Lewis is an insulting, self-absorbed, insensitive, boorish pig. And that's putting it mildly. I

*feel so set up. Things seemed to be going so well, but
then he yanked the trap door. Who does he think he is
anyway? Maybe he's like a three-year-old who shows his
love and affection by punching you in the arm. No, I
know who he thinks he is, but who is he? Maybe I took
Al's baloney too personally. And maybe he's testing me.
Maybe he thinks I'm smart enough to deal with his slams.
But, either way, if I don't stand up for myself, I'll lose
all my self-respect. Hmm. Give him a dose of his own
medicine?*

We were alone, just Al and me, waiting to be called into
rehearsal when I casually approached him.

"Hey, Al, I've got a question for you?"

"Yeh, Karen, what's that?"

"Where were you born?"

"Brooklyn."

"Brooklyn. Isn't that the blowhard capital of America?" And I
started to walk away.

"Whatta you been doing?" Al called after me. "Looking up
stuff in *Joe Miller's Joke Book*?" I reeled on him.

"No need to! I graduated from UC Berkeley! Remember?"
Now Al was laughing.

"Oy, that must be terrible, terrible for you!" He held his head
in mock sympathy, tittering, offering me his condolences! "I'm
awfully sorry!"

Goddammit, it didn't work! I didn't piss him off like I wanted
to.

The rest of the cast flooded in, loudly laughing at a story Jack
was telling them about his fate during a fraught audition. In a flash,
Al jumped up and into their conversation. Just like Bottom, the bossy
character in *A Midsummer Night's Dream*, Al had to be in every
conversation.

"Ya know how I audition?" Al asked, a rhetorical question.

"No ... Ah, how Al?" Jack replied.

"Heh. Well, you're only as good as your last performance,
right? What I used to do was go in ... Ever been to a Broadway
audition?"

"I have," I said. Resigned, I walked over to join the group. I continued, "The huge empty stage, a lone light bulb, faceless producers in the dark, calling out your ... "

"Yeh, that's right," Al cut in. "Anyway, I walk out onto the stage and state my name. Loudly. If it's a musical I tell 'em I sing passionately but poorly - and immediately begin my song." With zest, Al belted out a comic half-Yiddish song about camping in the *kukuleins*, those Borscht Belt Bungalows, perfectly disguising his faulty musicianship. "Meine Jeckule, send me the checkule ..." I had to admit it was pretty amusing.

"When I finish, I say, thank you for this opportunity to audition. My name is Al Lewis. I'd like to be part of this endeavor. If you don't cast me, it's your loss, not mine. Then I walk off stage." The room fell silent. Some punch line. The others scurried away from Al to the far corners of the room, apparently unable to handle his arrogant boasts of inappropriate rudeness. It was so silent you could almost hear the crickets. *Your loss, not mine!* he said? I was speechless! How could Al say such a thing! It certainly wasn't funny. What makes him think that he's not at the bottom of the heap like all the rest of us actors?

I had to ask. "Why'd you say that, Al? That it was their loss?"

"Cuz it's true. If you want Al Lewis, there's only one place to find him." Al patted his chest. "The director has the right to cast whoever he wants ... or she wants. But there's only one Al Lewis. That's me."

"It might work for you, Al, but it would never work for me!"

"Then you don't believe it," he said, talking to the group at large and not me. "You don't believe in yourself, that's all."

"That's all!" This ... scenery chewer was insulting me ... again. In front of everyone! Al must have seen my jaws clench.

"Look. You're letting them run the show." Al was looking straight at me but clearly orating to everyone else. "Either you believe in yourself or you don't. You don't have to say it like I say it. But you have to believe it, or get out of the business. You gotta have a spine like stainless steel. Otherwise, they'll eat you up. Alive." Thank goodness I was called back into rehearsal or I would have eagerly delivered a roundhouse karate kick to his ego. Oh crap, I think I have a date with my diary.

DEAR DIARY:

Guess who was talking at me today? Oh, you guessed it.
Why do Al Lewis's upsetting comments get to me so

much? I don't know if I'm coming or going. I'm worried about acting with this big jerk. Do I have to believe in myself more than I do already? New York is already tough enough. Do you know how tough it is when your co-star is making you feel you need to get out of the business? Am I being played for a fool or a naïve ingénue? Or is Al Lewis just an equal opportunity rude bastard?

"Hi, Karen, it's your mother." Mom always announced herself on the phone as if I might not recognize her voice. She was making her weekly call. Retired from Bell Telephone, she had free long distance service for life. "Guess what? Today's Crossword. 19 Across. 'Ancient Munster'. Seven letters. It's *him!*"

"Oh, wow." I feigned enthusiasm, wondering if I should burst her bubble and tell her all the trouble I was having with Mr. 19 Across.

Six

AL-LAGORIES

I was walking toward the rehearsal hall and I could already hear Al mid rant. "... so I always tell college basketball players, do your best. Then you're home free. When I talk to these guys, I tell 'em, Hey, man, you gotta sign your painting, put your stamp on it, make your mark, or don't bother. I tell 'em Vincent Van Gogh never sold a single painting in his lifetime. Can you imagine that? Never selling one painting. But he didn't give up. It doesn't matter what you do, paint, act, clean toilets. If you sign your painting, you're saying I did my best, and here it is. Can't expect more than that. Hey, otherwise you're a dilettante. Know what I mean? A dilettante." Al dramatically unveiled a cigar, the cellophane wrapper underscoring his point with a rolling crackle. Wonderful. Treated to another Al-lagory!

That cigar wrapper wasn't the only thing that crackled! My anger did too. I thought, I'm shy, Mr. Lewis, but I sign my work! I

25

must have physically expressed this feeling because I felt critical eyes drilling into my back. But I turned to see Al looking up like an innocent schoolboy from his perch on the studio's beaten-up couch. "You okay? Everything alright?"

My mother frequently told me that my face was an open book, and apparently Al was proofreading it! Calming my voice, I hid my anger with an emotional tap dance. "Yeah, Al ... say, what's a dilettante? Your definition, I mean."

"A dabbler. Yeah. Not a professional, a dabbler. And frequently they're the people in power!" With that, Al flicked his wrist, scribbling with an imaginary fountain pen, self-satisfaction rippling across his face. A dilettante? A dabbler? Is that how Al saw me? This is goofing me up. We've got to work together for a long time and we're not even on the same page yet.

The stage manager silently moved behind Al and pointed at his watch to remind Jack that there was no more time for listening to Al's "exciting, entertaining show biz tales." Al and I were excused for one hour so that Jay and Liz could go over some background business in the tennis scene.

"Come on, Karen, I'll buy you a cuppa coffee," Mr. Lewis proposed as he scooped up his winter coat. Every day this week Al has bonked me over the head with that rubber clown mallet mind of his, insulting me, pushing me, trying to yank the rug out from under me. Testing me! Maybe he finally noticed that I'm not one of his adoring fans and that's why he's working extra hard on me, trying to recruit me.

"Oh, no thanks, Al, I better pass. I need to go over some lines that ..."

"It's up to you, but fresh air always clears things up. Let's get some coffee and inhale some freezing New York air!" He laughed and patted my shoulder. Hmm. Now what does *that* mean?

I needed quiet time but I also needed a nice, warm cup of tea. Was I going to be in for it if I said yes? Oh, why am I making such a big deal out of this? "What the hell. It is freezing out and a hot cup of tea sounds pretty good right now. Thanks, Al." I don't need to get involved, I reminded myself, but just get along with him long enough to get through this contract and do a professional job.

There were only two of us in the cold, empty elevator, so I couldn't help but notice how his energy filled it up. I felt claustrophobic. "Good to take a break, no?" he smiled. Huh? Remember, Karen, this is the same man who just lectured us on how to audition.

As we marched in stride to the coffee shop, I breathed in some fresh air and realized how much I was anticipating that warming drink. Al swung open the glass door of the place and found us a booth in the front. I thought: I'll get my cup of tea, and by the time he gets through one of his epic stories I'll be able to write a letter to my dad, drop it off at the post office, make a couple of phone calls, do a load of laundry, take in a movie, and still be back in time for his boffo punch line.

"... so I said to John Wayne, 'You don't have a career, just a string of jobs.' And he *agreed* with me! Can you believe that? ... Karen?"

"What's that, Al? I was a bit distracted." At that moment the waitress appeared and Al leapt at the chance to entertain her. Of course. He seems to revert back to his compulsive entertainer mode at the drop of a hat. Is he trying to win over everyone in the world, one person at a time? Maybe he can't help himself. He's either totally insecure or his monumental ego is just hugely unstoppable. Utterly amused by Al's volley of friendly teases, the waitress was falling all over herself with TV star worship, giggling, face flushed, sputtering with delight, nearly dropping her pad. I hoped that she still managed to take our order; I needed that tea. I watched in awe as the waitress continued to make a fool of herself because she was in the presence of "Grandpa Munster." Does he expect me to be like that? Well, sorry to disappoint you, Al. I want a different kind of connection. A personal one. And anyway, I never watched TV and I don't know the drill.

The waitress had barely turned away when Al started in again working on me, the last hold-out of Munster Fandom. "During *Do, Re, Mi*, when the rest of us would go out for coffee and a smoke, the dancers'd be flat on the floor resting up for the next number. They worked their asses off. Remember Dick Shawn?"

"Sorry, who?" (Huh? What's this?)

"Dick Shawn."

"Dick Shawn? Oh Yeah, I wrote him a letter congratulating him after I saw his one-man show."

"Fantastic. Good for you. He deserved it." Half a kudo tossed my way. Hmm. Is this bait for his Munster Fan trap, encouraging fan behavior?

"Nice man. I met him once. Remember him in the Mel Brooks movie, *The Producers*?" Al laughed at the recollection of Dick's musical number, "Springtime for Hitler." "What a show stopper that was!" He laughed again. "What did you think of it?"

Maybe Al is ready for the thoughts of an opinionated woman. Shall I test him? "I didn't think it was funny the first time I saw it. I'd just returned from Denmark where they take World War II pretty seriously."

"Yeah?" Al looked surprised. "You couldn't laugh?"

"No, I didn't laugh. I cried. It cut too close to the bone. Ever see their Freedom Museum? In Copenhagen?" Al shook his head uncharacteristically at a loss for words. I continued, "It's a monument to the Holocaust. The Danish side." Al folded his arms across his chest and took me in. Then he shook his head again and laughed. Really looking at me for what must have been the first time. Had I finally captured his attention?

"You couldn't laugh at the movie, huh? You're a queer duck! Ya know that?"

What's this now? A tease? A moment of recognition? Then I exploded into cough-laughter that caught him off guard. "You might be right, Al! I've heard that all my life!"

"Maybe you had to be Jewish."

"Oh, I laughed the *second* time I saw it! Laughed till I cried."

"You converted?!"

"Didn't have to. I played Anne Frank! Doesn't that count? Jewish by implication?"

Al guffawed. "So the shiksa's a Danish Jew. Whadda ya know!" He sat stifling his laughter while he pretended to be confused and overwhelmed. It was terribly endearing, damn it. Did Al notice that I'm not just another one of his adoring fans? Or, is he actually wondering what makes me tick? Or just plotting his next ploy? Or, does he recognize a worthy opponent? Is that respect I see appearing in the corner of his eye? Or just more devilish mischief being cooked up? Oh shit, I think he's actually interested in who I am.

Now what do I do?

Seven

COURT JESTER

The entire cast was plopped down on the plastic seat cushions in a nearby Greek deli on a dinner break, drained and strained from a day-long rehearsal. Al, as usual, broke the silence. "Remember Princess Margaret?" Oh, God, not now, I thought, I hope this is one of his shorter epics. We wearily nodded and grunted, "Yeh, Queen Elizabeth's sister?"

28

"She came to visit us at Universal where *The Munsters* was filmed." Yeah, yeah, I silently grumbled to myself. I was tired and would have eaten alone if there'd been any way to get around this cast dinner and the latest installment of the on-going Al Lewis marathon-ologue.

"Princess Margaret, the sexy sister," he paused to make a face tormented by regal disgust, "was in love with Anthony Armstrong Jones. Remember him? The photographer?" Okay, Al's clown background came through when he made those faces. "The royal family didn't like Margaret hanging around with no commoners, that's for sure! Well, Universal got wind that the Princess was coming to Hollywood and invited her to the studio for dinner. And I mean dinner! A banquet. Champagne everywhere. Well, *The Munsters* was the big money-making show on the lot, so they transformed the studio, huge like a football field, into a ... friggin' castle with a stone walk-in fireplace and everything. They put tables everywhere and invited all the studio bigwigs, stars, and their families. Looked like one of those Douglas Fairbanks pictures where the king and queen sit up front at a great big table. Fancy-schmancies all around 'em.

"Since I was a star of *The Munsters*, our table was right by the head table. My wife, Marge, was sitting next to me, along with Ernie Borgnine and his wife. We're sitting there waiting for the Princess and Anthony Armstrong Jones." I stifled a yawn. When is our dinner going to get here? "Suddenly these big doors open up. Just like a palace. They got guys dressed up like medieval trumpeters. And they start blowing. Ta DaDah Duh Da Da Daah! Some poor schmuck has to roll out a long red carpet just ahead of the Princess. She and all the execs at Universal move along this flowing carpet, like the Red Sea parting. She's waving that little royal wave, side to side, you know... nodding." Al toggled his wrist to illustrate Margaret's regal hand. His outrageous impersonation was somewhat chuckle-worthy, but my stomach was growling.

"The place held hundreds of guests. Hundreds. I don't know what came over me. Too many Errol Flynn pictures, I guess. As she moved toward us, I grabbed my champagne glass and jumped up on the table. My wife looks at me like I've lost my mind. Well, my *then* wife. Ernie Borgnine's eyes were popping out. I yell, 'To the Princess! Hip! Hip!'... I wait for the crowd to yell back Hooray! Just like in the movies. Nuttin' happens." We gasped at Al-the-Court-Jester's incredible chutzpah.

"They look like they're in a painting, frozen in their seats. I try again 'Hip! Hip!'... Nuttin'. I couldn't stop. 'Hip Hip ...?' Then I took my champagne glass, raised it high and yelled, 'To the Princess!' and smashed it against the fake fireplace. I stood there, poised for a heroic response. Everyone just looked at me. Stunned. I heard Ernie Borgnine whisper, 'Oh, that Al. Not again.' He hid his face in his hands. Marge gritted her teeth and said *sotto voce*, 'Al ... Get ... Down.' I stepped back on my chair and then back onto the floor."

By this time, Jack, Jay, and Liz were in tears, they were laughing so hard. Begging Al to stop, blurting through hysterical laughter, Liz eked out, "Oh, no! Oh, no! You didn't! You didn't!"

"Unfortunately ... I did!" The laughter built to a crescendo that left them gasping for breath. Wiped out by Al's unbelievable tale, they dabbed their eyes with their paper napkins. I had been watching Al's performance and their increasingly amused reactions with the detachment of a sociologist. And it suddenly occurred to me that this embarrassing self-deprecating tale of Al's was told for <u>our</u> benefit, to cheer <u>us</u> up. What other self-important star would do that? The mood around our table had certainly changed for the better. It looks like Al might actually have some shred of empathy or feeling for the rest us after all.

Our food finally came. We warmed to it and relaxed, still chortling over the details of Al's Hollywood mishap.

Eight

GOOD RIDDANCE

Six months earlier, like a hobo clown, I'd moved to New York with just a bundle on a stick and the clothes on my back. Challenging myself in the theater, I was drawn to its epicenter. It was exhilarating to be free, to let the journey of my life unfold. But honestly, while proud to have endured the notorious slings and arrows of outrageous fortune as an impoverished actor in the Big Apple, the City's relentlessness distressed me, and without money, there wasn't much I could do to shield myself from it.

Neil Simon's *California Suite*. My ticket to North Carolina! Goodbye, loveable, smart-ass roommates! It felt really good to be heading out of town where I wouldn't always have to check my back, or sleep with earplugs in the sack. Yippee, a paycheck would soon be in my pack. Tra laa. Tra laa.

Nine

RUNWAY MODEL

SAVE, TOSS, GIVE AWAY

Wow, so many memories, but I can't keep getting distracted. I have to concentrate on this overwhelming job. So, back to the task at hand. Under a stack of magazines, nestled in the rear of my closet I find a dusty royal blue box, its black plastic handle flush against the lid. My make-up kit, a gift from Mom in the 70s. I created so many characters' faces with this kit. As I open the clasp and lift the top, my eyes look back at me, lined with sorrow, a reflection in the pop-up mirror. I shut the lid ... Save.

"Have to wait," Jack Hallett patiently advised the cast. We were loitering around bulging piles of belongings at the departure gate because nothing was moving in or out of LaGuardia Airport. North Carolina couldn't handle the record high snowfall piled on the runway at Raleigh-Durham, delaying our flight from New York.

Forced to wait, time was suspended. I sat alone in the middle of a row of fiberglass chairs. Since my arrival in New York, I had learned that auditioning was no longer about acting. It was about physical appearance, and a realization that I barely had the resources to play the game.

I scanned the outfits of my fellow thespians. Liz looked like she stepped out of a Bloomingdale's casual display. No doubt all of her commercials had given her the financial means to be a glamorous fashion plate. Jay, in his 1970's actor's uniform (pressed jeans, a crisp white shirt, and a sport coat with the sleeves pushed up), looked like the Marlboro Man. Al looked like he arrived fresh from a country estate in a tan herringbone jacket with elbow patches, heavy wool slacks, gloves, scarf, and chocolate brown Texas style ten- gallon hat. Jack, wearing warm winter togs, zippers everywhere, looked like a weekend skier.

But I wasn't in that same issue of Vogue Magazine. I was probably featured in an issue of Vague Magazine. I could almost hear the runway announcer. "And now here's Karen wearing a long, red-and-blue plaid wool skirt and matching, fitted vest, 5 years old, acquired by barter for an antique 1930s jacket that was too tight. A frilly Victorian blouse, at least 3 years old, a give-away at the Salvation Army Thrift Store. Blue leather resoled boots, 7 years old, a birthday gift from her former husband, the year before they divorced. And topped off with a brand new gray wool reefer coat, purchased at a student discount store near NYU for $79. Accessorized with a large vintage shoulder bag and a blue plastic make-up kit, a former fisherman's tackle box."

But didn't I have everything I really needed? My experience in the theater? The clothes on my back? And that blue make-up kit, my alchemical retort from which to create characters for the stage? I actually loved my look and could have tromped into my future proudly celebrating my perseverance and ingenuity. But, sacrifices for my art be damned, I felt embarrassed and self-conscious, and tapped my heel in frustration against my blue plastic make-up kit.

I looked up to see Al Lewis standing across from me, coffee cup in hand, smiling. "You look nice," Al said sweetly. "I like your outfit."

"You're joking, right?"

"No. No really, you look nice."

"Well then, you have excellent taste," I said. He chuckled and shook his head, then walked over to the group.

Jack was anxiously sorting through all our airline tickets. Al took advantage of the lull in the conversation and launched into - you guessed it - another saga. A rerun of his Circus Story. Al retold his tale almost word for word and he had everyone's rapt attention. "I followed the elephants. You know, elephants eat a lot, and leave behind a lot-to-be-desired. I was the kid that followed them and ..." At that point I joined him in unison to deliver the punch line. "... I swept up the lot-to-be-desired!" Everyone laughed. Al said, "You know, a lot of actors wanted to be in the circus when they were kids. Know what I mean?" With that he turned his head toward me and threw a private smile in my direction along with a sweet thumbs-up. That recognition felt good. My face flushed, so I pretended to be looking for something in my purse.

At long last we boarded the plane for Raleigh. I was seated in the rear next to Liz. Al was all the way up front with the boys.

"Weird leaving my husband behind," Liz admitted as she ordered a drink.

"Sorry to hear that. I sort of feel that way, too, about my roommates. But I said goodbye to my husband ages ago!" I laughed. With that, I saw Al stand up in the aisle and stretch. He strode down to our row and stopped. "Enjoying the flight?"

"You bet, I'm enjoying it," Liz toasted with her plastic cup, "I just left my old man back home!" She grinned wickedly.

"I left nothing behind!" I jested. "How about you, Al? Didn' t you say you were married?"

"Ha! She divorced me years ago!" The airplane lurched and Al scurried back to his seat, waving to us all the way.

Ten

PRUDENCE

"Good Morning, Ka-ren!" Al stretched my name out, loudly filling the dining room of the Royal Court Motel with his voice, starting my morning with hilarity. Come on, Karen, I coached myself, you don't need a snappy comeback, he only said hello. And using my hands like a foghorn, I honked back, "Good-Morning-Al!" He reached over to one of the chairs at his four-seater and rocked it out a few inches so I could sit down.

"Order some breakfast," Al urged. "Rehearsal's in about forty-five minutes." Then he leaned back and crossed his arms across his chest. We were holed up in this motel for a few days until our apartments became available. What with the storm conditions outside and our new surroundings, I sensed a family feeling emerging.

Al asked me if I had slept well. I had. I asked him the same question and his ambivalent response sounded more like grunts than words.

"Dream anything good?" He teased, as if I'd gone to a movie

33

and could deliver a review.

"Can't remember, but I love dreams. For years I wrote them down."

"When you were asleep?" Al sounded surprised.

"I taped butcher paper to my headboard and had a pen on a string. My system worked pretty well unless I was so sleepy that I wrote on top of what I'd already written!" He shook his head as he laughed.

"I talked to my brother Phil last night. I had to make sure his friend got paid for running lines with me." What? Paid? Oh, so that's how the big stars learn their parts so well!

"I have to rely on the 'kindness of strangers,'" I joked, quoting Blanche du Bois. "That's the only help I can afford." Al clown-winced. "By the way, how come your brother Phil's called Meister, not Lewis?" I asked.

"Changed mine. You should change yours!"

"What's wrong with Ingenthron?" Al began to chuckle and worked up into a full fledged laugh, until his shoulders heaved up and down like pistons.

"No, I mean it," I added defensively. He faked earnestness. Then we both started laughing simultaneously. I added, "What's wrong with a long Scandinavian name that people routinely stumble over?" Al laughed again.

"How about Prudence Pennywhistle?" He forwarded this moniker with mock sincerity, a vaudevillian solution to my problem.

"But don't you know this is the era of ethnic names!"

"Yeh, when I changed mine, it wasn't! Go down the cast list of any play in New York City today. You can't pronounce any of 'em. Yeh. Like Herschel Rodriguez Jones-Wong. It's stupid. Name recognition is very important and who can remember a name like that. You artsy-fartsy types don't know nothin' about marketing." Stupid? Artsy-fartsy? Marketing?

"I happen to love my name. It's also my father's. That's how you get a name, you know, from your dad," I jabbed back. "Anyway, after a few times, people never forget it."

"After a few times? It could be too late!"

"A great man once said, 'There's only one Lewis, and that's me.' Trouble is there are dozens of Lewises in the theater."

"Yeah, yeah, very funny. But you can't possibly know what it was like to have an ethnic name back then."

"Maybe not. But I have a feeling I'm about to find out."

He shook his finger at me and muttered, "You're catchin' on, kid. Anyway, I used to go up to Bedford. That expensive bedroom community with all the mansions." He rolled his eyes in a comical

34

half-circle that clearly articulated "fancy." "I used to visit Fred Gwynne - you know, from *The Munsters?* - and his wife, Foxy. His mother lived there, too. Same horse face like Fred. Boy, did I love to tease her. I'd go up on the train. When you got to the area where they lived, there was this huge sign. 'No Jews or dogs allowed.' Heh heh heh." His laugh was musical, but filled with sarcastic venom.

"What did you just say?" I whispered, stunned. "What year was this?"

"No Jews or dogs allowed," he repeated, proffered without a blink, as if it were as common as a no parking sign. "When I arrived at the house, I'd greet his mother. I knew she loved me. And say, here I am, your Jewish houseguest! She'd run up stairs so fast, trying to get away from me. She'd cluck. 'That Al! Cluck, cluck, cluck, oh that Al.' And up the stairs she'd go. Fred's face was exactly like hers. Exactly."

"How could you keep visiting them there?" I stammered. "How could there possibly be a sign like that in America during my lifetime?"

"Huh. That was nothin'! Tip of the iceberg. But, hey, I wanted to see my friend." I sat quietly not knowing what to say.

"Well," I finally said, looking at my watch, "we'd better go, Albie." Al froze. With palms pressed down on the tabletop, he stared at me for a few seconds.

"Why'd you call me Albie?"

"I'm sorry. It just came out that way. I opened my mouth and out it came." He looked so stunned, I was afraid I'd offended him. "Did I ..."

"No. It's just ..." He paused, looking down at the table. "That's what I was called as a kid, that's all. How'd you know my name?"

"I didn't know. Things like that happen to me sometimes."

"Yeh. That was my name. As a kid." He softened, and as he stood up, grabbed the check from me, and purred, "How'd you know that?"

DEAR DIARY:

Al Lewis and I were in the hotel restaurant eating breakfast this morning when I called him "Albie". What ever possessed me to say that?! What nerve! Then he told

*me it was his nickname as a kid! It did feel kind of, well,
intimate. Did I stumble on it by accident, catching my foot
in a pothole I should have walked around? Have I blown it?
I hope I haven't chased him away. I'd like to hear more,
other chapters from Al's past. And what about the future?
How the hell did I know his childhood name?*

Eleven

NOTHING BETWEEN US

During the next rehearsal a debate arose about the propriety
of my First Act Call Girl character's costume. "Before we run this
scene, the costume department wants to know what you're wearing
underneath the teddy," Jack announced. "What do you think, Karen?
They need to set it." There wasn't much to this costume and now we
were homing in on the details. "No pantyhose," I said. "A call girl
would wear a garter belt or bare legs."

"I don't know ..." Jack had concerns about the close proximity
of the audience.

"I think you're right," Jay chimed in. "I've played this theater
for years and the audience is, well, pretty conservative."

Al quietly added his opinion to ours. "No need to lose the
audience by forcing them to look at something they don't want to see.
Hey, this is a comedy!" *Say, what's wrong with my butt!* I thought,
feeling a teensy bit insulted.

But majority rules. So, underneath my provocative underwear
- a red lace teddy with black satin ribbon threading through it, and
little red lacy panties - I would wear industrial strength pantyhose to
assure the audience that this was not *Oh, Calcutta!*

"Since we're focusing on propriety," Al continued, "I'd like to
cut that *fuck*. Cut it right out." There was just one in the text.

"But, Al, this is Neil Simon!" Jack blurted out. Neil Simon was
the current King of Broadway and his words were considered
sacrosanct.

"Didn't we just agree that the audience is conservative? This is
the Bible Belt. Those blue-haired old ladies will throw up!" Al held his
head, miming one of those offended women.

"But it worked in New York!" Liz interjected.

36

"This ain't New York!" Al buzzed back.

Jay and Jack looked back and forth at each other, weighing the argument for and against, then agreed that there was no benefit to be had from offending the public either with swear words or nudity. And The Word was cut.

I'd been quietly fretting about being half naked on stage, but never thought this controversy might dominate our rehearsal. I'd worn lingerie in a play before – but NEVER with an Al Lewis or in conservative North Carolina.

"In costume. Karen and Al. We're taking it from the top!" Jack called out.

I was pretty nervous and literally got cold feet. Stanislavsky be damned, I was feeling vulnerable, skin to skin with Al. My character, Bunny, is not aware of Al's character, I thought – she's drunk! Pull yourself together, Karen, and be that character. Be oblivious. Clothing has nothing to do with anything! Fortunately, Al was a real pro, and to diffuse any embarrassment, he behaved as if it was "normal" for me to be dressed out of Frederick's of Hollywood. As a consummate professional, he never said a word.

The theater was chilly without the audience to warm it up. So I bundled up in a blanket and Al and I stood on the second floor by the elevated stage waiting for our cue. When it came, I dropped the blanket and jumped into the bed followed by Al. My feet were icy cold and I ran them up and down on the bottom sheet trying to heat them up. "Got cold feet? Huh? Huh?" he teased, grinning at me with a huge clown face. "Har de har har," I said sarcastically. "There is nothing I love more in a man than a great sense of humor." Kidding aside, I could see that he was trying to make this awkward moment easier for me. Still, hopping scantily dressed into that stage bed next to Al in his boxer shorts and t-shirt played havoc with my fantasies. I dove over those feelings and plunged deeper into my character who was in a drunken stupor.

Twelve

GRANDMA'S EYES

Walking into the hotel restaurant on our lunch break, Al held the door for a man using a walker. The man gave Al a grateful smile.

"You know Al, you remind me of my grandmother." He nodded his head appreciatively, then added, "Poor lady!" He cackled gleefully for a second or two. We seated ourselves and I continued. "I loved this woman who taught me so much about life. The tramps that came through town on the train put a mark on her house. They knew she'd feed 'em. She always found a chore for them to do in exchange for a full plate served on the back steps. Saved their dignity that way. People said she was a fool, a mark, a target. Know what she did? Shrugged her shoulders as if to say, if that's the way you see it, okay. But she wouldn't let a man go hungry."

Al looked at me for a long moment, nodding his head. "Then I'll take your comparison to her as a compliment." Al cocked his head, looking into his own past.

"My mother, may she rest in peace, was born in a little shtetl outside Odessa. Polish Russia. Sometimes it was Polish. Sometimes Russian. She was the oldest of six sisters. When things got bad for the Jews ... you know pogroms?"

"I played Anne Frank, remember, Al?"

"That's right, the Jewish shiksa. So you know. My grandfather ... everyone says I look like my grandfather ... sent my mother to America by herself at sixteen. Why?" Al wrapped a growl with laughter. "Because she was the toughest one in the family. Wasn't afraid of nuttin'."

"I could never do that. I crossed the Atlantic at sixteen, too! Going the other direction. But, it was on an ocean liner with chaperones, tons of food, and dozens of other American Field Service exchange students like myself, heading for comfortable homes in Europe. But that seemed difficult enough for me."

Al continued, "Yeah, she didn't travel in no luxury liner!" This time he laughed a staccato heh heh heh, sounding like a round of caps from a cap gun. "Nope. Steerage. You know what that's like? Like sardines in a can!"

"My God, that sounds intolerable."

"Yeah, she was down below listening to her fellow passengers' mournful Yiddish songs and the creaking of the ship. You know how big she was?" Al moved his hand toward the middle of his chest, making his mother about as tall as mine.

"Five foot two?" I ventured.

"Ha! More like four foot eleven!" The juxtaposition of this big six-foot tall man with his petite mother tickled me. "Her father sent her to America to scout for the rest of them. Went through Ellis Island by herself, my mother, and made her way to the largest Jewish ghetto in the world. Brownsville, Brooklyn. Got a job in the garment district as a seamstress and brought over every single member of her family. Heh. Tough? You don't know from tough."

"Wow. Every single one. It's hard to believe that she could survive all that. My grandmother is a tough cookie too. She was born in 1892. Yeah, she'll be 87 in April. Mayme."

Al smiled warmly and said, "You don't hear that name any more."

"Nope. I wrote a song for her once. She's the one who told me a life without love is an empty barrel." Al looked stunned, and then his face seemed to soften into admiration. Had Grandma's sentiment struck a chord? "This is how it goes." And I started to warble:

I look into my grandma's eyes

I see where I come from

I see the chain of ladies' hands

Reaching back to mine.

Oh Earth, hold me and keep me

Safe in your arms

Oh Earth, hold me and teach me

Show me your powers and charms

(Chorus)

Women and their daughters

Go together like Chinese dolls

Women and their daughters

Fertile ground and waterfalls.

Women and their daughters

Fertile ground and Chinese dolls.

"Beautiful. That's just beautiful," Al mumbled. He looked like he was going to cry. I think we both felt vulnerable with the intimacy we were sharing. "Hey Al, I've got a funny Mayme story for you!" Al looked relieved.

"Grandma comes for a visit when I'm in high school and I

want to show her around San Francisco which was very different from her small town in Pennsylvania. There are six of us, and we take her to a famous ritzy downtown Japanese restaurant. One of those places where you have to take off your shoes and sit on the floor."

"Where there's a little pit for your legs and feet?" Al asked. I nodded.

"A geisha in full regalia escorts us to our private room behind a Shoji Screen. She bows and points to our feet. You know, get the shoes off! Well, Mayme was a big lady. She weighed in at about 180. In order to take off her high heel oxfords, she grabs onto a tall, expensive looking decorative vase to balance herself. Well, it starts tottering, wobbling in circles, threatening to crash. We're all frozen, watching a disaster about to happen. But Mom catches it just in time. Then we're all giggling. You know, at Grandma destroying the temple! We're all shushing each other in that quiet atmosphere. The more we try to be quiet, the harder we laugh as we're bending down, bumping into each other, trying to pull off our shoes. That floor is very slippery and Mayme starts to slide in her nylons, and tries to aim her body in the general direction of the table. But her feet go out from under her. Her legs fly up into the air and her body seems to hover a brief second over the table until she floats down like a feather."

"What happened? Was she alright?"

"Grandma bounces when she lands, but ends up, somehow, feet extended into the pit, sitting erectly at the table, hands folded in front of her as if nothing had happened. Then she turns to us and says ... 'Oh, I always do it this way!' We laughed hysterically, completely out of control. Mayme was a natural physical comedian." Al drummed the table with both hands to accompany his laughter. "I think it's genetic, that's where I get my graceful moves." Al guffawed for a long time, then wiped his eyes and smiled at me.

DEAR DIARY:
I think I'm starting to like this guy, Al Lewis. He surprised me with his depth, the way he listened to my Mayme story. Well, the way he listened, period. Maybe I cracked through a couple of layers there. We'll have to see how this goes. But, now I've got to go buy Opening

Night presents for this odd bunch of people, or is it this bunch of odd people? Wish me luck.

We'd all snuck around the many shops of the nearby mall looking for opening night presents for our cast. Liz looked like she'd just swallowed a canary. Eyes flashing, she declared, "Mission accomplished!" I wondered what she'd found to put that twinkle in her eye. Inspired by the third act's tennis motif, I purchased fluffy little towels like tennis pros drape around their necks.

DEAR DIARY:
Now I've got second thoughts ... everybody's covered if I go with this theme gift I just bought for the cast and crew. But is a tennis towel what I should be giving the lead in our play? Should I be thinking cast member present, joke present, or friend present?
We did just have an intimate talk, so if I give Al this goofy towel, he may not get that I'm interested in our friendship. A real theme present would be what? ... Lingerie! Noooo! And then there are the cards to go with the gifts. What do I write in his card? Help! What do you say to a big star that you're very quickly getting to know and like? I suppose I could write him a poem. That'll amuse him. Then again, he could take it the wrong way! I don't want to risk offending this great guy. And how do I even address it? "Dear Albie?" There's a narrow line between insult and intimacy and I might have already stepped into that pile. Only thing to do is to be simple and direct.
Here it is: "Dear Al, thank you for all your helpful ideas and support. It's already been wonderful working with you in California Suite. Have a great show and break a leg! Karen."
P.S. Did we know each other in a former life?

AL LEWIS

starring in

CALIFORNIA SUITE

Also Starring

JAY HUGUELY

with

KAREN INGENTHRON   **LIZ OTTO**

DIRECTED BY

JACK HALLETT

Thirteen

OPENING NIGHT!

I slipped into Al's dressing room, the big one, with a huge
silver star on the door, and placed my gift on his makeup table beside
the others that were already piled there. I slipped out and continued
my deliveries. In the ladies' dressing room that I shared with Liz, gifts
were stacked by my chair, including a huge bouquet of flowers. I read

the attached card, but I couldn't tell who sent it. There were telegrams from my parents and my friends in New York. I tried to meditate to contain the excitement, but it was impossible. It threatened to overwhelm me, and I feared that I would forget my lines and belly flop on stage.

Liz came in and found my gift. "How adorable! Thanks, Karen!" She artistically arranged the little tennis towel I'd given her, decorating the makeup table in front of her. "Liz, do you know who sent these flowers? Management, my parents, my friends in New York?" She didn't know. I owed someone a huge thank-you and I didn't know who.

From down the hallway we heard footfalls and trumpeting laughter, rather like a stampeding elephant approaching our door. It was Al blaring loudly, "Hip! Hip!" He banged on our door then entered. There he stood, wrapped in a red plaid dressing gown, clumsily tied around the waist, holding up a maroon t-shirt, emblazoned with the words *Hip! Hip!* hilariously recalling the punch line of Al's Hollywood party story about climbing on the banquet table to toast Princess Margaret, when he never got to hear the resounding *Hurray!* he'd hoped for. Liz had remembered how good that story he told on himself made us all feel. Al waved his gift t-shirt like a pennant as he laughed in delight. And Liz was tickled pink by his response. She'd clearly hit a home run in the gift department. It <u>was</u> a great present, but then again, why wouldn't he love it, it was all about him! But he didn't acknowledge my present or even my presence for that matter. Maybe he didn't see it yet. "I haven't opened anything else," Al yelled as he waltzed out the door, closing it behind him. "Break a leg!" Well, I guess that answers one question. I have to wait until he gets to it. I'm not going to ask him directly and make an embarrassing faux pas.

This theater was unique in that we climbed onto the stage right by our dressing rooms and a hydraulic lift lowered the entire set right into the middle of the dining audience. The Stage Manager called "Places! Ladies and gentlemen, places please for the premiere performance of *California Suite!*" My place was in my skimpy costume under the covers on the bed in the middle of the set. I felt scared as the stage hit the dining room floor and the lights went up. The play had begun. The opening night audience seemed quiet, expectantly waiting for us to entertain them. With the first laugh that Al got I relaxed and knew they were with us. And when Al pulled me out of the bed and threw me over his shoulder like a rolled-up rug, they went wild. He had to stand and wait, mid-sentence, his shoulder bone digging into my belly for quite a stretch, until they settled down and he was able to continue his lines. They roared with laughter at the end of Act One and all my fears were dispelled. At the end of Act Two, the Academy Award scene, they pounded their hands together as if Jay and I had taken them to the heights of "legitimate" highbrow theatre. And at the end of Act Three, when we decimated each other with tennis rackets, they leaned into each other, hee-hawed, guffawed, and slapped their thighs. It felt great as we took our curtain calls to hear wave after wave of resounding applause.

When Al took the last bow, the audience rose to its feet in a standing ovation, acknowledging his stardom, eagerly letting it rub off on them. After all, they'd made the trip to the Country Dinner Theatre to see Al Lewis and he seemed to have exceeded their expectations. I had never played with a performer of this caliber and as my heart filled with pride, I couldn't help but wish that my parents had shared this moment with me. Lining up to join Al in an encore, we had the pleasure of bowing numerous times, waiting for the audience's clapping hands to tire, before we could exit the stage. Maybe the opening night audience was special, top-loaded with supporters and season ticket holders, eager to adore us. But the ice was broken and we knew we'd be fine – probably better than fine. We might even have a hit on our hands. I'd never seen Al's TV performances, but now I'd seen him acting live from six inches away, and I'd heard the uproarious audience response. Al's acting certainly improved in the last week and making him look good was easier than I thought. He'll be fine. I won't have to mentor him any more. Maybe now I could relax and unwind a little and celebrate.

Raising my intoxicating glass of apple juice as the cast party danced around us, I was jubilant and merrily placed my bottom on Al Lewis's lap, put my arm around his shoulder and toasted the play. "Here's to a successful run! Hip! Hip!" Al groaned comically and sputtered, "Nuttin'!" I tried a second time, raising my voice, "Hip! Hip!" and this time all the revelers yelled, "Hooray!" I stood and bowed in Shakespearean fashion. "Wouldst thou dance, my liege?" I asked, playfully swaying side to side, but Al took me seriously and pulled me close with a quick tug.

"I can't, or I'll have to dance with every lady here," he whispered seriously, then released me with a knowing smile. I'd been suckered in by my own assumptions. What else hadn't I understood?

"Were those beautiful flowers from you?" I smiled, wanting to thank him yet hoping I hadn't made a mistake in asking. He raised his eyebrows and tipped his head in a gesture that challenged: Figure it out! What's he saying to me? Yes or no? Why doesn't he tell me?

Embarrassed, I felt flushed and turned away, and pretended to inspect appetizers on a passing serving tray. When I turned back I saw Al happily talking to a female supporter in a fancy dress, probably a board trustee or major donor. Something icky fluttered right through me, and landed in my stomach like a nest of angry butterflies. Now, where did that come from?

What is this about? Oh, no. I had had enough of this with my Ex. Why should I feel like this? Al's a free man. It's a free country. And I won't tie myself in knots to suit a man, ever again. So, I'm not going to go there. Enough! I checked in with my stomach! Oh, shit, it's still there. That old twisting internal pretzelation. I'm JEALOUS ... He gave me those flowers, I know he did. Why won't he admit it? He's acting nicer to a stranger than to his own co-star. Get over here, you jerk, and admit you bought me that huge bouquet!

The party swirled around me. I tried to enjoy the snacks and the happy chatter, but that dark emotion had taken hold, discoloring everything. I would have given my right arm to be back in my apartment, but I had no ride. Fortunately, when I looked around, there were signs that this party was about to end.

Suddenly, there Al was in the center of the room, inviting everyone to join him in further merriment at some fancy bar he'd discovered. He looked expansive as he slapped people on the back. The goodwill of our star was creating excitement as folks ran to get their coats and bags while he gestured toward the parking lot. Al patted me on the back. "Hey, Karen, you ride with me."

"Nah, sorry, Al. I've got important business to attend to. I gotta get home and rearrange my sock drawer." Al smiled, "Suit yourself!" As the room emptied, I said to myself, I don't need anybody. And found myself standing alone. I grabbed my stuff in a hurry and was waiting by his car when he arrived to unlock it. Al or no Al, I didn't want to be left out of my opening night party.

At the designated high-end establishment, I stood next to Al and watched him as he skillfully made arrangements with the maître d'. He was a manipulator. He patted the seat next to him and gestured for me to sit there. Now what? Oh, right, I could use a little more punishment tonight. I soon discovered that Al was only playing social director, hoping to encourage the others to join us at his table by planting me at his side. Nothing personal. I continued to feel jerked around as I considered my newest role as a decoy duck. Sure enough, they slowly flocked to me and found places to put their things and derrieres. There was lots of loud talking, loud music, and more drinking. By that time, to drown my sorrows I had graduated beyond apple juice to sparkling apple juice. Finally, there was a lull in the racket and I hoped Al and I could converse, but it wasn't to be. The evening quickly ended and we all piled into cars and drove "home."

When I heard Liz on the phone to her hubby in New York raving that our exciting first night smelled of success, and heard the tension slip out of her voice, I shut the door to my room and slid down the other side to sit on the floor in the dark. I was too exhausted to cry. I felt emptiness creeping in. The push to opening night was over and I was just another actor on the road.

Fourteen

WHAT'LL IT BE?

Liz and I were eating breakfast in our apartment, sunlight and draft creeping into the room through glass panes ill-prepared for an unexpected northern chill. "What's that?!" Liz called from our kitchen window, redirecting my attention from my bowl of granola and yogurt to a blur that looked like a giant, dark bird. Double-take. A large man. A large man grappling with the buttons of his navy pea coat, as the wind flipped the front panels out of his fingers. Then one hand pressed down on his Greek Fisherman's cap before it could be whipped from his dark-haired pate. Liz looked startled. "It's Al Lewis!" Shit. Now what?

We both stared at the man charging toward our door and waited for the inevitable knock. Liz answered it and welcomed Al into our home-away-from-home. His nose was red and we could see his breath hanging in the air by the doorframe. Al thwapped his sides with his arms and sputtered the cold air from his lungs, "Ahh, oh, whoa ...," as Liz and I watched this unexpected apparition attempt to speak.

"Anybody want breakfast?" He was grinning through cold clenched teeth. I just sat there on a mismatched dining room chair swallowing the last bits of cereal wondering what brought him to our door. Fortunately, Liz took control.

"Nah. Just had my last cup of coffee. Thanks." Then Al shifted his gaze to me. "What about you, Karen?"

"No, I'm just finishing my cereal. Yes, no, wait. Yes, let's go. I've got some questions for you."

"Okay! Get your coat. It's freezing out there." I got my coat, pausing at the doorway to test the temperature, laughing at its icy welcome. The frosty Raleigh morning caught my breath. The apartment building was set at the bottom of a shallow knoll facing a gentle slope, twenty feet or so from the parking lot where Al's car sat as if dusted in powdered sugar. There were still patches of snow on the green-brown sod, like individual meringues, lightly browned on top. Inhaling again, I wondered where I stood in Al's cast of characters. Probably just an Extra. Maybe that's what the opening night party was really about. Sorting out the hierarchy. Or was he just showing off his exclusive "star car"?

He had found a breakfast shop and in we went. He was relaxed. I was tense. At the party there had been other people around. When we shared a meal during rehearsals, we were always on the clock. Now this was open-ended. We settled into a booth. He was ready for a full meal, the works. And I was about to give him the works. I ordered a muffin and tea.

Before I could hit him with the big question, he started in: "Opening night parties are work for me, Karen. I gotta play the room. You know, deliver for the management." He smirked and then laughed. Was that an apology, or just an explanation, I wondered? I wanted to tell him how I felt last night, but instead I said, "Yeah, sometimes I forget you're famous."

"Famous, Shmamous. It's part of the job." And he laughed again, shrugging off my statement.

"Hey, look at this. Kinda achy today." Splaying his fingers out on the table, Al showed me how arthritis affected them. It was an intimate thing to do, but also totally ordinary. I felt relieved, as the conversation was spread out on our table with his fanned fingers, inviting me in.

"Ever use comfrey? To soak your fingers, I mean. We use it in karate for bumps and swelling."

"Karate, huh? You can get pretty bruised up. I know the feeling," Al replied. "I used to work out at Gold's Gym in Brooklyn. Boxing. Oh, yeah. Don't laugh. Don't laugh. I helped some young fellas work out. Build their careers. Let's face it. I was never going to be a boxer." He took a moment to light up a skinny cigar. "So, how are you doin' with the karate?"

"I'm feeling out of shape! I'm not used to going this long without class. I tried to find a karate studio around here, but the closest one's in Fayetteville. That's miles away," I said disappointedly.

"I'll ask around. Some of the best teachers are hard to find."
He smiled warmly, and his heat spread to me. It felt like I was, well,
not quite Guinevere, but championed nonetheless.

"Oh, wait. I almost forgot. There's one more thing, Mr. Lewis,"
and I reached over the table and grabbed Al's shirt, startling him.
"Did you or did you not give me those flowers?" He placed both hands
over his heart as if I'd shot him and groaned, "You got me! Nice work,
Sherlock."

I could feel that this lucky breakfast was about to be over, but
I wanted to continue the contact. "Al, a bunch of us are going out
tonight after the show. Would you like to join us?"

"Who's that? Actors?"

"Yes," I uttered with sunshine in my voice, assuming that Al
would want to come, too.

"No. I don't hang with actors, Karen."

"I'm an actor."

"Yeh, but you're not me-myself-and-I'ing. If you weren't here,
I'd find someone on the tech crew to eat with. I don't like that actor
bullshit. I don't want to be around it. They're only concerned with
themselves and their ca-reers."

"Huh? You're an actor, Al."

"Sure, and I'd fight for any one of 'em. I just don't get off on
telling theater stories." I nearly choked on my muffin at that one. "I
like real people."

"Well, I'm real. Just come. We'll have fun."

"Not interested." Guess I hit a sore spot. But hopefully, it's
just a bump in the road.

When we returned to the apartment complex, I got out my bag
of comfrey root to dole some out.

"Here, Al. You take about half a handful ..."

"Nah, show me later." He grabbed it eagerly. "I gotta get goin'
on your case. Find that karate genius who's going to whip you into
shape!" He scrunched up his eye like a comic book detective on the
case, tracking the scent, and left.

That was a lot to take in and I wasn't sure how I felt.

That night the entire cast, minus Al Lewis, that is, went out to
a bar. And I watched what was going on around me with new eyes.
Almost everyone got a little tipsy and just as Al predicted, the evening
was spent commiserating. You stroke me, I'll stroke you. Lots of great
theater stories, even some I'd never heard before. It was really fun,
but I was self conscious the whole time. So now my socializing and
drinking with fellow actors was ruined by that bastard, Al "I Don't
Hang with Actors" Lewis, the actor.

48

Fifteen

READ 'EM AND WEEP

After a few performances, Jack Hallett called a rehearsal. Fine tuning, he said. When I walked in he shook a rolled newspaper at me, a huge grin nearly distorting his face. "Karen? Did you see this!" I felt uncomfortable. I had read it, a glowing review for *California Suite* and especially me. The only way I knew to handle this was to smile, nod politely, and deny its personal significance.

"I hope it will sell lots of tickets!"

"But did you really see what it said?" Suddenly there were three people, Jack, Liz and Jay, in a circle around me pointing at the newsprint.

"It says you're the real star of the play!"

"Come on," I parried, nonetheless giggling in satisfaction, as I pushed them away. "You can't act in a vacuum. I'm not doing this play alone."

Then Al walked in. Jack was eager to share the excitement with him. "Did you see the reviews, Al?!"

"No. Never read them. Once you start believing your own PR, you're dead." Why was he raining on our parade? Had he read the reviews and felt slighted? Had he seen the part about me being called the real star? All the newspapers instantly disappeared and for the cast the subject was dropped. No one would confront the elephant in the room. But me.

"What if we read them but don't believe them, Al?"

"That's your call. I don't read 'em." Why couldn't he allow us the pleasure of being praised?

"Okay," said Jack, raising his voice to get our attention, putting this difficult moment behind him. "I brought you all together to tighten up the play. We have to do it today, see, because I've got to get back to New York."

"Ohh? Auditions?" We were eager to find out.

"Yeh, yeh," Jack shrugged shyly. "There are a few ..." and unable to admit his success, he actually blushed. "Back to business. The play's running a little long and I need you all to pick up your cues. Let's start with Jay and Karen. Take out all the dead wood! It's slowing everything down." We read through our scene making it move twice as fast, and Jack seemed satisfied. Jay and Liz huddled together nodding boldly in agreement with Jack.

Then he called Liz and Al together to speed through their act. "The play's becoming short skits," he said. "It needs to be a unified piece." But Al ran through his lines exactly the way he always did them. Jack quickly stopped them. "Tighten up your shtick, Al. This is ensemble work." Liz was delighted at that. Al wasn't at all. They started up again, but Jack held up his hands. "Hold it, Al. Come on, let's speed up the pace ..."

"Of course ensemble is great," Al interrupted, his voice booming. "But the people come to see me, Al Lewis. And that's what I'm going to give them. Al Lewis!" The room froze. Jack was speechless. The rest of us were stunned and embarrassed by what we took to be a blatant Hollywood hissy-fit. I was ripped in two. Al was my pal and co-player, but Jack was the director, and he wanted us to work as a team.

Jack tried to make his point clearer, but Al loudly countered every argument and utterly refused to take this direction. "No!" Al yelled. "I'm not going to flatten out my business! I worked hard to create it!" Was this about Al fighting for his art, or just ego? I'd never witnessed anything like this kind of squabbling in my 12 years of professional theater. Finally, Jack retreated. The other two actors waited for me to join in a united protest against Al, to storm out in a huff with them. But I didn't. I wanted to know why he'd said those things, and I wanted accord in our cast. I waited for Al as the others packed up and left. My heart was clenched. Why had Al blown his top? My background was in ensemble work where I learned the importance of supporting each other on stage. If he just hadn't ranted and raved, maybe we could have all worked something out together.

Al grabbed his stuff and stomped out. I followed him. The situation was unresolved. I wanted to understand his position. And besides, he was my ride. When we got into the car, he continued to blow off steam. "Damn. They couldn't stand it. I got all those laughs. I didn't miss a single one!" he fumed.

"But are they honest laughs? Or are they breaking the flow of the story?"

"Whaaat!? What story!? There isn't any! It's performance! The whole thing is performance!"

"But, Al, you know about Stanislavsky and his approach to plays. It's all about ensemble and ..."

"You're so classically trained you've got your head up your ass! This is a comedy, for God's sake. It's barely a play even. It's a scenario that you gotta fill. Go back to Berkeley."

"What?! Gee, thanks a lot, Mr. Lewis. Drop me off at my place, please." I said dryly through clenched teeth. That's what I get for standing by him?! I'm glad I'm not his enemy. My throat swelled into a lump as big as a golf ball. I wanted to open the door and jump out - after slapping him first, of course.

"Yeah. Sure." Al mumbled. I was hurt and furious ... and speechless.

Oddly enough, my complete silence must have pulled him up short because he calmed down. "Listen," he said almost contritely. "You gotta approach each play differently. *California Suite* is not *Uncle Vanya*, for Crissakes. The audience comes to see me! I'm the star. I don't think of myself that way. I never have. But they do, and I gotta be there for them, show them a good time. Stanislavky'd know this piece requires clowning, you know, big reactions. If I do the first act like ... Jack ... wants me to ... Shit. You know?"

"I'm sorry, I didn't hear you. I have my head up my ass, remember?" Al scowled. I continued, "Does this have anything to do with the reviews? I got a great one today ..."

"Why should you care what a critic says!?" Ouch. "If you believe them when they say you're great, you have to believe them when they say you stink. I know what I'm doing on stage and I don't need a newspaper to tell me!" We drove on in silence for a while. "Jack wants me to cut my business in Act One. That's stupid. I kill the audience with my walk to the bathroom." More silence. "Jack said the play is disintegrating. Oh, yeah? Well, the audience reviewed the show with their hands. Their applause. I'm here to please them."

I'm in trouble. I still have to act with this overbearing control freak eight times a week for ten more weeks. What am I going to do?

Al dropped me off at my apartment. "Thanks for your apology," I mumbled as I slammed the door. I sought out Liz and Jay to try to bring the cast together again. I played devil's advocate to feel them out. "What do you think about Al's performance?"

"The guy's an egomaniac!"

"A stubborn egomaniac!"

"Isn't clowning essential to his part?"

"Oh, pluh-eese!"

"In the Third Act, we're all clowning!"

"Yeah. That's the Third Act ..."

"Maybe he was just blowing off steam today. Don't you think he had some good ideas ..."

"We have one director. That's Jack, and he has final say. Period."

"Okay, I just wanted to hear both sides."

DEAR DIARY:

~~That Al~~

~~What am I~~

~~This is~~

Oh, hell. What can I say ????

Sixteen

MUENSTER ON A ROLL

I found myself in the middle of a theatrical ego battle and I didn't like the feeling of being pushed and pulled from both sides. There had to be a way for me to find my own peace in all of this, to find that middle ground between the two opposing extreme opinions about the play. I still had a long way to go on this contract and I just wanted to do the job I was hired for, remain politically neutral but still contribute to the ensemble. And I was getting great reviews, so why change anything?

Shortly after opening night, management asked Al to add his "encore." This wasn't a musical! What was that about? Curiosity got the best of me. I had to ask.

"Karen, I don't do jokes. I ad lib, play the audience. That's what I do," Al plainly informed me. "Yeah, it's part of the dinner theater tradition. The stars do a turn after the curtain goes down." He shrugged his shoulders as if to minimize its importance. "Some performers sing, I go out and talk to the people. Management was waiting for the show to open before they added this extra bit. But I been gettin' ready, checking out our audiences. Looking for a few marks!" He tittered gleefully.

I decided to see if Al was all he claimed to be: the main attraction, the big cheese, the man everyone came here to see. That night when the play was over, we finished our curtain calls, cleared the stage, and, as the applause built, Al returned to center stage in a welcoming round of cheering and clapping. I ran upstairs in my final act tennis shoes, to find a spot where I could watch him unseen from overhead.

"Thank you, thank you." He brought his hands together in prayer position and acknowledged everyone for coming to see the play. He worked his gratitude as a theme to include the young, middle-aged and older theater-goers alike. When he had the coals amply heated, letting the audience bask in collective warmth, he quickly changed course, and went hilariously on the attack.

Al zeroed in on an audience member. "Oh, hello, Baldie!" The mark giggled and his wife poked him in the ribs with her elbow. Wow, they loved being singled out, I thought, but they're pretending to hate it. How did Al figure all that out? He obviously loves people and all their foibles. I could never walk out onto that stage and talk to the audience like he is doing without studying human behavior for months. I wonder if all that social analysis comes naturally to him?

"Yeh, yeh. We're all getting a little older!" Al declared in an affirmative tone. The audience nodded. Then he whipped his body around 180 degrees to verbally nail another man he had already located, who trained his hair into an ersatz toupee covering his baldness. "What are you laughing at?" Then looking at the audience, blurted, "He combs it over!" which precipitated torrents of laughter that Al rode briefly and then topped. Wagging his index finger, he admonished, "Trying to cover it up, huh?" Al madly pantomimed combing his hair from one side, up over the top of his head and down the other. More laughter. Al's timing. It was outrageously on point.

I'd seen the Stage Manager conferring with Al before the show. Now I realized that he was pointing out a couple celebrating their 50th Anniversary. Al gestured to them as if he was a tour guide for Mount Rushmore. "Now look at these ancient wonders. Fifty years! You should be ashamed of yourselves, not getting divorced 25 years ago like the rest of us. What are you? Nonconformists?" They roared. And Al finished up with praise. "The rest of us'll never catch up with this lovely couple! Aren't they wonderful! I want to be like you folks when I grow up!" It was all pretty sweet and the audience lapped it up.

"He's so relaxed out there!" I gasped, and the assistant stage manager tapped me on the shoulder. "Shh ..." Al was working very hard, serving that audience. Maybe I shouldn't have watched this. It was hard for me to accept that he was justified in his ego rants, but I just saw it with my own eyes. He is a master at his craft. Have I just taken sides, like I swore I wouldn't do?

Al ended his encore by stating, "I've been running up and down these aisles for 57 years! On April 30th I will be 69 years

YOUNG!" He goosed the word, making it sing with exhilaration, then leapt into the air like a twelve-year-old cheerleader. The crowd roared with excitement and delight. From this high point, he quietly started an epilogue, "The Irish Blessing," a prayer which he wanted to impart.

> May the wind be always at your back,
> May the sun never set upon your doorstep,
> And until we see each other again,
> May the good Lord keep you in the palm of His hand.

"Thank you, thank you, thank you." He nodded with his palms together, like an Indian guru, as he backed off, then waved goodbye. Tissues came out of handbags. A soft murmur of heart-warmed satisfaction rippled through the crowd as they padded their way to the exits.

The Assistant was jumping up and down, squealing into the audience applause. "Did you see that?! That man's outrageous! Just awesome!" He pushed me away from the elevator as he pressed the lever to raise up the stage. "Oh, wow, not in a million years! Ever see anything like that!? I never ...!" I stood in the shadows watching his reaction. Was this how our audience felt? Did everyone feel that way?

When Al stepped off the elevator, the Assistant couldn't resist hugging him full on. "Mr. Lewis, you were great! You were just ...! Oh, my God. We're so lucky to have you here in North Carolina!" Al hugged him back. "Glad you liked it. Thank you." That's when he spotted me in the half light and said in a warm and jovial tone to the assistant – but for my benefit: "Heh, heh ...You can say whatever you like about Al Lewis, that he's loud, opinionated and smokes stinky cigars, but damn it, he brings the wagon home!" Covered with sweat, Al accepted a towel from the Assistant who, bouncing all the way, escorted his idol to the dressing room door distinguished by the huge, silver star.

I've got to admit, Al really knows what he's doing! He's doing it his way and going against Jack's direction, but he's making it work. Despite what Jack and the others say, he's still honoring the play and getting extra laughs, which Neil Simon would probably love him for. What's so terrible about that? Can he really be considered an egomaniac when he's just being true to his own talents? And what does this all mean to me? Have I been seduced by those rave reviews into continuing to follow the party line, believing that was the "right way" to do the play? The thing is, I wouldn't even know how to do it my way. Is this what Al meant when he told me I didn't believe in myself?

I got great reviews for doing what the director wanted, but Al didn't do what the director wanted and he's out there doing his job pleasing the audience anyway. How can Al be considered not a team player when he's doing what he believes is best for the play and getting standing ovations to confirm it? I'm seeing it pretty clearly now. I wonder if I have the courage to follow through and change my ways.

In the green room before the next show, Al asked, "Anybody want to do an encore? You sing, Jay, and so do you, Liz."

"That's very democratic of you, Al, but no thanks," said Jay, walking quickly away as if saving himself from disaster.

"Me neither. Thanks though," said Liz swiftly backing out. "The encore is the star's domain."

"How about you, Karen?"

"Thanks for the invitation, Al, but the audience comes to see you, remember? Thanks anyway."

"Hey, Karen, you change your mind, just let me know. It's a good experience. It can expand your acting abilities ..."

DEAR DIARY:

Does Al really want to share the limelight, or is he just trying to prove he's a team player? Is he trying to patch things up after that big blowup about working together as an ensemble? Jay and Liz ran away from his offer like rats from a sinking ship. So why am I even considering it? Maybe this would be the first test of my courage.

Seventeen

NO EXIT

Al's challenge to perform an encore was tempting. Was this the devil calling me or the seductive voice of opportunity? I was probably taking myself too seriously, but I felt that getting cast in this production with an actor of Al's distinction was leading me upward in my career. But what was really bothering me? Al's comment that I had my head up my ass. Am I so classically trained that I can't understand what the average person likes to see in the theater? Only one way to find out.

"Is the door still open, Al, on that offer to do an encore?"

"What? You got something? Of course!"

"Okay, I'll try out the performance piece I wrote. Try it out in Raleigh!" I was suddenly excited and scared. I rehearsed a piece that I'd written, trying to bring it up to performance level for my encore moment.

After the Wednesday matinee, the curtain went down and I walked out onto the empty stage. It immediately felt strange. "Good afternoon!" I announced. "Mr. Lewis has kindly given me this opportunity to share my performance piece with you." The audience seemed baffled. Where was Al Lewis? And, what the hell's a performance piece?

I set the scene for them. I'm in my dojo, and I bow like I'm in karate class. I quickly realize as I launch into my "turn" that I might as well be explaining Pirandello's *Six Characters in Search of an Author* to Raiders Fans. But I have to go on with it even though it feels like a slow scratch down a blackboard. Over my kicks and punches, I roll out a spoken narration about a woman getting shafted by her boyfriend. The audience stares at me in stunned confusion, clueless, but I plunge on anyway to my knockout finish: a front kick, a roundhouse, and spinning back kick. "Take that, Lover, take that!" And finally … Scene. The audience sits there like the proverbial oil painting. I bow, thank them anyway, and say goodbye. I beat a hasty retreat to little hiccups of applause.

I heard people mumbling in disappointment as they headed quickly for the exits. Oh, that was a great idea, Karen! Why hadn't I quit while I was ahead with those great reviews? Now headlines appeared in bold print in front of my eyes: SHE BOMBED IN RALEIGH. Hip, hip, nuttin'. And damn him. That Al Lewis had made it look so easy!

In the dressing room, Liz quickly took in my despondent face. "Well, you tried it, kid!" and she actually looked proud of me, but in the same way that people view plane crash survivors. I quickly changed out of my costume and ran into Al in the hallway.

"Hey, how do you feel?" he asked.

I felt like I might throw up. "I feel rotten, Al."

"About your encore?" I nodded. "Why don't you try it again?"

"No way. At first I thought I'd bombed. But then I realized that the audience really wanted to see you out there and I disappointed them."

"Aren't you glad you tried it?"

I took a deep breath before I was able to answer. "Yes. Yes, I am."

"I'm proud of you, Karen. No one else had the guts to go out there." His eyes rested softly on my face and then he gently held my chin, straightening my head until I looked directly into his eyes. "It ain't easy. I'm proud of you." He meant what he said. I had taken that risky leap. There is nothing like the experiential. I'd tried, alright. A trial by fire -- I saw how hard that little ole star turn could be, how brilliantly Al had managed it, and that I hadn't actually died.

Eighteen

EMPATHY

Liz heard me yell as I hung up the phone: "My dad's coming. He said yes!" Recently retired from his job at a textile research lab, Dad was reluctant to travel because he suffered from Parkinson's disease with its concomitant good days and bad days. He finally surrendered to my pleas and booked a flight.

The night my father attended the performance, I took him backstage and introduced him to Al. Several days later Al surprised me. "Ask your Pop if he'd like to go out one night for a bite to eat. You know, after the show." He wants to see more of my father?

"Thanks, Al, I'll ask him." Dad was thrilled. My discrete father and this loudmouth? That'll be interesting. Desperately wanting the evening to go well, I was a bit nervous sitting in the restaurant beside these two men. Why had Al extended himself this way? Was he just bored with our quiet life in the boonies? Yet they seemed to understand each other perfectly, and happily, they shared ideas and enjoyed our meal together.

Later, shaking his head with awed respect, my dad enthused, "That Al has lots of energy! Especially when he comes on again after the bows!" I cringed. Good thing Dad wasn't there for my ingenious catastrophe. "Quite a character, that Al. It was wonderful to meet him, Karen. Wait'll I tell everyone back home!"

The next morning, my dad called. "I can't meet you today, Karen. I don't feel up to it," and he insisted on staying alone in his hotel room. The following day he called to tell me, "I changed my return flight. I can't stay, kid. I just don't feel well."

This sudden downturn of my father's health and change of plans rattled me. I tried hard to talk him out of it, but he was adamant and left the following day. A gray cloud surrounded me as I took in how much Parkinson's disease controlled him.

Later Al caught up with me. "Hey, is your dad still around?"

"No, he left. He went home. I feel awful. Damn Parkinson's. You know, he loved to work, but this was the official company line: 'A hazard on the job and to himself.' Early retirement. The Golden Handshake. He's only 63!"

"I feel sorry for your dad, Karen," Al said softly. "It's a terrible feeling if you think you can't care for yourself or your family. I'm sure your dad's going through something tough like that. He'd probably like to spare you, now that you're in this show and everything."

Hell, Al was trying hard to brighten my day, so I unconsciously grabbed his hand and stroked it, just as I was taught in massage class, working each finger and pressure points on the palm. When I finished, he pulled me into a hug then quickly clasped my hand in his and pumped it up and down, a clumsy embarrassed handshake. "Thanks a lot. This massage stuff really works. I feel bettah! How about you?" I shrugged my shoulders. Was Al giving me the old sympathy routine? Suddenly I thought about my father telling everyone about his dinner with Al Lewis, the star of his daughter's latest show. Yeah, the actor who played on *The Munsters*! Over the lump in my throat, I croaked, "Thank you, Al. I feel much better, too!" I did.

DEAR DIARY:
There are things, like my father's health, that are more
important than cast ego fights and encores. I tried mine.
I got my reaction. Al seems to be proud to know me.
Maybe I should just lighten up a bit and concentrate on
getting through the run of the play. Hopefully the
others can follow my lead and lighten up.

Nineteen

BREATH OF LIFE

Al called to see if I wanted to take a drive with him. "I'm tired of hanging around this apartment gargling. Wanna go to Chapel Hill? Maybe there's a health food store over there where I can get something for my throat. It's sore."

"I like health food stores. Let's go!"

Chapel Hill was an exciting college town with its bookstores, bicycles and surplus of university-driven energy. This stood in stark contrast to the staid suburban neighborhood where we holed up in Raleigh. We walked down the aisle of a health food store and Al looked for slippery elm lozenges while I searched for arnica, an herb my karate friends and I used for bruises. Al seemed to have a shopping list in his head, and already three people had volunteered to help him -- two store employees and another excited shopper who'd all sighted Grandpa Munster. When I caught up to them, Al was holding up a bottle of garlic capsules, shaking it like a mariachi musician.

At the cash register, Al started in. "Did I ever tell you my garlic story?"

"No, I don't think so."

"Remind me when we get outta here."

"Oh, yeah, as if I have to."

Al put the key in the ignition and stepped on the accelerator. "It was really an Actors Studio production, but we performed it on Broadway. It opened December 2nd at the Golden. I remember!" With that, Al tapped his temple. "Ya see, Mike Gazzo had written a new play and we wanted to do it. *The Night Circus*. It takes place in a bar. I'm the owner, the bartender. The star was Janice Rule. Remember her? What a lovely lady. Married to Ben Gazzara at the time and he was in the play, too. Totally brilliant, that Janice Rule."

"Yeah, yeah, go on." I looked at my watch for emphasis.

"Anyway, I decided I needed the garlic cure. I read an article about it, how good it was for your health, so I started eating garlic. Raw! I was building up. You know, started with a few cloves, and by the time we were into rehearsals, I was eating a whole head a day."

"You weren't! I tried to eat half a clove of raw garlic. The fumes made me cry, and it burned my mouth!'"

"Oh yeah. You get used to it. Peel it and chew it up. Wow, did I stink! You know what happens, don't ya? It starts coming out your pores. When you sweat. Phew! So, in the scene, as the bartender, everyone has to come up to me and order a drink. There's no way around it. First, Janice Rule. She comes over, leans in ... you could see it on her face! The smell. She leans in and recoils, like she bumped into an invisible shield." Al, reliving the experience, was stifling his laughter.

"Then it's Ben Gazzara's turn. He comes over. Recoils. Same thing happens to him. Janice, she was my friend. She takes me aside and begs me, 'Please Al, just for now, can't you stop with the garlic. Please!' I say no. This is for my health. I need the garlic cure! The next day she comes in with a bottle of garlic pills. You know, the perles? She says, 'Look, Al, odor-free!' I tell her I'm on the garlic cure and I'm not taking those fake pills."

"What happened?!"

"Well, she tries everything, asking me nice, the pills, tough love, the whole nine yards. But I won't do it. Then the director, Frank Corsaro, asks me, sternly but kindly, on behalf of the entire cast, would I please stop with the garlic. I tell him the same thing. It's a matter of my health, so no. Then I hear nothing. I figure the whole episode's blown over. We rehearse. Everything's fine."

"Uh huh?"

"Then what happens? I get a letter in the mail from Actors' Equity. I'm up on charges! I'm up on charges for creating a toxic environment for my fellow actors!"

I started screaming with laughter. "Aren't those charges usually for toxic chemicals and leaky boilers?"

"Right. Ever hear of anybody being up on charges for eating garlic?"

"Nooooo." I sobbed with laughter. I suddenly realized that I was laughing my head off over the very trait that frustrated me most about this otherwise loveable man. His stubbornness. "What sign are you, Al?"

"Oh, are we going to start with that crap!" He shook his head in disapproval, then added, "Taurus. What's it to ya?" and laughed, throwing his head back just like a braying bull.

"Taurus? They sling the bull. Need I say more?"

"You could!" he added to get in the last word.

"How does *stubborn* strike you?" I tried to keep a straight face.

"Yeah. Yeah." He was nailed and he knew it. "What else is new?!" Al laughed, a man who could take his punishment ... if he deserved it. And almost as well as he could dish out! I felt I was with a standup guy. There had been enough weasels and wrigglers in my past, and I liked the solid feel of this man. Plus I'm a sucker for a sense of humor.

"Karen? It's your mother."

"Hi, Mom. Everything okay?"

"You won't believe this. The whole puzzle's about *The Munsters*! How do you spell Gwynne?"

"G-W-Y-N-N-E."

"Then that's right. Listen to this. 48 Down. Flappable senior Munster. Al Lewis! Flappable. Get it? Like a bat?" I could see her shaking her head over that silly pun of a clue, referring to Grandpa Munster's vampire past.

"Mom? I'm starting to like that flappable Munster."

"Oh?" she asked, a gossipy note clinging to her question. "Is he nice?"

"Actually, Mom. It's hard to tell. Al is one of the kindest people I've ever met. And he's got to be the most stubborn person I've ever met. Does that explain it?"

"Oh, Karen." I could imagine her shaking her head.

"Plus, he makes me laugh."

Twenty

OVERBOOKED

SAVE, TOSS, GIVE AWAY

I've got to press on, deal with this mess, and clean up my home. But the memories keep pouring out. Come on, Karen, buckle down to the task at hand. More books to deal with. Shelves and shelves of them. Oh, I haven't seen this book for years. I've taken it with me through every move. I can't part with it now. Save.

Al picked me up at my apartment and told me he had found an independent bookstore listed in the Raleigh phonebook and invited me to investigate it with him. "Write down the address," he said. I discovered he had a sorry sense of direction and I speculated that that might be the reason I was ferried along in his big boat-like Mercury. Another star perk from the theater. He hated getting lost. From the passenger seat, I navigated with a local street map and we arrived at the establishment in no time. Al gave me the thumbs-up.

At the shop door, Al lunged ahead of me like a kid released into F.A.O. Schwarz. He almost knocked me over in his excitement to harvest his food for thought. I wandered quietly up and down the aisles, carefully considering the store's offerings. I spotted Al with his reading glasses perched low on his signature nose, standing in front of the Mystery section. He'd begun assembling a small pile on the shelf at chest level, now he picked up his finds and moved on. The cost of books slowed me down to a crawl, but I felt the delicious pull of them and wished I could buy every one I wanted.

The smell of the place, dusty paper and incense, the kids sitting on the floor surrounded by open books, the shaggy proprietor, made me feel like I was back in Berkeley. I didn't dare tell Al this, given his outspoken opinions, but he fit right into this little Berkeley-like scene. He was grazing along on this literary field trip in total contentment. Holding to my frugal budget, I chose one lone book and bumped into Al at the register. He'd collected several K.C. Konstantine mysteries, one Ngaio Marsh, a "Covert Action Quarterly," and a few other books I couldn't identify, their titles hidden by the clutter of his stack. Just as the sales clerk was about to bag Al's, he nabbed one of them and asked me if I'd read it. *Love Stories by New Women.* As I reached for it, he placed it in my hand. The cover had a shiny black lacquer look, inscribed with a square that framed two porcelain dolls, their moveable eyelids flirting, their mouths pursed for a kiss. Why is he giving me this? What message is he trying to send me? It's making me uncomfortable. Why can't he just tell me what it is about this book that he wants to share?

I went home and opened it. As I moved through the chapters it dawned on me that all of the short stories were about women. There they were in my two hands, strange little pearls of literary love written by women, which poured out onto each page. Then I noticed that the book was edited by women, too. I trembled, knowing that he gave me a book by, for, and about women. Again I have to ask, who is this Al Lewis? He has so many sides to him and I feel differently about each one.

Twenty-one

BREAKFAST IN BEDLAM

Al stood in my doorway, tossing his car keys. "Ready to go out for breakfast?"

"How about I make it for us this morning?" I ventured. I'd finished the book Al lent me and wanted to talk with him about it ... privately. Besides, I was feeling awkward about going out to eat so often with him.

"Too much trouble. Don't worry so much. Let's go."

At the diner, it slowly dawned on me that his foraging for breakfast was not just about food intake, it was about noise, people, news, action. Sitting in our booth, Al was at peace with himself. He had his newspaper, folks around him, and me. And what was I? Assurance that he wasn't alone? That he deserved attention? He had that. An audience? He certainly had that. He appeared to be totally content, in the world he'd devised, and I wondered why I'd accepted his invitation. At one point I looked over at him and another one of his many facets came into view. His eyes played off of the folks eating in the diner, flashing them an unspoken message: "Yeah, I'm Grandpa Munster and look what I've got!" His boyish rapture at being seen with a shiny fish in his net? Yeah, a "trophy" girlfriend to show off in public. Do I mind that? Not really. I have to admit that it kind of tickles me – the She's-Wit'-Me routine!

"Hard not to like people who like you," Al mumbled. At first I thought he was referring to me, and flinched at the thought that he'd read my mind. Then I realized he was talking about some annoying fans anchored two booths down. They wanted his autograph – big time – just as his eggs arrived. He told them kindly, "Not while I'm eating. Come back when I'm done and I'll sign everything you got!" They looked ruffled, but reluctantly returned to their seats while Al chopped up his breakfast with the side of his fork. Aha, his mouth was full! An opening to ask about the book.

"Al, the book. I read it."

"Ya like it?" He wiped some scrambled stuff off his chin. He was a delightfully free, messy eater, shoveling in his "two cackle berries on a raft".

"Yeah. Why'd you give it to me?"

"No reason. A new book by women. Everywhere you go, you're

63

writing stuff down, that song about your grandmother, kinda like a poem, and you wrote that piece you performed. Hell, maybe you could write a story. Or a book, for that matter."

"I noticed that every story was written by a woman ..."

"Boy, do they have trouble getting published. But there they are, in print! You can do it, too, you know."

"What do you mean, Al?"

"It's about passion. How much are you willing to stand up for yourself? Ever get arrested?" I nodded but he wasn't looking at me. He was keeping his eye on the autograph hounds who looked ready to rush him. "Two years ago 1500 of us stormed the nuclear reactor at Diablo Canyon. Trying to shut it down. We went right over the fence. The cops weren't too nice! Arrested 47." What guts, I thought. "Last year, we did it again. Five thousand of us demonstrated. Nearly 500 got hauled in." He was clearly pleased with the improved numbers.

"Wow, Al." I looked over at the family in the booth holding their pens and papers, waiting for Al to finish breakfast. Do they know how long this might take?

"Ever been arrested?" He asked again, then added in a mocking Muppet voice, "Oh no, not Prudence Pennywhistle!"

"Yes, Al, I did get arrested."

"What? You?!"

"On the UC Berkeley campus."

"Why? For what?"

"For demonstrating against the Vietnam War. Remember the Blue Meanies? Named after the villains in the Beatles', Yellow Submarine."

"Oh, yeh, Karen, the Oakland Cops. Mean racist bastards."

"Just thinking about that day gives me the shakes. Those thugs herded us onto an old bus, filled it up to the top with students, and locked us inside," I quietly confided. "A very bumpy ride to Santa Rita jail. The metallic clang of the place." I shuddered. "The terrifying notion of being lost to my known world."

"They were trying to scare you. So you'd never demonstrate again," Al stated matter-of-factly. "You know. 'Teach those kids a lesson.'"

"Well, it left its intended threat imprinted on my soul." As I spoke, Al's body language changed and he looked softly into my eyes. Was getting arrested for your political beliefs romantic to this guy? My eyes hung on his for a second, searching for a clue. But we were rudely and amusingly interrupted by the flapping paper sounds generated by the family with the autograph-hunting kids. They had seen him lay down his fork and took it as a sign to eagerly peek out of their booth, pen and papers at the ready, hoping he hadn't forgotten them. Resigned, Al smiled and waved them over. Then he turned to me. "Why don't you write about that, the Vietnam War?" he whispered confidentially. Before I could say anything, Al was engulfed by this bubbly family. "Thanks for waiting!" He cajoled. "Gotta eat your breakfast, right?" he kidded. "Right? Just like mama says!" The pen flew across the paper as he autographed his name boldly, and child-like. The result looked almost like a sketch.

"Put my name?"

"Don't do names!" Then turning to one of the parents, he gibed, "Once had a paternity suit! I'll write love, but no names! I ain't tellin'!" They mellowed to Al, started laughing, shook his hand and sincerely told him how much they were entertained, how they still enjoy his performances. They exited the diner, smiling and hugging each other. Al had sprinkled their lives with magic. I felt giddy for a moment, as if skipping in the stardust that they'd kicked up, rolling around in it like a kitty in catnip.

DEAR DIARY:
What a conversation with Al! The way he handles things,
deftly, sleight of hand, he had to have been a juggler,
not a circus clown. We talked about writing and he
encouraged me. Does he have more confidence in my
ability to write than I do? Do diary entries count?

Twenty-two

BUYING INTO IT

A couple of days later, Al showed up at my place. "You wanna go to the mall? I need to pick up some things for my kids."

"The mall? I forget what town I'm in when I shop at a mall. They all look alike."

"Let's go!" Al urged, sunshine radiating from his very being. He was moving quickly, so I grabbed my purse and sweater, and tripped over myself trying to keep pace.

Once inside the mall, Al walked briskly down the long

corridors, taking great pleasure in being recognized and interacting with fans. I struggled to keep up. "What's going on, Al?" I panted. "I thought we were here to shop. And take a break from show business."

"I'm selling tickets," he explained, shrugging off any importance implied by the public attention he was receiving. He grinned, "You gotta promote, promote, promote." And Al the walking billboard did just that, drumming up interest for our show. But, I could see it was just an excuse to do his usual Grandpa schmooze and was totally unnecessary. Had he really sold any tickets? He just wanted to have some fun, while I, his anonymous co-star, waited and watched. After all the attention died down, Al said, "Come on, let's go!"

"Where to, Al? Another crowded mall full of Munster fans?"

"No, I'm on a hunting expedition for my kids."

Al entered a high-end store and began shopping like there was no tomorrow or no limit to his charge account. "Dave needs Extra Large, he's nineteen. Ted's a large, he's 14. And Paul's skinny, so he needs a medium. What's wrong? You don't wanna help? That's okay."

I answered, "No, I can make myself useful!" So I followed him around helping to pick out just the right thing for each of his sons. Al dumped a massive mound of clothing on the counter, paid for it all, and had everything boxed up by an obliging sales clerk, of course another high-five'ing Grandpa Munster fan.

Later at his place, I surveyed his closet which was piled high with earlier purchases, still tagged. He'd already been shopping – a lot.

"Help me pack this up?"

"Okay, sure," I said, still awed by the amount of stuff he was sending. In tandem, we began taping up the heavily laden boxes. He turned them and I rolled the tape. Surprisingly, we were a well-oiled machine. Then he asked me to hand him a ball of string. "What are you doing?" Al was reinforcing the packages with the string, weaving a web which made each box look like it was caught in a fisherman's net, the way my mother used to do. He beamed with pride. "Hey, I got a reputation to keep up. My boys'll know these are from me!" We made labels: DAVID, TED, and PAUL. "They're the jewels in my crown," he whispered tenderly.

Al looked so happy. His parental dedication warmed my heart which seemed to open a little, like a flower in sunlight. I was trying to remain objective about Al. But when I saw how much he loved his sons, I started to feel more for this man and his family, too. He was thousands of miles away from them plying his trade to earn money for their welfare. I wanted to reach over to hold Al's hand at that moment, but it was only a moment, because thoughts of my own failed relationships of the past sobered me up.

DEAR DIARY,
What went on inside me at Al's place? An emotional switcheroo. How could I feel lonely, when Al had been right there beside me talking about his family? I felt so close to something good and right, and in a flash, afraid that I'd never have it. I sank into a lonely place, sad and left out - aching for that special someone.

Twenty-three

KISS TO BUILD A SCHEME ON

The next chance I had to have an intimate conversation with Al was after a light meal at Denny's following our show. Too many Grandpa fans at Denny's. We parked in front of my apartment. "Is anyone waiting for you back home in New York?" Al questioned, trying to sound casual. Then he touched my hand. Oh, God. Now what? The thing I want most, but can deal with the least.

"No one is waiting," I uttered so quietly that he couldn't hear me and I had to say it again a bit louder. "I don't know where I'll go after the run. Maybe back to New York, maybe not."

"What do you think about the difference in our ages? That's a lotta years." The following thoughts all occurred to me in the next second and a half: Oh no, is this a proposal? What is he saying to me? Difference in ages? What is he getting at? Why is he asking that? Is he asking me if I like older men? Is he telling me he likes younger women? What has he got in mind, a January-December romance? Is he going to tell me he's going out with an older woman? I opted for comic relief.

"You can say a lot of things about me, Al, that I'm loud, opinionated, and smoke stinky cigars, but I've never been called an ageist." Al chuckled. "Seriously, it's never been an issue with me. In fact, I think we're both lots of different ages. I can't help when you were born!" Al laughed again, relieved by my response. "How old are you right now?"

Al answered, "Maybe thirty-five? More like seventeen." He looked terribly shy, yet inched his hand over to mine and closed his fingers softly around it and said, "Funny, isn't it?" We sat in our stillness for a few minutes, his hand still wrapped around mine. I was not quite in fight or flight mode, but the adrenaline was definitely rushing though me. Was Al lonely? He was literally reaching out to me. But, why? For what reason? Did he actually feel something for me? In any case, this was starting to feel very tender.

"Well ... I'm a dad before everything. You know my kids come first." There we go! That's it. The Anti-Intimacy Alert. Still, my face smiled acceptance and approval of that fact, even though it would have been nice to hear something else. About us, perhaps. About our hands, which were still cradled between us, until ...

"Goodnight," he said and kissed me gently ... on the lips! When in doubt, get out! My inner Crossing Guard shoved me out the door. I shut it, kissed my finger, and tapped the window. He smiled through the glass and took off. I stood there for oh I don't know, 45 minutes, going over the recent events.

All night I tossed and turned, running the replay, trying to make sense of what happened, angels and devils getting equal time.

DEAR DIARY:

That was the weirdest kissing scene I've ever played! Smooch. "My kids come first..."?? This is ridiculous. Well, I have got to get through this show. I, Karen, promise to take this as it comes. No expectations. No anticipation. No speculation. Signed on the dotted line. (My signature:_____.)

The following day, I hadn't slept very well and was tired and nervous. I was afraid to talk to Al, but kill-the-cat-curious to see how he was feeling. I anxiously avoided contact until the evening performance. Since I usually greeted everyone back stage before the show, I started by knocking on Al's dressing room door. He was sitting in front of his makeup mirror when he invited me in.

"Hi, have a wonderful show, Al."

"How are you?"

"A little tired."

"Couldn't sleep last night?"

"I had trouble falling asleep. Why?"

He took my hand and pulled me to him. He hugged me and laughingly said, "So did I!" If this is what I think it is, I don't want to think about it right now. I have a show to do! As I backed out, I said, "To be continued, Al. The show must go on!"

Twenty-four

YOU'RE AN OLD SMOOTHIE

SAVE, TOSS, GIVE AWAY

I'd barely begun to deal with the kitchen. There are piles of bubble wrap and unfilled boxes in the corner. It's sobering to see how much stuff Al and I had collected over the years. I don't think this blender even works any more. Should I keep it? When did we get it ...? Oh, yes, I remember. Save.

The next day after the show Al drove me home. We didn't talk much. He clicked off the ignition, reached over the expanse of the front seat and pulled me to him. We shared a little peck on the cheek, but as I opened the door to step out, he pulled me toward him again for another peck. Then I felt my resistance melting away, as our lips led us into a tender delicious kiss. After that sweet kiss, I was lost. I kicked my diary under the seat. We continued to smooch like teenagers until the lights went out in the apartment building in front of the car. Al got out, walked around and opened my door.

"Goodnight, beautiful Karen." We floated hand-in-hand to the front door. We kissed again. I said goodnight and went inside. That was nice, I thought. Al's so respectful. We hadn't been drinking but I sure felt high.

Every night for a full week, that scene was played again. We sat in Al's car talking and kissing before we parted, as if our parents were waiting up for us. On the eighth night, we'd gone out for a snack and returned to our usual parking spot. We kissed playfully at first, kisses like fluttering wings. We both knew at the same time that our emotions were deepening and our kisses filled with longing. Al took my head in both of his hands, and looked softly into my eyes for what seemed a long time. Then he gently stroked my hair as sweet sigh-sobs lifted from his throat.

I pulled back. "Al? Is everything alright?"

"You're so lovely, and it's been ... well, it's been a long time, Karen." He laughed in soft rolls.

"Me, too. I think I've been waiting for something like this." He offered a tender, open smile. And pulled my forehead to his and gazed into my eyes. I gazed back, letting myself fall into his eyes. I saw a shy, sweet boy, a hilarious, devilish jokester poised to shock and astound, a warm but tough parent, a serious man, as bold as a flamenco dancer, and, his feminine side, a seemingly patient, earthy goddess. Perhaps it was her idea to steadily court me for a week! Al pulled me close so that I filled his arms, and we kissed again, slowly and deliberately.

Caressing my cheek, he questioned, "Do you want to say good-night?" I wanted his arms around me for a long time. I needed that. I knew there was some reason I should be resisting Al, but at that moment I couldn't think what it was. Before I could decide, just like a scene right out of a romantic comedy, Al shifted the car into reverse, and sped backwards up the 200 yards to his parking lot. His spontaneity was like intoxicating champagne. Wait, did I say yes? There he took my hand and kissed each finger and asked me seriously, "Are you sure this is what you want?" So I told him, nervously to be sure, "I want to stay with you." I felt my body-spirit being tugged by him. He didn't have to tell me what he was thinking because his eyes were spelling it out like a lit up marquee, and he said, "Oh, good, I can't think of anything more wonderful."

Thus it was that in early April of 1979, with my hands locked around his neck, Al and I literally danced in large, laughing sweeps from his car to his front door.

We were very happy in bed. We laughed repeatedly in sheer surprise that this could be happening to us. We were so different from each other. How could it be that we were together? That we thrilled each other? I wanted to curl under his arms, to be close to the warm hearth of him, and felt right at home in his embrace. It seemed that for both of us, a dam had broken, where pains of the past were being washed away.

"I never thought this could happen to me, Karen," Al whispered tenderly. I smiled into his gratitude. "After that divorce ... it was rough." I was experiencing a new feeling myself. My divorce had been tough too. We loved each other well into the night. I reveled in being both the contented lover and the one who pleased. The next morning we did it all over again.

I grabbed my t-shirt and followed Al's voice toward the kitchen. "Hey, Karen," he called out, "I'll make you a blender drink! Want one?" He was standing in his undershirt and boxers, arms stretched overhead, pulling tins off the shelf. How I enjoyed looking at him reaching toward the cabinet, the sunlight shimmering on his back. What a handsome man, I thought, so relaxed and comfortable in his underwear! He turned and saw me standing in his kitchen naked. He laughed a loving, accepting, excited laugh, as I pulled my t-shirt over my head, and yanked it down. Another surprise. I hadn't been the least bit self-consciousness about standing there in the buff! I threw my arms over his shoulders and leaned into his back, hugging him. He turned to kiss me on the nose, then said, "I got protein powder, molasses, and ... brewer's yeast." We kissed again, making twisted faces to celebrate the brewer's yeast! "Look in the fridge. See if there's anything you like."

"Are you going to make it for me?" I was radiantly surprised, as I grabbed the refrigerator handle to check out what might be inside.

"Any way you want it!" His short-order cook imitation tickled me. I watched Al take in my happiness as if it were a rare and beautiful thing. And it was. I could feel it on my face. He absorbed it, tenderly, like a butterfly visit. I grabbed a large yogurt carton from the refrigerator and watched as our breakfast items were tossed into the belly of the blender.

"Most people travel with a toothbrush. You always travel with a blender?" I teased.

"Don't leave home without it," he said, imitating Karl Malden's American Express commercial. "Come here!" I danced over to him, using the quart of vanilla yogurt to flirt with him. He opened the lid, stuck in his finger, painted my mouth with a huge dollop, and kissed it off of my lips. After that, he tossed a glob into the machine. When he pressed "Start," I felt our lives were being blended into something brand new. Al and I were a Lovin' Smoothie Delight.

Twenty-five

LOVE BONKERS ALL

"Come here, Al! I've gotta test you!"

71

I sat on the bottom shelf of the newspaper rack a few inches off the floor at the local Winn Dixie Market with a coloring book in my hands. My captivating literature was titled, "How to Improve Your Sexual Prowess," and featured pop quizzes guaranteed to miraculously transform you from inexperienced dork into an accomplished lover. These questions needed to be addressed. Okay, I admit it, we were behaving like juveniles.

"Test me? On what?"

"Your sexual prowess, of course!"

"Yikes! Well, okay, shoot!"

"Which of these – I guess they're people - is pregnant? You get lots of points for the right answer," I challenged, like a game show host. "This one?" I pointed to "A", a skinny guy, who looked like a debauched beanpole.

"I'm not sure. What else you got?" Al struggled to keep a straight face, but I wanted to crack him up.

"Well, here's "B". I showed him a transvestite dressed as an old lady in a housecoat.

"Maybe." Al feigned making a difficult decision, almost cracking up.

"Okay, or ... this one. "C" was a twenty-something beauty, wobbling like an elephant with the weight of what appeared to be 18 months of gestation in her mid-section.

"I dunno, I'm stuck!" Al burst into uncontrolled, tear-spouting laughter. "Gimme that!" he demanded like a crazed kid, snatching the magazine and pretending to need another go at it. We suddenly became aware that we had frightened off all the clientele at the Winn Dixie. Of course, we bought the book so that later Al could test everyone he encountered.

That same day Al accosted Liz. "Hey, we've got a question for ya." She took one look at the page Al held open and glared at him in stupefied disbelief that we could find this interesting, let alone funny. Liz stared at Jay as if to say, Can you believe this?! It was clear they thought we should be institutionalized, which made it all the funnier. In this way, Al and I bonded like two giddy demented teens.

Two weeks later Al approached me, his face a grim mask of fear. "Do you think it's cancer?" He was pointing to the inside of his hip crease, the groin area. I rubbed my fingers along his lower belly and asked him to move his knee toward his chest, the most rudimentary check for muscle involvement. He groaned as his knee inched upward, so my guess ran toward a pulled muscle.

"Talk to a doctor, Al. Unless you're hiding something, like other symptoms, I don't think it's cancer." He looked scared, so scared that any speculation on my part was out. I could understand why Al would fear cancer. Ida, his immigrant mother and best friend, languished for over a year in a cancer ward, disappearing -- until she was, in his words, "A twig. This big." Holding up his baby finger for emphasis, his eyelids fluttered with wonder at how she faded away. Just the thought of being in the doctor's office set off Al's fears, so he asked me to go with him.

"Cancer?" He nervously whispered, raising again this fear into consciousness as we sat in the doctor's waiting room. I shook my head no, but he remained unconvinced. After he was called in to be examined I sat there reading a magazine, confident that Al's medical complaint would be positively resolved.

Thirty minutes later he emerged beaming, picking up speed like a runaway train, the white-coated doctor tripping after him like a pet trying to keep up. "Karen," Al boomed, "the doctor wants to say hello." I shook the physician's hand as he assured me Al was fine, he just had to rest a groin muscle. It was pulled and would heal itself. I thanked him, invited him to the play, and we said our goodbyes.

"See!" I ribbed on the way to the car. Al started laughing and patting his body like a newly released prisoner. "The doctor asked me if I was into any unusually heavy physical activity, something new, or that I hadn't done in a while. Hey, you can't lie to your doctor! The only new activity is sex!" Then pausing to really trap my attention, he added, "The doctor wanted to meet the perpetrator!" He grabbed me and kissed my hair and forehead, then resumed chortling to himself. Once inside the car, behind the wheel, he shot his eyes over to mine. "Do you think we can ease up? Doctor's orders!" We both shook our heads No and burst out laughing.

Oy vey, I had a real Neil Simon character on my hands. "Hey, Al. Did you hear about the guy who goes to the doctor with a pulled groin muscle. He's 68 and his girlfriend's 33. The doctor says, 'Too much sex! You keep going on like this, it could be fatal.' The guy says, 'Doc, if she dies she dies!'"

Choking with laughter, Al punched the air above the steering wheel. "To the moon, Alice!"

73

Twenty-six

LOVE IN BLOOM

SAVE, TOSS, GIVE AWAY

A box of half-used stationery. Tucked inside it, an azalea, rosy brown, pressed and dried between sheets of the Raleigh Classifieds dated 1979. Toss, awready! Toss.

Determined to fill the doctor's Rx, we decided to spend our day off from the play taking in the local sights and force our renegade bodies to focus on the external world for a change. Our first step toward Al's rehabilitation was a day trip in his car to the Carolina Tree Festival to view the highly touted local arboreal splendor.

We weren't exactly sure where we were going, but we thought we were close to the designated area. Then we turned a corner and were suddenly knocked out by the sight of intensely colorful dogwood trees and fruit trees whose foliage, like gigantic doilies strung at varying heights, created magical patterns of light and shadow several blocks long. The vast height of the blooming towers sucked the air out of us. We gasped at the lacy beauty rising in pastel sheets above our heads. North Carolina's spring, when Mother Nature puts on a show of reawakening, fed our own giddy sense of renewal. We stopped to get out. Bending our necks back, we found it hard to see all the way to the treetops. And the waves of heady scent seemed to bring tears of wonderment to Al's eyes. Or was it just allergies?

Speechless, we returned to the car and continued driving through this phenomenal display. When we reached the end, we turned around, and drove back under the spectacular canopy for a second time.

"Well, what do you think?" I said, in awe.

"Geezus," was all Al could muster. Then he covered his mouth with his hand and whispered, "This is like stealing!"

Twenty-seven

THE PLAY'S THE THING

I leaned against the pillows at one end of the couch, while Al was at the other, our socked feet touching in the middle. We'd both been reading for a spell when I broke the silence. "What part did you want that you never got to play?"

"I always wanted to play Alfred P. Doolittle in My Fair Lady." I woulda been good in that part." Then bursting into song, Al belted, "With a little bit of luck, with a little bit of luck, with a little bit of bloomin' luck!" He was slightly off key, but sounded great, his gusto passing for brilliance.

But I didn't want to let Al off the hook that easily, so I goaded him. "But wait, Al. Isn't My Fair Lady a <u>love</u> story?"

"Love story? Ha!" retorted the well-spoken Mr. Lewis. "Shaw wrote the original. He was getting back at stupid men, male chauvinists. Professor Higgins is doin' a makeover. He wants to change Liza Doolittle."

"And you? Aren't you a bit of a Henry Higgins?" I mock argued.

"Yeah. You could say that. But there's a major difference here. I have no personal stake. I'm in it for the greater good." He beamed at me like the Cheshire Cat, a real shit-eating grin.

"The part I always wanted to play was Lady MacBeth. You know, Shakespeare? You've heard of him?!"

"Terrible!" Al's face went sour.

"What's wrong with Shakespeare!"

"Over-rated," Al insisted, flipping me into mental turmoil.

"I was in thirteen Shakespeare plays," I asserted. "Some of them more than once. He's lasted for centuries."

"But does anybody really understand what he's saying? Wait three hours for a great, quotable line. People pretend to love him. Why? Cuz he's Shakespeare!" I knew when I'd been had. My laughter chugged out like pieces of shattered statuary. "Hey Al, if the audience members in the Pit at the Old Globe got it, so can you! Maybe it's a question of who's directing."

"Yeh, directors are important alright. Do you know Jose Quintero?"

"He's a great director."

"You ain't kiddin'." Al paused for a second and asked, "Ever want anything so bad you behaved like a caged tiger?" My eyes grew wide.

"No ..."

"Ever read Jose's book? *If You Can't Dance, They Shoot You*?

That sums it up, doesn't it! I'm in that book. I auditioned for Jose when he was directing *Iceman Cometh*, by Eugene O'Neill. When I learned Jose was directing, I said nothing's going to stand in my way. I've gotta be in that play. So did all my actor friends when they got word. All those wonderful character parts. I went down to the theater immediately to see if they had a script. No dice. But one of my friends got hold of a copy and he passed it around. I couldn't believe all those amazing parts, losers and dreamers, down and out at Harry Hope's bar. There was a police officer by the name of Lieutenant Pat McGloin, a tough New Yorker, part crook and part cop. Something I could sink my teeth into. The more I read, the more I wanted to be in it. Then a friend of mine told me, 'No reflection on your acting, Al. I think you'd be good in that part, but Jose Quintero is one tough hombre. It's impossible to get in to read for him.' So, what good's my talent and desire if I can't even audition?"

"Ain't that the truth," I agreed. "That sums up my last months in New York."

"You know then. I got so worked up about playing McGloin that I decided nothin' would stop me from at least talking to Jose. So I sneaked in the front door and barged right into the theater yelling at the top of my lungs, 'Where's Mr. Quintero? I gotta see him! Where's Mr. Quintero? Where's Mr. Quintero?'"

"A bull in a china shop."

"That's what I'm tryin' to tell you. Finally a lady came out, his secretary, I think. She looked like she was going to have a heart attack, I was makin' so much noise! She tried to calm me down by telling me to wait, she'd be right back, but I followed behind her right into the office. Suddenly there I was in a room full of people. What could I do? I started shouting! 'I want to meet this Quintero guy, the director!' When this little man said he was the director, I was sure he was protecting the real Jose. So I said, 'You're not Jose Quintero!' He said, 'Yes I am.' 'Well, you don't look like Quintero!' What could I say to save face?"

"Oh, Al, how could you barge in like that?" I asked in astonished disbelief.

"Well ... Jose asked me the same thing! What was I doing in his office? So I told him I love this play. And I pulled out the beaten-up script I'd rolled up in my pocket. 'I fell in love with the character of Pat McGloin, the police lieutenant. I want to play that part more than anything. I guess I blew it. But it was a pleasure to meet you, Mr. Quintero. I saw the plays you directed and you are the genuine article. You rate pretty high in my book. You see, this friend of mine told me I'd never get to see you otherwise. Well, I'm gonna find him and kick him around the block.' I went to shake his hand and that's when he looked me in the eye and said he liked me! That I had the kind of energy he needed for his play. He asked me to show up for the first rehearsal in a coupla days! Can you beat that?"

I just looked at Al. "I don't know if you're a genius or a maniac, but your pluck ... amazing, Al."

"Karen, it's hard to explain how it feels when you're part of something that explodes. In the positive sense, that is. The play focused on the marginalized people that society gives up on. Each one of them hiding behind a dream so he can get by. You know, saving face through the lies he tells. Up till then, heroes in plays were all noble or noble gone sour, but in this play ordinary people were considered important. Not heroes exactly, but human beings who struggle with life."

As he spoke I saw in Al the Everyman ready to fight for the little guy. I felt tenderness humming in my heart.

"I had an exhilarating ride during the Bay Area Theater movement of the '60s and '70s and I can understand your excitement, Al." He nodded. We just sat there in the hilarious wreckage of his wild success story. Emotionally exhausted from telling me his most personally meaningful theater tale, he grabbed my hands and mumbled, "I can't believe you know all these plays ... You know what I'm talkin' about, don't you?" I was high on our shared feeling that the theater was absolutely essential to our lives.

"You understand my life as performer, Al. There were men who dated and dropped me as soon as they discovered I was an actress with a crazy performance schedule." He looked up at me aglow, and I saw for the first time that this entrance into each others' lives was bringing a mutual hope.

Twenty-eight

DOUBLE TAKES

In yet another greasy spoon, Al was leaning back against a taped-up vinyl cushion, patched to keep the stuffing inside. His right arm rested on the seat back, while his left leg was stretched out on the seat cushion. "Ever meet Neil Simon?" he asked.

"No," I said.

"Ever see *The Sunshine Boys*?"

"No."

"Ever read it?" I got the feeling that this was important, but there was no fudging with this guy. I'd have to take it on the chin.

"No, I haven't."

He rolled his eyes and waved his wrist in my direction. His comedic over-reaction declared, Why am I talking to you? I'd been dismissed and sat quietly like a comedy foil waiting for the other clown shoe to drop. The leg came down. The arm came down. Al now sat squarely across from me. He'd decided to let me in after all.

"I knew Neil Simon. He told me he wanted to talk with me. Neil wanted to hear my vaudeville stories. If you knew *The Sunshine Boys*, you'd know that one of the characters is named Al Lewis. That's me." His eyes darted around the stained soundproofing on the ceiling. The rest of him was still as a mountain.

"You're right, Al. I don't know *The Sunshine Boys*. I was busy wasting my time playing in these little unimportant make-believe skits. Oh, you know, *Hamlet, Uncle Vanya, Electra, The Duchess of Malfi* ... "

"Yeh, yeh, but read that sometime. It's full of my shtick. Neil noticed that I use my index finger a lot!" Al started laughing at himself.

"Yeh, I saw you poking Jay and Liz in the breastbone with that digit!"

"Apparently Neil Simon picked up my characteristic gesture to use in his play."

"What else did he use?"

"All my stories, my way of tellin' 'em. Hey, my past. He stole my identity."

"Why didn't he just cast you instead of ripping you off?"

"If I knew the answer to that ... I thought he would cast me. That's why I gave him all that material."

"Gee, Al, how'd that make you feel?"

"Heh. Well, Karen, I'm over it now, but it brought up the whole Show Biz system, how it'll bleed you dry. Simon called the play's comedy team Lewis and Clark. After me. Ever hear of Bobby Clark?"

"The guy with glasses?"

"Okay, score one for the thespian! Yeah, he used to paint those glasses right on his face. It was his personal hallmark. I trained with Bobby for, huh, about a year, I guess, maybe more. Brutal. Just brutal. Pratfalls and double takes. What am I saying? Double takes? Triple. Quadruple-takes, until I thought my neck would fall off." Al guffawed loudly.

"You know double-takes?" I nodded in the affirmative. "But do you know how to do one? Really pull it off?" I quickly jumped into a little double-take inspired by my bird-like, old lady character from *Arsenic and Old Lace*. I stared at the swinging kitchen door, then back at Al, and then focused my eyes on the door a second time, as if the kitchen was on fire. "Not bad, huh?"

"Nah!" griped Al. "One you can see!" Al showed me how it was done. The set up is a road accident and he's an old lady rubbernecker cruising past. She's holding a huge handbag. First she stares at the accident and covers her eyes with the bag. She looks again, grasps it despairingly to her heart. She looks a third time, and sinks her teeth into it!

Every gesture was clean and huge, and I was sure I saw her in her car moving slowly past the accident! Al was hilarious, a skilled and dynamic clown.

"Ya know how long that took to master? Huh. About a year. Three hours a day for a year. Shit. Nobody does physical comedy any more." Al's eyes softened. He seemed to be drifting back to that studio, having his act whipped into shape by the autocratic Bobby Clark.

"Yeh. Either you do it right, or don't bother. Unfortunately, most people don't do it right and they do bother. They bother me."

I agreed. "You have to go way back until you can find someone who did it right. What do you think of Charlie Chaplin?" I questioned, hoping I wouldn't be slammed down.

"Charlie? Charles Chaplin? No one could touch him. I used to take my kids to see his movies. One of those wonderful dads in the neighborhood would hang up a sheet and project Chaplin films right there in his backyard. The kids loved them. God, they would laugh. He was a master. If he didn't get the scene he wanted, he'd stop filming until he figured it out. Did you know he'd let everybody go, all the actors, while he went back to the studio and reworked everything? But they were still on the payroll! Hollywood hated him for that. Hated him. Do you see what a precedent that would have set? Paying actors when they're not working! Fortunately for the studios it never caught on."

Al's colorful, entertaining (albeit longwinded) stories touched me. It was the passion behind them that got inside me and stirred up my thinking.

Twenty-nine

HARD CASE

SAVE, TOSS, GIVE AWAY

It has a slash in its dark chocolate side, and it takes a helluva lot of shoving to get the metal closings to line up, but the American Tourister luggage is still with me. We've been through a lot together. Maybe I should have it bronzed. Save.

We were 8 weeks into our 14-week contract and I was restless. Although I really wanted to know what Al thought of my acting, I feared what he might say. Fortunately, I spent several years of my life engaged in certain transformative, grounding experiences, such as psychotherapy, meditation, and Tae Kwon Do. The most difficult method was Gestalt Therapy, developed by Fritz Perls and his powerful technique called the hot seat. It was a kind of psychological firing squad against neuroses. When you sat on the hot seat, you agreed to listen to what others in the group really thought about you. It wasn't easy hearing their scathing critiques, but I got through it. Asking Al for his opinion couldn't be worse than that.

So I closed my eyes, took a deep breath and jumped in. "Al, will you watch my Academy Award scene in the play tonight?" Al said, "Sure."

That night I performed my scene and was conscious that Al was watching. So I did my best and really put myself into it. I met him in the hallway backstage and, anxious to hear his critique, asked him, "So, what'd you think?

"Sorta mechanical."

"Go to hell, Al." And I walked away.

For several days I questioned Al's statement and my reaction to it. I felt angry, but with little stabs of conscience about not sticking around to hear the rest. Was I really going to let fear and defensiveness hold me back? Of course. But at last I worked up enough courage and went to Al to hear his critique. "You sure?" said Al. "I lost a coupla friends this way."

"Including me," I said, "But I'll give you another chance."

"See, I don't do this unless the other person asks," Al said, looking directly at me, his face open and soft, sitting in the living room of his apartment where we would not be interrupted. "You know, for most people it's too icky. You're kinda thin-skinned."

"Just get on with it, Al. I'm trying to better myself by being open to objective criticism."

"So you really know who to believe, huh? There's only one person. Yourself. You gotta have hide as thick as a rhinoceros."

"So why'd you say you'd help me?" But he didn't bite.

"I want to know what you're going to do with my response," he said seriously.

"If it's good you get my eternal devotion. If it's bad, you can fold it five ways and stick it where the sun don't shine!" My cockiness made him laugh but didn't impress him like I hoped it would. I surrendered, "Okay. I'll try to separate the wheat from the chaff. Just go easy on the chaff."

"Try! You'd better DO IT if you're going to get along in this business."

"Alright. Semantics. I am doing fine in this business. Play after play. Great reviews. Audience acceptance. A paycheck every week. The longest I was ever unemployed was six months. Once!" Al was into evidence so I thought my response was convincing.

"And you believe in yourself." Al paused, giving me time to react, but I couldn't figure out where he was going with that statement, and fell silent. He continued. "All at the same theater?"

"Basically. Three or four others. To fill in."

"How long were you there?"

"Ten years at The Berkeley Rep." I said with some pride as I was somewhat of a local celebrity. "I stayed for the Tenth Anniversary!"

"And you say you believe in yourself?"

"Huh? Well, sure I do. I left Berkeley because they were giving me the same kinds of roles over and over again. Yeah, difficult character roles, but I wanted to try my wings."

The epitome of calm, Al said, "Ten years in one place ... I'm just asking ... why you didn't leave before now?" He sounded different, rather like a sympathetic ... what? Attorney?

"Well, I was married, part of the time. I got great roles. I was building a reputation."

"In Berkeley?!"

"Yes, in Berkeley. Remember? 'The Rape Capital of the World'?" My pride took a hit so I countered. "It's right near San Francisco, you know, California?"

81

"Calm down. I'm just saying that if you're good and you believe in yourself, you'd probably get out of a little place like that to get into the action."

"Geez. Well, dammit, here I am in Raleigh! And you are too."

"Let's forget this."

"No. I came for your opinion and I want it."

"Awright, but don't get so upset. This is nothin'. Nothin' compared to the real shocks you can get in this business." He waited until he saw my face muscles relax a bit. "So, you all right?" Then he looked into my eyes and hugged me. "I care about you, or I'd never agree to this."

This is caring? I consciously took another deep breath and pressed on. "So. Did you watch my scene?"

"I listened to it."

"Listened to it?"

"Yeh. It sounded like a bad radio play. So I didn't really watch it. I caught a coupla minutes."

"A bad radio play??" Damn you, Al. A lump was forming in my throat.

"Yeh. First Jay talks loud and full of import. Then you talk loud and full of import. No spaces, no breathing, no listening."

"Well, the director told me to pick up every cue. I had to ..."

"Well, what if the director is wrong?"

Oh, here we go. A rerun of all the trouble he caused Jack in rehearsal. "I follow my marching orders!"

"You don't get any of this," Al quietly declared.

Now he's criticizing my intelligence. "Jack really likes what I'm doing," I retorted defensively. "He said that I was the best actress to audition, the best thing to 'come down the pike.'"

"Okay, you were the best he saw. Sometimes people – in life – don't know what they're doing. That's what I mean you gotta trust yourself. There aren't any rules. Nobody says you're going to jail if you take a pause, like a real person takes a pause."

"Well, he drilled us and drilled us. 'Take out all the slack,' is what he said."

Al began to shake his head. "Take out all the slack. Take out all the slack." Then he actually rolled his head heavenward. "Take out all the life, the passion, the heartbeat. White Bread. Oh, you fell for the message." Al breathed deeply. "Look, honey, I just didn't believe you."

"Well, the audience did. They clapped and clapped."

"And that's good enough?"

"Isn't that the point? To entertain the audience?" I began to feel like I was back in Acting 1-A. Al went on. "For example, you're

82

supposed to be married to that guy. I didn't believe that relationship. He coulda been the super of the building!"

"The super of the building ...!" I huffed.

"Don't be melodramatic. Tell the truth."

Still indignant, I whacked him with a killer excuse. "We only had six days to get this play on its feet!"

"So did I. So did everybody. That's no excuse for lying on stage."

"Lying? I'm lying now?" I felt like I'd moved from acting class to a police lineup, only the police were Lee Strasberg, Stella Adler, and Alligator Al, the Believability Squad SWAT Chiefs of the Stanislavsky Gestapo.

"Well, there's not much I can do about it now!"

"Yes, you can. You can think about it and see what happens on stage."

"It's set. It's been set since opening night. I can't change things without rehearsing with Jay."

"You don't have to. It's his job to stay alert. The scene doesn't have to be frozen in time, like you're going to the freezer every night just in time to thaw it out before the show starts. Instead, you can start over each night with the idea that this is happening to you for the first time. It's liberating." Al was cheerfully optimistic.

"Don't talk down to me. You're raking me over the coals because you didn't like the reviews ..."

"Reviews! Look, young lady, I've never read a single review of a play I've been in and I don't intend to start now. What does it say over the Moscow Art Theater?"

"Heck, I don't know, Al. You're changing the subject." That really fired him up.

"It says, TO ACT IS TO DO! It doesn't say, to act is to comment. And I don't need some critic to tell me what's good. I know. I'm there on stage!"

Then he looked at me with burning, infuriating warmth and said, "You're making too much of the wrong things and not enough of the right things."

"Well, the review said I was the best."

"If the best mark in the class is a C+, does that make it good?"

"Yeah, if you grade on a curve."

"I'm saying, if all the actors in the play are bad and you stand out, does that make you good?"

"Gee, don't you ever let up? Now you're saying I'm a lousy

83

actress." I was so frustrated that I lost it. I began to growl-cry. Round fat tears rolled down my face as if my head was a giant sea sponge. Every exhalation squeezed out more salty drops.

"So I say it ... or somebody else says it. But only you know if it's true or not. It only matters what you think is true."

"Do you have any friends? How could you? Why can't you let people be? Always prodding and poking ..." He moved toward me with that index finger extended, but he didn't poke me with it. He put his arms around me. But that didn't quell my anger!

"All I said was I didn't believe your performance. I didn't say you were a bad person." He chortled, actually warmly chortled, like he was making light of a scraped knee, then pulled me closer.

"Take your hands off me!"

"If I didn't care about you, do you think I'd spend all this time and effort on this? Giving you my opinion?"

"What kind of crazy caring is this?" And I actually pounded on him!

"Thatta girl. Get it out. Get it all out."

"Oh, go to hell. Don't patronize me, you bastard!"

And he gently let me go. "None of this would bother you if it wasn't the truth. A little tiny bit of the truth." Goddam Fritz Perls wannabe bastard! Al simply lit his cigar and picked up the paper while I was crying, sitting in the slightly worn chintz-covered club chair. Even that made me mad. Worn out chintz! Pink flowered cloth that had seen better days. So goddamned apt, I cried again and left.

For several days I was guarded and spent my time evaluating my desire to be near a man who behaved like Al. In other words, questioning my sanity. Knowing that he'd pushed me to the limit, Al quietly waited to see how I'd process our conflict. Deep down I knew that he was right, that I could uncover a more honest performance if I wasn't so defensive.

During the next performance, I let go and made small, achievable aims, like pretending the Academy Award scene was happening for the first time, and – damn you, Al - the show did get better!

On the surface, that painful critique appeared to be about the art of acting, but it was also about being courageously present in my own life and committing to the truth. Like sighing out a breath of relief, I felt myself entering into a powerful state of equanimity. I figured if Al and I were meant for each other, wonderful. If not, so be it. I had to honor the truth.

It was Al who reached out first.

"Being with you is like walking on egg shells, Miss ... I mean, <u>Ms.</u> Pennywhistle!"

"Well, being with you is like getting sandblasted, Mister ... I mean, Doctor Freud!"

"I love you, ya know."

"You express it kinda funny, Mr. Lewis."

"Well, you wanted the truth."

"Yeah, I did. Thank you. But it's not always easy to accept." I smiled and closed my eyes, relieved at having had the conversation that I'd been afraid to face. I felt a flutter like flighty wings on my cheeks. Al was kissing my eyelids, so tenderly. I felt him going in for The Kiss ... then moving away.

"You need some good luggage," he said. Huh?? What just happened? He was about to kiss me and then pulled back. Oh, Mr. Critic has intimacy issues. "You know, luggage that'll last. Not fall apart on the tarmac!" Al sputtered gleefully. "You remember your duffle bag when you arrived in Raleigh? Your underwear popping out of the seams? Heh heh heh."

"Why are you talking about luggage right now?"

"You didn't see the paper?" Al produced from his inside jacket pocket a ripped-out ad for American Tourister. A big sale.

"Let's check it out!"

"What? You mean right now? Weren't we going to do something else just now?"

"Yeh, let's go look," Al insisted. So, I guess the make-up kiss would have to wait.

"Why don't we just go to an Army Navy Store and get another duffel bag?" I asked.

"You kiddin'? Miss out on a sale?"

At the luggage store, sure enough, Big Sale signs loomed everywhere. The store staff instantly stormed Al, going happily berserk greeting Grandpa Munster. "Hey, it's him! It's Grandpa!" They'd seen the play. They'd seen every episode of *The Munsters*. They were high-fiving him, throwing him favorite "Grandpa" lines, and shaking hands. I looked around and realized that I couldn't afford anything there. My heart began to sink. Even with a discount, I was in a pauper's panic. What am I going to say to Al?! 'I need to think it over'? Then Al really put the screws on me. "Tell 'em what you need, Karen!" Then he stepped back, chewing on a dead Avanti, to look at wallets and leather suitcase tags, while I moved toward the sale display and smaller (read: cheaper) bags.

"You travel a lot?" The salesman glanced at Al, then at me, and putting two and two together, quickly opened a deluxe model. Al surged forward like an iceboat on the East River, bellowing, "You'll never get all your stuff in THAT!" Okay, Karen, MasterCard. Just think MasterCard. You can pay it off over the next year. Keep smiling.

"You don't know how to pick out a suitcase," Al grumbled as he rushed back into the conversation he'd sidelined. "Show me what you got." After viewing three examples, Goldilocks Lewis picked one that was – not too big, not too small, but ju-u-u-st right. I had to admit to myself that it was very nice.

"We'll take this one!" Al proclaimed.

"Nooo ..." I stammered. "I can't ..." Al reached into his pocket, producing a roll of bills.

"You get the next one," he murmured in a soft throaty voice, and pushed me aside to accompany the item to the register.

"Al, it's beautiful. I can't afford it ... Why?" I felt bewildered and grateful.

"Because I can. When I'm doing well, then those around me should do well," he mumbled humbly, as if he'd bought me a piece of chewing gum or an ice cream cone.

"Al bought you luggage? Tourister! It's so expensive!" Mom was oooh'ing into the phone, obviously impressed by his generosity. To her it meant he cared.

"It is spectacular, Mom." All the same, I felt ashamed that at my age I didn't have money to buy my own. And I wondered, was this a guilt-gift for raking me over the coals about acting? Or ... maybe he really loved me!

Back at the theater, the stage manager reminded us, "We're moving to Charlotte on Monday!"

"Oh, boy, packing. You'd think I'd get used to it." Al looked like he'd received a detention slip from his teacher. Grinning, Jay zinged Al, "The old nomad hates packing!"

"You don't like to pack?" I stood gaping at him in disbelief. "I'll help you. I don't mind." After years of travel, I rather enjoyed the challenge.

"Yeh?" Al looked relieved.

Al sat on the couch in his living room pretending to read while I lined up his luggage and then his clothes. Hmm? So this is payback for the expensive suitcase. But I really didn't mind. Folding one of his suit jackets, he stopped me, gently grabbing my wrist and taking it out of my hands. He swiftly turned the garment inside out, folding it

86

in half along the back seam and adjusting the sleeves. Then, with a magnificent gesture, he folded it in thirds.

"Oh, so you don't know how to pack, huh?"

"Boxer," he said, "in Howard's Clothing Store, Brooklyn. My after school job!" He recalled the sweet days of tissue papered suit boxes, tied professionally with string and little wooden carry-handles. I loved the way the jacket's collar was protected by Al's folding technique. A new travel tip, straight from the Stump Al Lewis Show! Was there anything he hadn't done, or any subject he wasn't an expert on?

Thirty

NO FRILLS

"Just follow my van!" yelled the stage manager, hanging out of the driver's side waving us on. "You won't lose us. We're takin' it slow. Don't want our scenery scattered on the highway!" he said with a puckish grin. The drivers lined up their cars, creating a caravan heading toward Charlotte and the new venue for our play.

We passed through the lush southern counties of North Carolina like a wagon train, in time for a second viewing of Mother Nature's spectacular display of blooming trees. We drove through a virtual wonderland of spring petals fluttering from their branches, creating the illusion of snow, banked on low green hills, piled at the roots of the trees. I think we all got a little high and goofy from the visual orgy of spring, our movement through the verdant countryside, gliding in our spacious vehicles, windows rolled down, inhaling the scent-filled air. The blossoming had a profound affect on my wellbeing, sending me into a state of bliss, filling me with positive feelings for humanity, particularly for my partner, Al. Partner. That was my word for our relationship. I couldn't help wondering what Al's word was. I drifted into the most open part of my mind, floating above my insecurities.

"Snake oil."

"What, Al?"

"Snake oil. I was here before, you know. During the Depression. Selling snake oil." He watched my head snap backwards and my eyes bug out. Here we go again, I thought. He loves to hook me in like that. "I'd follow the revival meeting preachers," he excitedly continued. "Why? I knew they'd gather a crowd! I know the entire Oral Roberts spiel by heart. Heard it a million times.

"'I'm here to save yer soul. Hallelujah! Come to Jesus.' I cut a deal with the preacher. Then I could set up next to the revival tent, where people would be streaming out of the meeting. I had concocted a brew in a rooming house bathtub and bottled it. Little Alfie's Snake Oil, to fix whatever ails you! As soon as the revival meeting ended, I began my pitch. 'The preacher saved your soul! I'm here to save your body!' Of course, most folks always felt better after a single dose, with alcohol as its primary ingredient."

"Al, you've told me a lot of amazing stories like this about your past, but what about our story? How do you feel about us, Al?"

"Judge me by my actions."

"Okay, you're the man who fools people into buying snake oil! You mean that action?"

"You can't interfere with anyone trying to make money for his family, Karen."

"But that was illegal!"

"You use what you got to get what you need."

"Yes, but ..."

"It was during the Depression, Karen. And in the South."

"Well, what difference does that make?"

"Heh. The South ain't nice to Jews, blacks, gays, or ... divorcees!" he cackled, comically including me.

Master of the snappy comeback, but still no emotional commitment from Slippery Al. Was this his technique for pushing me away? Or waking me up? I looked out of the car's open window at the romantic Southern view, the hot spring air swirling around my face, and wondered if I was under a spell or just plain deluded by a charismatic snake oil salesman. A relationship like that was certainly nothing to write home about.

At The Pineville Dinner Theater we were given schedules and orientation. "Al's apartment is here," said the Administrative Assistant, pointing to a spot on the Charlotte map she'd copied for us. "The other actors will live over there." The star's apartment was about five miles away from the actors' complex.

"Gee, that's terrible," Al said softly into my ear. "You forget your toothbrush, I ain't goin' back for it!" he humorously leered.

"That's fine, Al, because you're not making snake oil in my bathtub!"

I was startled by the loud ringing of the phone in my new apartment.

"Karen? This is your mother."

"Hi, Mom! I just sent you a postcard."

"I got it. I was wondering where you were. Listen to this. 78 Across. Pacino and Lewis."

"Als," I hollered.

"Right! Good, huh? How's everything? Still in love?"

"This man is so interesting, Mom." I didn't mention Al's reluctance to commit. I told her what a wonderful raconteur Al was, avoiding the word *storyteller*.

"Oh, you. Uranus in Gemini! You always love eccentric men."

"Mom, you don't know the half of it."

Al drove the five miles from his apartment to mine. "Hey, it's almost your birthday. Whadda ya want?"

I gulped. Nobody except my mother had asked me that in years. "I don't want anything, Al. Just share the day with me."

"Okay, but don't you want a present?"

In one and a half seconds, this part of my life flashed through my mind: In all my years struggling in the theater, at the edge of poverty, I shared my life with similarly situated artists. Friends gave token gifts, and surprises, such as custom made songs, poems or dances, flowers or food. Those were presents that were fun and easy to reciprocate. But now Al's giant gifts were overwhelming and impossible to match. His enormous generosity put me in a position of feeling indebted to him.

"You already gave me a present. I love my suitcase," I said.

"I'll take you to the mall and you can pick out what you want." Al insisted. Well, you can't say no to Big Hearted Al because he'll never let up.

"Okay, I'll do it for you."

"No, it's for you!"

The Mall. I heard Al's impatient voice in my head as I wandered around wondering what I could comfortably ask him to give me. "Pick something out, anything you want ..." The whole situation was too loaded. Then I thought, Lingerie! Maybe that would please him and pleasing him would make me happy. After sweating over the price tags, I selected a slinky nightgown, relieved that my task was completed. I found Al sitting in the food court and told him I was all set and I'd take him to see what I'd picked out. He followed me through the department store as we made our way along aisles of shimmering undergarments to my rack of frilly nightwear. I lifted out the item I'd chosen ... for him. A look of innocent shock crossed his face.

"What do you want that for?" he stammered incredulously. My heart stopped, and then dropped into my stomach. Fight or flight? Flight; period. I turned on my heel with karate precision and flew out of the store, my feet barely touching the carpet. Outside the door, I tried to catch my breath and gather my thoughts. I turned to see Al loping toward me, looking confused.

"Didn't you want it?"

"No. I changed my mind." I jetted down the mall esplanade, cheeks burning, eyes straight ahead, Al right on my tail.

"What's wrong?" he huffed. "I thought you wanted the nightgown. You don't want it? What?" I bit my lip and kept moving.

"Forget about it, Al. I never wanted a nightgown." It wasn't a lie. I never wanted it. I thought the icky feelings about picking out the gift would go away once I'd chosen something I thought he would like. I was too embarrassed to even speak to him. My brain was on overload and starting to shut down. He walked beside me now bemused and a bit forlorn. "How about some ice cream? That sounds good, doesn't it?"

I numbly followed him to an ice cream vendor, then robotically picked a flavor. Licking it, cold and creamy, grounded me and cooled my overheated synapses. A Feminist Failure, that's what I felt like. Did I fall on my face on my own? Or did Al pull the rug out from under me?

Still licking my wounds along with my ice cream, I was finally able to speak, but not about my feelings. "Peanut Butter Brickle! Thanks, Al." It was delicious and bumpy. The ice cream was Al's idea and it was working wonders to bring me around. I was almost myself again, the woman eating an ice cream cone with her friend, Al Lewis, the guy who never lied to her.

"Happy Birthday! It's your birthday! Hey, birthday baby, open your presents." Al charged through the doorway of my apartment with two large bundles bobbing in his arms. He tossed a padded package to me! With great trepidation and anticipation, I gingerly tore off the pretty wrapping paper and a thick layer of newspaper to discover a large ceramic mask depicting Tragedy.

"Oh, my, oh my." I touched the cool, marbled surface of the mask. "Al, did you know I studied Greek Theater at Berkeley?" and holding it near the light from my window, continued. "I even played

Electra. Thank you! Wow, where did you find this!" Al looked so pleased I had to rib him. "Hey, he looks a bit like you!" That was funny but also true.

"Don't scare me," Al kidded. "I'm the other guy, Comedy!" This mask offered a glimpse into this complex person who had gone to great lengths to find it. A gift that suited me perfectly. "You're a very special person, Al."

"One more!" Al yelled, hiding his delight. The second gift that Al tossed into my arms on my 34th birthday was a mesmerizing drawing by Evie Chang, a landscape which appeared to magically shimmer. It was filled with dense shadows of trees and clouds, and grasses that fluttered near a path and a pool.

"Oh, I love it. I now own Real Art!"

These gifts, though smaller than a suitcase, were overwhelming in their own way.

"Thank you so much." I started to cry. Al quickly brushed away my tears with the side of his hand, and began softly laughing.

"Like 'em?" He smiled.

"Oh, my God, yes."

"Good. Here's the bill! Nah, just kiddin'."

"You rat!" I teased, punching him in the shoulder.

After the show that night a bunch of us went out for drinks and my birthday was toasted. Hospitality flowed like mint juleps in Charlotte. "Tell 'em what you got! Go on, tell 'em!" Al, like a proud grandfather, wanted me to produce a show-n-tell. But I felt awkward, afraid that this feeling of love would evaporate if I displayed the teensiest amount of hubris. I cautiously described Al's presents, humbly downplaying their significance. I'm sure it was not the performance he wanted. He had been angling for a joyous explosion. A young costume assistant whispered with excitement, "Only Al Lewis would know exactly what to get you. See! He's brilliant and kind and thoughtful and ... penetrating! He even knows about Greek Theater!" Her eyes glowed with vicarious pleasure, the face of a true fan, enjoying my good fortune and the cleverness of her beloved idol. This world was new to me, and I found myself floundering uncomfortably, surrounded by people who eagerly engaged in star worship. But wasn't she right about Al? Hadn't he gone to great lengths to find the gifts that perfectly suited me? And he certainly was a giver! It seems that gift-giving is Al's special way to express love and intimacy.

Thirty-one

LOST IN THE SHUFFLE

"Yeah, good morning to you too!" Al had rolled to the side of the bed to grab the ringing phone. It was barely seven o'clock. "Thank you. Thank you very much. Yes, I'm now officially 69 years young!" It was the local radio station wishing him Happy Birthday.

"Seven o'clock," I grumbled with a pillow over my head. "What's next, Al? Are you going to open our bedroom to reporters?"

"It's Drive Time. Those guys start early." Al was always in professional mode, but this morning he was in high gear and he hadn't even brushed his teeth yet. Then the broader media from New York and L.A. called for interviews and photo ops were requested by our theater and the local paper. So much for the intimate birthday breakfast I had planned. Al's day became so public that my participation in it was lost in a tidal wave of affection from the theater staff, city officials, fans, reporters, family, friends and strangers.

"I gotta go downtown. Newspaper office. Wanna come?" Well that's that. I tossed my heart-shaped strawberry pancakes into the trash.

"I don't really feel like tagging along, but hey, it's your birthday."

"You can make good contacts," Al enthused.

"Yeah, right, that's gonna happen." I dressed to go with him, choosing a more professional looking outfit instead of the clown pj's and colorful toe socks I was going to wear for our intimate party, before my plans were wrecked.

I was surprised to see the scope of Charlotte's newspaper office with its many floors and doors. After the reporter greeted Al, she turned to me.

"Who are you? What are you doing here?" Oh no, what had Al dragged me into now?

"I'm in the play, too," I stammered, and could think of nothing else to say. I didn't have a label for my relationship with Al and he wouldn't supply one. If Al was teaching me to swim in his world, he'd just thrown me into the deep end.

"Ready for the next one?" Al chortled, heading for the door, pleased with his progress, and not waiting for my answer. After that hour of hovering at the newspaper office while Al held court, I saw no purpose in sticking around any longer. I ducked out and went home. I sat down to write all the letters I would have already written if Al

Lewis hadn't been absorbing most of my leisure time. I felt left out of all the excitement, curled up alone in my room. At least I didn't have to explain to anyone that I couldn't find my place in Al's public life. And maybe by walking out today, Al would view me as an independent woman with her own agenda. That is, if he noticed I was gone.

That evening, we were costumed and waiting by the stage elevator when we heard over the PA system: "Pineville Dinner Theatre proudly celebrates the birthday of our star – Al Lewis! Who is 69 years young tonight! Join me in wishing him a very Happy Birthday!" That announcement set the tone for the rest of the evening. Rustling into the excitement, the audience lapped up the news. They'd clearly picked the best date to see the show! Geez, did everyone celebrate Al Lewis's birthday? Everyone? Everywhere? Around the world? Wherever they got a TV signal?

Like a reporter sidelined from the action, I observed Al from the shadows working the crowd. Sixty-nine? Impossible. I'd never met anyone with as swift a mind or with so much stamina.

After all his bows and encores, Al finally made it back to his dressing room. "Help me with this stuff. You got a bag?" Al needed a huge shopping bag for all the presents that had arrived. We then hustled off to an after-theater birthday toast.

Earlier, when Al told me he wanted nothing for his birthday, I went through quite an inward struggle. I kept thinking about my birthday and all that I went through. I didn't want to repeat that for Al. So, do I take him literally, or get him something he would really like that I could afford? I settled on a poem, a homemade certificate for a massage, and a breakfast invitation, which I artistically organized into a birthday card. I slipped my card into the stack of other cards addressed to Al. After cake and drinks with the cast, we got back very late that night. This was the first time I got to speak to him alone. "Al, did you see my card?"

"It must be in the pile with the others," he sweetly replied. Ouch. Still, I wanted to share my birthday poem with him before the day ended. So I dug through the foot-high heap of commercial Hallmark cards to fetch my little homemade one.

"Here it is." And I read: "Al in a clown suit, zoot suit, paternity suit heavenly nose discloses roses ..." In the moment it took me to read those words, Al had fallen fast asleep with his clothes on, his face lost in the couch cushions. I felt hurt and quite lonely. I put a blanket over him and went to bed alone.

Early the next morning, Al questioned, "Didn't you give me a card? Where is it?"

"Right here," I groaned still disappointed and hurt. Al shook open the envelope and all the contents fluttered on the bedspread.

"You wrote this?! For me? Wow. That's beautiful. Funny, and beautiful," he beamed. "Get over here," he grinned, happy as a clam, and kissed me. "I got a Certificate right here, so get busy! Are you a masseuse, or not!?"

"I can't massage you right now. I might wring your neck!" Al laughed.

"Yesterday was brutal, Karen. Work had to come first. I'm building audiences. It's business."

"Yes, it is Al, and you work very hard at it. But now I've got to go take care of my own business." I went back to my place and made myself some heart shaped strawberry pancakes and pulled out my diary.

> *DEAR DIARY:*
> *My feelings are hurt. That's right, hurt. Al seems to*
> *know his business really well. But, what business do I*
> *have being with Al?*

Thirty-two

SCHOOL OF HARD KNOCKS

SAVE, TOSS, GIVE AWAY

More clothes to take to the thrift store. I'm making headway,
clearing out the bottom dresser drawer. There it is, a bundle
wrapped over a broken board and tied in a square knot with a Black
Belt. My old karate uniform, my gi, tied up with the first board I
ever broke ... Give away.

Settled in Charlotte, Al called me from his apartment. "I got one! Yup, I got one. Wanna go test it out?"

"Got what, Al?"

"A karate school for you, that's all!" He was pretty proud of himself. I'd even forgotten that he said he'd look for one. Well, Al did say I should judge him by his actions! Was this the only way he expressed his love and affection? But he really was into helping me. He seemed to love my passion, and he did offer to drive me to the new dojo every Monday on our day off.

It had been nearly six weeks since I'd had a real workout, and after that first scary introduction into a new school and an intense class, challenged by other aggressive Brown Belt punks and protected by spiritually-minded Black Belts, I could barely walk. My performance in California Suite on the following day was painful. I ached all over.

Every Monday, until the end of the run, Al drove me to the dojo for an hour and a half of pure prideful terror as I moved forward with my goal. I challenged myself and took some falls. Was romance so different? Could you get a Black Belt in Love?

DEAR DIARY:

Transformation into a Black Belt has me in its grip. My new karate class has me all charged up. I'm driven! When we practice self-defense I'm empowered. We enact those ugly scenes in dark alleys, of women getting banged around or abused. We fight back! I don't ever want to be hurt like that or be put down because I'm a woman. How do other people view me as a Brown Belt? Is it affecting my relationship with Al in a good way? Well, maybe I can hold my own a little better. I can break a knee cap, Al, but only in self defense. However, I have the power to make you talk, Albie. I know where to apply pressure.

Thirty-three

STATE OF AFFAIRS/AFFAIRS OF STATE

"Now do a hundred," Al smirked comically from the comfort of his couch.

"Forget it," I said, "twenty-five sit-ups are tough enough. I'm pooped. It's going to take me a while to get back to the fifty I used to do without any huffing and puffing."

"Want an idea?" He questioned, picking up his cigar from an improvised pickle jar lid ashtray. I turned over onto my stomach to start a set of push-ups. It was hard to talk.

"Yeah," I grunted.

"Why don't you make an exercise video like Jane Fonda did?" He challenged.

"Cuz-no-one-would-buy-it," I said, gasping for breath.

"Who knows? She's one smart cookie. You could follow her example." I hoped he'd go back to reading and let me finish my calisthenics in peace, but instead, he tossed the book over onto the couch, and took off his reading glasses, rubbed his eyes and leaned back, spreading his arms wide like eagle wings. Uh-oh. Those were the distinct signs of an impending Al story, one of Al's "Tales for Captive Audiences."

"I met Hank Fonda a couple of times. Jane took me to his house. I liked her father. As an actor? Phew. You couldn't touch 'im. Like Spencer Tracy. That kind of realistic actor." Al's voice was filled with awe. "Fourteen weeks on *They Shoot Horses*. Boy, did I love that. That's a long time to be getting a steady paycheck, you know." He paused. "I guess you could say we were an item during that period. Jane and I." I sat bolt upright.

"What?! An item? You and Jane? Barbarella and Grandpa Munster? It's hard to picture."

"She knew she was in trouble with her part. I think she overheard me talking to Gig Young. Gig didn't understand his part either and both about to be immortalized on the silver screen."

"Did you feel sorry for them?"

"Yeah, they were clueless. I told Gig, 'You always play the nice guy next door. Look,' I said, 'in all the other movies you've been in, you're clean-shaven and get the girl. Here you've got this terrible five o'clock-shadow and your clothes are all rumpled up. This part will get you nominated for an Academy Award. I can't promise you'll win. But if you play it right, I know you'll get nominated.'" Al puffed on his cigar and looked at the ceiling, his eyelids fluttering. "Gig took it in. He still didn't know how to play the part. I had to show him."

At that point it was impossible to continue my workout. Noticing that I was now paying close attention, Al went on. "I told him, 'Gigger, you're not going to play the scene like THAT, are you?' Gig looked at me like I was nuts. How could I criticize him, a star? He asked me what the hell I was talking about, so I got my chance to tell him." Al paused briefly to enjoy his own chutzpah. "He was so used to playing the nice guy that he didn't know how to shade the character. Remember how he cheats Jane out of her pay? I'd give him a line reading, and he'd parrot it back to me. We'd spend time every day drilling until he got it down."

"That's amazing. No actor I know would ever ask for a line reading, let alone give one. Theater etiquette. The actor's holy ground."

"Yeh, but Hollywood's all about money. That kinda thing happens all the time. They got dialogue coaches, all kinds of coaches, if they think it'll help the actor deliver the goods. Gig called me right after the Academy Awards. You know me, I never look at the Oscars. Political garbage."

"Political garbage?!"

"A no-brainer," Al responded. "It's all about money. The producers with the greatest clout get the nominations. For everyone else? It's hopeless."

"Who nominates the candidates?"

"Heh, heh! Who do you think? The Academy, of course!" Why does he have to ruin everything? "So, right after the Oscars, damn phone rings. It's four in the morning. Who the hell calls you at four in the morning? A drunk, that's who. I pick up the phone. 'Hello, Al!'" Al warped his words, imitating Gig Young on a bender. "'You were right, you bashtard, you were right. You knew all along! I got the Oshcar. I got it right here, Al. It should be yours. Never could'a done it without you.'" Al shook his head, moisture forming around his eyes. "Nice guy. Too bad, though. Suicide, after shooting his wife. Rest in peace, Gig."

I dropped back to the floor stunned by Al's schmaltz bomb. Then I felt tightness in my chest. Jane. "But what about Jane? You didn't finish telling me about Jane."

"Yeh. I did the same for Jane. But no line readings for her." He smiled. "Most people look at *They Shoot Horses* as a story about endurance and romance. No way! It's about economics, what financial hardship forces people to do. Dance until you drop dead! Jane appreciated my interpretation."

"Wow, that's a pretty clear take on the script, Al," I said, "but what about Jane?"

"Movies. It's a director's medium. If the actor can't do the emotional transition, the director cuts away to your eyeball or something." Al shouted, "Close up on her iris, Charlie!"

"But what about Jane?"

"Jane had tough transitions. I helped her with 'em." He shrugged.

"Is that all you helped her with?" Al scowled and gave me "the wrist".

We were sprawled on couches in the Green Room when I brought up the touchy subject again. "You know, Al, I was really proud of Jane Fonda when she went to North Vietnam. She was so young! I admired her political courage. I demonstrated against the war, too. I even got tear-gassed from a helicopter on the UC Berkeley campus right here at home. We were attacked from above with no place to hide. That was scary. We scurried like bugs to the only bathroom we could find to wash out our eyes. I was terrified. So when I saw that Jane had flown into 'enemy territory' as an anti-war protester, I knew she had real guts."

"She was gutsy alright," Al replied. "That's the system. The big guns get to shoot and gas the peons."

"Vietnamese peasants or protesting students. All the same."

"Jane's very political. I talked to her about the Black Panthers, you know, their breakfast program, taking care of the kids. I wanted her to visit and maybe give them some money. She never went, as far as I know."

"Wait, you knew the Panthers?" I found this information staggering. "Are you talking about the Black Panther Party in Oakland? Grandpa Munster meets Huey P. Newton??"

"Yeah, I taught a Black History class for 'em. So what? If you believe in something you support it."

"We were peaceful. The Panthers were militants."

"Oh, yeah. Feeding kids breakfast. I guess that was too militant for Hoover and Reagan," Al remarked in disgust.

"They had guns, Al."

"You get more with a kind word and a gun than you do with just a kind word!"

"Al, what are you saying?!"

"Al Capone said that. Just like that other gangster, Uncle Sam."

Comic relief, but the image of this big white Jewish comedian clown TV actor teaching Black History to the Panthers, tough, armed, no-nonsense resisters, seemed so incongruous that I had to laugh.

Al reacted, "What's so funny?"

"Well ... Grandpa Munster? With the Black Panthers?" And I giggled again.

"I had something they needed, Karen. It would have been wrong to withhold it," Al stated plainly, almost sweetly. But he'd said all he was going to say on the matter. He reached over to pick up the book he'd tossed face down on the couch, flipped it to the page he'd marked, then patted the seat cushion next to him, hunting for his glasses.

In this way Al continued to amaze, amuse, and aggravate me. But, as the man himself would say, "Two outta three ain't bad, kid."

Thirty-four

THEMES LIKE OLD TIMES

"Do you like jazz?"

"When I was a teenager, my older brother, Jon, dragged me along to little East Bay jazz clubs and we listened to artists I'd never heard of before like Thelonius Monk. It was fun."

"So you like jazz! Great," Al answered.

A few days later, Al flashed some tickets. "It's a black jazz club. You wanna go?"

"Sure."

Al took me to a small dingy club in Charlotte where we were ushered to a tiny, wobbly, cabaret table for the late-night seating. I noticed that we were the only white people present. After the first number, the lead singer/horn player made an announcement from the tiny crowded stage.

"Ladies and gentlemen, we are honored to have a celebrity in our midst. Put your hands together for Grandpa Munster! Mr. Al Lewis! Stand up!" Al slowly rose to his feet and everyone, including the band, applauded and cheered.

I shouted at him above the din, "Oh, come on. No, you set this up, Al! You're 'selling tickets' again! " He smiled and shrugged his head innocently, and shook his head no. When the cacophony of shouts and cheers died down, the bandleader announced, "Our next song is dedicated to Grandpa!" It was a very jazzy version of the Munster theme song. The familiar theme catalyzed a delightful ripple of laughter through the audience. How did these jazzmen know it? Why did they even learn it? Again my boggled mind concluded, everybody <u>does</u> love Grandpa. That's everybody. No exceptions. Every single person. Around the world. In the universe. And beyond.

The band then launched their set like a brightly lit party cruise boat. My thoughts drifted into the music, and the silence of listening offered room for meditation.

Yes, Al's fame clearly was established and celebrated wherever we went, even in this tiny, shabby North Carolina club at midnight. But it could have been anywhere in the world.

In the theater world, fame was highly sought after. But I could never imagine handling being known by everyone everywhere. Sure, I wanted recognition, but also a private life. How do you accomplish that? Al with his notoriety; he seemed to seek it out and even self-promote it. He teased fans and made them laugh. It was outlandish and fun. But it took a lot of energy and time. Time away from our relationship and time away from me developing my own career. My choices? Go along for the ride ... or bail out. I'm getting my emotional parachute ready.

The band was riffing again. "I Did It My Way", which was apparently Al's personal theme song. He was enjoying the hell out of it, as if it had been written for him. The audience clapped and Al whispered in my ear, "Like it?" Before I could answer, the bandleader called out, "Any requests?" Al's loud voice cut the air. "'Funny Valentine'! Can you play that?" Without missing a beat, the music flowed out, zigzagging between sweet and hot. The singer crooned: *My funny Valentine, sweet comic Valentine, You make me smile with my heart ... But please, don't change a hair for me, not if you care for me. Stay little Valentine, stay! Each day is Valentine's day.* Al grabbed my hand and mouthed, "That's what you are." I shook my head "No!" and pointed my finger at his chest, ready to tell him off. He grabbed it and pressed it to his heart before discovering how I meant it. I felt his body heat through his dress shirt and knew that he had sensed my questioning doubt and reeled me in just when I'd contemplated bailing out of this relationship. Al got me again. Stay little Valentine, stay.

After the show, I let Al grab my hand, hoping he would continue the romantic momentum that he had started. But the musicians crowded around our table and Al bought a round of drinks for everyone, ignoring me completely. Al, the fisherman. Reel me in. Then cast me out. Suddenly Al verbally attacked the trumpet player.

"You think you're Dizzy, don't ya!" My God, what was Al thinking?! I held my breath. Startled at first by this arrogant white man's verbal assault, the trumpeter smiled broadly and struck back. "Who you foolin,' man? I had more in mind Miles! Yeah, Miles!" he said, with a straight face.

"Miles? Miles?" Al fired back. "You can't play like him! <u>Look</u> like him maybe. Yeah! That'd be an improvement. Wouldn't he look better like Miles?!" The split second of silence that fell over the room seemed like an eternity to me. Then all the band members broke into uproarious howling laughter. I breathed a sigh of relief. Everything had turned out alright. Better than alright. Hilariously alright. I hadn't realized that Al was just "doing the dozens," a traditional trash-talking game of one-upmanship among African Americans. The band loved it.

"Aw, Grandpa, you're too much."

"Whooo! The man is over the top!" More laughter.

"Hey, Grandpa, you're from New York. Ever hear Lester play?"

"Hear him play?! Lester Young? I taught him how to play." More explosive laughter.

"No, for real, Grandpa."

"I wouldn't lie to ya'. Lester and I shared an apartment up in Harlem. I heard him even when I was asleep! Yeh, we were roommates, saving money on rent." I rolled my eyes and sighed. <u>Another</u> famous friend. Should I be keeping track? His imaginary address book must read like The Who's Who of Twentieth Century Celebrities.

"You knew Mr. Porkpie Hat, Grandpa?"

"Oh, yeah, one of the greats. God, he could play."

Totally comfortable, Al challenged each musician with his mastery of jazz history, speaking of crossover styles and those that rose from specific cities. Al surprised me again with this display of ease in yet another field of knowledge and experience. This perpetual state of surprise which he created in me made him magnetically attractive. Al was indeed a very "funny" Valentine. Funny *ha ha* and funny *peculiar*.

Thirty-five

"MARITAL" ARTS

"You know Dick Gregory?" Al asked.

"Yes. The black comedian activist with all the kids."

"Well," Al lit his cigar with a loud sucking sound, "he's in town and I'm going to see him. I know him."

"Of course you do. You know everyone."

"Right. Good one, Karen. So you wanna go? Here, take a look." With that, he tossed me the newspaper.

Hmm. Dick Gregory, the anti-nuclear and civil rights activist, the 1968 Peace and Freedom Party presidential candidate, and expert on the John F. Kennedy assassination, was doing his one-man performance at the Johnson C. Smith University's Brayboy Gymnasium. That was not far from where we were staying. A date with Al. To see Dick Gregory? "Sure, I'd like that!"

We pulled up into a vast parking lot where people, moving in animated flocks, migrated toward the venue. It looked like a river after a snowmelt. Al jumped out of the car, locked it, and took off without a word, like he'd forgotten I was with him. What the hell? He just raced off like a kid running to his best friend's birthday party! When I finally caught up with him, he was already standing at the box office window picking up the comps which Dick Gregory had left for us. "Hey, what's going on, Al?" He handed me my ticket, and once again, without a word, took off like a shot leaving me to find my way through the crowd entering the hall. I was pissed. Is this going to be the future of our relationship? I must have missed that meeting. Wasn't I his Funny Valentine? "Stay little Valentine, stay."? Stay by the car, maybe.

I moved along the aisle of the auditorium looking for Al. I found a seat with a decent view of the stage and sat down. I admit I felt confused and manipulated. Al had invited me on a date to see Dick Gregory. So why wasn't he with me? In fact, where was he? Then I saw him in the crowd in front of the stage, shaking hands, slapping backs. Was this what he was trying to ditch me for? Or did he expect me to join him up there? Well, here I am in a gymnasium, an appropriate place for a painful high school flashback, my date taking off with his pals.

Then Al moved back up the aisle, his eyes scanning the crowd until he found me. He grabbed me by the hand, and pulled me closer to the front, grumpily scolding, "Where were you? Why didn't you come down to meet my friends?"

"Well, for starters, you didn't ask me to. I wasn't invited. And anyway, I was hanging out with *my* friends." He glared at me but located seats for us near the stage, where presumably Dick Gregory could spot him and know he was in attendance. That's Al, always "selling tickets," always in the middle of everything, always the center of attention.

Al wagged his head, trying to shake off his apparent frustration with me.

"Why are you so angry with me?" I asked. "You ran off. What did you expect me to do?"

Al growled, "What made you so damned scared of everything? What kinda childhood did you have?"

"What's that got to do with your rude behavior?"

"Are you just gonna stay in your box like The Man tells you?" Al continued.

"No, Al, I'm not. In fact, I'm not even going to stay in my seat like Al, The Man, tells me." I got up and found an empty seat.

Just then, Dick Gregory walked out on stage. The unpleasantness between us was temporarily eclipsed by this brilliant man and his rare brand of articulate insights. Gregory's analysis regarding the war on the oppressed was a festival of truth-telling. A health enthusiast who helped Muhammad Ali diet before Ali out-boxed Leon Spinks, Dick even took on pantyhose manufacturers, as part of his presentation, admonishing them for not protecting women's health. "That ole nylon crotch captures moisture creating the perfect, insidious environment for yeast infections!" I was moved. It was refreshing to hear this *man* looking out for us women. The oppression that Dick was roaring about brought me back to my conflict with Al. What was it about this setting that unsettled my date? Was Al embarrassed to be seen with me? Wasn't I cool enough or politically correct enough for him? No, he was up to something, but what was it? Maybe he felt obliged to invite me, but figured he could lose me once we got here, which he did. But blame me for it? I don't get it.

Dick Gregory continued to score big with the audience when he spoke about the system's impact on African Americans. How they were forced to feel personally responsible for negative results, like being redlined if they tried to buy a house when it was actually "The Man" who was stripping them of their rights. Any mention of loss of power in Mr. Gregory's satirical style brought down the house in raucous laughter. How could that be? Was it gallows humor? Laughing at adversity helped oppressed people survive. Maybe I could use a dose of it myself if I was going to survive my relationship. I suddenly pictured Al as The Man, The Oppressor, but he came out looking like Bluto from Popeye. And I fell into side-splitting laughter.

After the show I saw Al pushing up stream to get to Dick Gregory. I also decided to make my way down to talk to him on my own.

When I got there, Dick was hugging Al to his chest, like a long lost friend. I stepped forward to congratulate Mr. Gregory. Seeing this, Al jumped in and introduced me, successfully high-jacking my moment. He quickly told his comrade why he was also in Charlotte, and invited him to our show. Then in a flash, the conversation went deeply political and I was instantly excluded. I would have liked to have joined in that conversation. I wasn't completely ignorant about those issues and wanted to ask him a few questions myself. But Bulldozer-Al was hogging the discussion.

I walked back to the car and waited. When Al got there he was still visibly angry with me. "Why can't you act on your own, take some initiative, get involved? You act like you're waiting around for permission!"

"Wake up, Al. I didn't wait around at all. I took the initiative to find my own seat and to introduce myself to Dick Gregory. I made my way back to the car. All on my own."

Apparently I called his bluff because he glared at me in frustration and continued his nonsensical rant. "I'm sorry but I just can't be hemmed in by your expectations. They're your expectations, not mine. They're too narrow for me."

"That's just ridiculous, Al. It doesn't make sense. All I expect is a little honesty."

"Okay, then. I can't play a role in your romance novel or anyone else's."

"My romance novel?"

"Just look at the word *courtship*," he said. "Who do you think made that up? You're getting warm if you think the *king*." I felt bewildered. He's not telling me the truth. This isn't the issue. He set me up. But, why? It's like he just wants to dump me for some reason, but he's not owning up to it. Then he added, "I bet you go on *dates*. I don't go on *dates*."

When we arrived at the apartment, The Man went inside, but I sat for a moment reflecting on what had happened. I'm not some hubby-seeking debutante. I'm an honest independent working woman. How can he use those stupid arguments against me? He

104

knows I'm involved, self-reliant, politically conscious, and gutsy. I thought that's why he was attracted to me. I'm in the world dealing with life. He's calling me a needy, clinging, dependent adolescent and it's just not true and he knows it's not true. So that can't be what's on his mind. If I thought about him, the way he seems to be thinking about me, I would have to call him a pathetic bullying chauvinist. That he feared intimacy, like every other guy, and was too scared to be honest about it.

Why should I ever talk to Al again? ...

... Because maybe I need to tell him a thing or two.

I stormed into the apartment and found Al sitting calmly smoking and reading the newspaper. I opened my mouth to let him have it and he beat me to it. "I want no part of that, Karen. You know, the man does this, and the wife does that."

"What weird planet are you tuned into!? This is absurd, Al. We're not even married. What the hell are you talking about?"

"You're a nice person, Karen, but your behavior... well, what happened to you? You are so backward!"

"Backward? Backward? What the hell do you mean by that?!"

"I'm not going to patronize you by discussing this."

"What!?"

"You want me to patronize you? I won't do it." Al stubbornly held to his ridiculously inexplicable position.

"Don't patronize me. Just tell me what this is all about."

"No," Al said softly.

"Spoken just like The Man! I thought you were a feminist."

"Is a feminist a person who supports women?"

"Definitely not in your case, but yes!" I shot back.

"Well...? If you won't stand up for yourself, who the hell do you think will?" Al pulled up his newspaper, snapping it open dramatically, burying his face in it, thereby ending "the conversation."

I stood there and felt my blood pressure rising. I started to shake. My muscles quivered. My eyes bulged. I was like Bruce Lee when he's pushed too far. The music swelled. I coldly took aim at the center of his outstretched sports page and "KI-AAAAHHH!!!" Riiip! deftly split it down the fold with a lightning karate chop, revealing the stunned look on Al's face. Priceless.

Thirty-six

50,000,000 FANS CAN'T BE WRONG

The next day's show went off well despite the tension I felt between us. It was a testament to our professionalism that our private emotional turmoil wasn't evident. I was hoping for a word or two of apology from Al, or at least a little respect for me for standing up to him, even if that would have been emotional hush money. But we barely said anything to each other that day. After the show I was still hoping for some gesture of acceptance from him, but sure enough, there was a sudden tidal surge of eager Grandpa Groupies in the lobby who had patiently waited for Al to appear. I watched from a distance as their elder ringleader stepped forward and enthused, "Mr. Lewis, you were wonderful. Just wonderful!" They all hugged and kissed their favorite TV star, and Al was having a ball hugging them back. It would have been like moving a mountain to change this natural phenomenon that was Al and his fans. "I always loved you, Grandpa, you were the best! Wasn't he the best?!"

Beside themselves with excitement and appreciation, they had their programs autographed by him and photos taken with him. Al quipped, "I know, I know. You watched *The Munsters* every night. Why'd you have to put your stinky feet right in my face!" Laughter exploded through the little band of fans.

As I watched this scene unfold I saw once again the childlike joy that this insufferable man engendered in other people. If they only knew what I knew.

But I was just an observant fly on the wall, realizing that I was only guessing at what Al was all about and what I meant to him. This dual personality where fans come first.

When the groupies made their exit, giggling and nudging each other, hugging their signed programs to their breasts, I took control of myself and confronted Al. "They love you, don't they!"

Al looked absolutely shy. "Yeah, those are my people, Karen."

"And lately, it seems that I'm not ..."

"Huh?"

"I feel like you're angry with me and want me to be someone else."

"Oh, no! You're just like my former wife. 'Why don't you accept me as I am.?' All that EST crap. Geez," he uttered grimly.

I think I hit a nerve. "I've thought about it, Al, and sometimes when you talk to me, it feels like you've got someone else in mind. Some kind of projection ..."

106

"Oh, now with the armchair psychology!"

"Yeh, maybe. But I really don't believe I am the way you say I am, that's all. And I don't like getting yelled at."

"Ah, white bread. What's a little yelling when you love somebody?" With that he threw his arm around my shoulder and gave me a hug, the kind a coach gives his star player. "What? I'm not supposed to tell you to wear your galoshes when it's pouring out?!"

"I'm sure you meant that as an apology, Al. Thank you."

A few days later, Al said, "Hey, are you ready for the Seniors' Luncheon?"

"Ready for what? I wasn't invited to a luncheon."

"At the Senior Center. I told management to call me anytime for opportunities like these."

"For more 'audience building'?" I interrupted. "PR?"

He glared at me. "You got it all wrong, Karen. I care about these people. I care about the welfare of ordinary folks. It's in the wood." He shrugged. I had to concede that I admired him for that, if it was in fact true. Al said, "They serve a lunch. It'll be fun." He seemed to be anticipating an exciting excursion and not in the least bit concerned about actually resolving things between us, as he apparently felt that he had already done.

"You don't need me tagging along," I said, just to see if he'd refute it, but he sat mutely smiling at me. "I'm not going," I went on. "Heck, I'd be the only one there who isn't a fan or a senior. I'd be a tourist."

"You're smart. You should get this one easy. Wherever I go, I feel like I belong. If I don't feel that way, I don't go. Fake it till you make it. You'll get it. Yeah. Walk through every door as if you are making an entrance to a place where you are always welcome."

"Fake it till you make it? What's that from, your New Age Seminar?"

"Alright. If you insist ... but you can do it. You could feel welcome."

"That's easy for you. You _are_ always welcome!"

The food at the senior center was delicious American fare: hot dogs, macaroni and cheese, greens, sweet corn, popovers, and tossed salad. But I was very uncomfortable in that setting, as if I'd crashed their party. Was Al uncomfortable? Of course not. He loved these elders, and they could feel it. He asked them about their kids and grands, where they grew up and what their passions were.

I didn't think Al knew anyone was watching when he lovingly guided an elderly woman to her walker and planted a smooch on her forehead. Hmm. Okay. Was that a rare glimpse into the real Al? Does he genuinely *like* these people? The rundown lunch room and their mac 'n cheese?

Several friendly seniors came up to me and thanked me for my performance. "Will you sign my program?" one elderly lady eagerly asked. "Miss Karen was in the play, too!" she announced to her sidekick who immediately dug into her tote looking for her program. So this wasn't just the Al Lewis Show after all. I signed my name with a flourish, trying to remember if I'd ever done this before. Signing autographs wasn't a regular activity at regional rep!

Just as the energy in the lunchroom crested, and right on cue, Al made his exit. As we drove back to the theater for the evening performance, Al asked me, "Did you enjoy yourself?"

"I felt awkward at first. But, once those lovely folks recognized me from the play ... ha ha! I had a great time! I caught Al Lewis fever."

"You're so smart and charming. All you had to do was turn it on."

"When I turn on my little light it's drowned out by your 1000 watt klieg!"

"Kleig, huh! That's pretty good. But you know I care about you, too, Karen."

I thought about that day for the next two days and decided that I also cared about Al. This second-hand fame business was very sticky.

Thirty-seven

YOU NEED BALLS

More messages started piling up in the administrative office of The Pineville Dinner Theater where we were still performing *California Suite*. Invitations, mainly, requesting Al's presence.

"Wanna go to a game?" Al grinned like he'd been given tickets to the Kentucky Derby. The question is, am I ready to be tested again?

"I don't know, Al. What game?"

"Basketball. High school. Not far from here." Al went on, "Coaches all over the area want to meet with Al Lewis to talk hoops. They want me to speak to the kids." After a quiet moment, he added for my benefit, "I won't be able to spend much time with you there, so you'll be on your own." Either he was being condescending to me or my karate chop to his sports page had gotten his attention.

"Then why are you asking me to go?"

"It might be fun." He watched my head nod as I considered his invitation, then he added, "We can go out for something to eat after!"

"Okay. If you need me, Al, I'll be ten paces behind you."

"Har dee har har."

We drove up to a nondescript gymnasium. Once inside, it took just seconds for the voices to rise. "Al! Al! Over here! We're just getting started!" the coach yelled out, then rushed to Al for a big embrace, followed by the assistants who swarmed like happy hornets, trying to get in a hand shake. They seemed to be giving him carte blanche to address the team and within seconds he was warming up. He paced around, pulled on his wrists to stretch his arms, as if to also stretch and order his thoughts. He then sent up his antennae, scanning the kids. They were lanky, with adolescent athletic feet, mix 'n match limbs, aching to become basketball stars.

"I'm not here to bullshit you," He began. "You don't need me for that. The fans'll dish out plenty!" The kids giggled. "I love the fans. Don't get me wrong. But personally, I don't like that kind of blind devotion. I study the game. To do that, I gotta be critical and objective. So I love the fans, I just don't wanna be one!" The entire stadium -- parents, kids, and coaches -- burst out laughing. Al had their attention now. "What motivates a player?" he questioned. A murmuring rumble of recognition rolled through the crowd. Then like a hell-raising preacher on a roll, he shouted, "The truth or ego?!

"I am here to tell it like it is. How hungry are you? Just how much do you want it? Huh? Huh?... But if you're in this only for yourself, forget it! This here's a team sport that requires the passion of each and every one of you – as a team. Every single position on the court is equally important. But you gotta have each other's back and work together. And no holding back! You don't just put out for a single game, but at every practice. You give it your all. Now I been talking to you for twenty minutes. But there's really only one thing I have to say... You gotta believe in yourself!" Slam-dunk! There was wild applause and cheering. Some players had tears in their eyes.

Some looked down at their shoes. Even the coaches seemed to be holding back their feelings. Even I felt my hair stand on end. I'm sure everyone in that room, including me, believed Al Lewis was talking directly to them. That's why Al Lewis, "sports expert and motivational speaker," was in great demand.

Al had done what the coaches couldn't do: inspire their players. So maybe Al was applying those same motivational principles when he was picking on me, and harassing me, and pushing me to improve my performance. Maybe he saw my potential better than I could see it and was encouraging me in his own obnoxious way to be the best Karen that I could be.

"Thanks for all your guidance, Al."

He looked at me. "Huh?" His face, a question mark.

"Maybe you do believe in me more than I do myself," I said softly, lacing my fingers around his neck. "Maybe I might even win a few games if I apply myself."

"Better late than never!" he beamed, lifting me off my feet. Swirling me around, I felt this spark of understanding igniting passion between us.

Shortly after our post-game burger and fries, we found ourselves entwined under the covers in his bed following a joyous tumble in the hay. My newly discovered understanding of Al's ardent coaching style, on and off the court, had led to a new kind of closeness. Perhaps gratitude *is* the greatest aphrodisiac? Now we lay sunning ourselves in the afterglow.

"You have a great laugh! Ya know that?" He was beaming at me. It made me giggle and he enjoyed the sound. I felt truly warmed by his comment, pleased that he liked the music that fell out of me when that funny bone of mine was struck.

"There are good laughers in my family, Albie. You might say I descended from two strong lines of laughers."

"Laughing stock?" he quipped.

"Get out!"

"That's all I ever wanted to do in life, Karen. Was to make people laugh. Yours is like a goddam orchestra. You got whistles and bells in there." He tapped my chest and laughed. I snort-laughed, one of my obnoxious specialties.

"What about snorts?"

"How'd I forget that!" he bellowed, hugging me so tightly that I farted. We both roared.

On our next day off, we found ourselves in the bleachers waiting for a baseball game to begin, a local league game that Al had sniffed out.

"I loved the way you talked to those kids last week. I played softball when I was a kid, but I never got that kind of coaching."

"What position, Skinny Minnie? First base?"

"As a matter of fact, yes. That and pitching. I was always the first one on the mound after lunch. I couldn't wait to play. Don't you love the sound when you hit the ball in the center of the bat?"

Al smiled. "That's what it's all about."

That sweet warm evening in the South arrived right out of a Tennessee Williams play. A baseball diamond shimmering in the late sunset, just before the sun disappeared, blinding the players behind home plate. The half-uniforms, where the pants didn't always match the shirts. The kids screaming cheers to their ball-playing dads. The food vendor, shirt riding up over his belly, hawking his homemade fare of chilidogs. The peeling paint on the bleachers. The Southern breeze wafting through the kudzu. It all added up to …

"A nice way to spend our night off, don't ya think, Karen?" He looked at me like a happy kid, the age he was when he started rooting for the Brooklyn Dodgers, and walked with his buddies to Ebbetts Field. "I never missed a game as long as I lived in Brooklyn, or the Dodgers did! When they dumped us for L.A." Al said, "What can I tell ya. *Braaaat.*" He gave that town a loud raspberry.

"Aha! So you were a big fan!"

"Oh, no. I was a follower. I don't use the word *fan* for myself. I don't like that kind of allegiance that knows no bounds."

"Like all your Grandpa Munster fans, you mean?"

"They're the fans, not me," he defensively retorted. "I want to study the game, help the players. I don't want to be a blind cheerleader. I want to be critical and objective. What motivates a player?" Al bit into his chilidog and mumbled, "The truth or ego?"

"That's kind of like acting," I responded.

He smiled and said, "Hey, you're getting the hang of this, kid!"

Thirty-eight

CLOSE BUT NO CIGARS

"Whatsa matter?" Al looked genuinely concerned as he sized up my mood. I felt tired, and there were purple circles under my eyes – physically out of kilter and bottom heavy. My period was late. Should I mention it? I'd been very careful and didn't think I was pregnant.

"Huhh?" He questioned again, an intensification of his effort to know how I was.

"Okay, my period's late. I feel lousy." Al got the truth out of me once again!

"Late?" He smiled warmly. He's happy, I thought, quite suspiciously. No former lover of mine had ever been happy about those words, "It's late."

"Think you're pregnant?" He sounded eager! I didn't respond. I wanted to curl up under a blanket and zone out - a blob of jelly.

"How would you feel if you were?"

"Well, you'd like me to be, wouldn't you! I've led my life in avoidance of getting pregnant so I could get a college education, perform on stage, be financially stable." Al stood there with a shit-eating grin on his face. Ralph Kramden with a winning lottery ticket. I think he did want to be the father.

"If we have a baby, Love, I want to roll out the red carpet for it and I don't think we're there yet."

"Huh," he said. "You're probably right." But he was deflated. I think he wanted me to want that baby more than anything, and ironically, on his account, I was being sensible.

"Al, we're not married even! You wanna be?" He took a deep breath.

"Karen, there's somethin' I should tell you from, oh, a while back. You know, about my family."

"Oh?"

"I got one of *those* phone calls during *The Munsters*. Hope you never ever get such a call." Al sat with his arms folded over his chest, as if reining in his heart.

"What happened, Albie?"

"They called me on *The Munsters* set. My wife, Marge, and our kids were in Florida visiting her twin sister, Marion, and her family. They were all out taking a drive. Marge was behind the wheel when a drunken driver smashed into her side of the car."

"Oh, no!"

"All I knew at that point was that they were alive, but Marge, Dave and Ted were in the hospital in bad shape. Yeah, bad." *Bad* lingered on Al's tongue, a million shades of disaster folded into it. "Then they took me to Marge. I never saw anything like it. Her head was three times the size of a normal head, and totally covered in

112

bandages. She lost an eye, broke her jaws, and her leg in several places. I told her, 'Marge, don't talk. It's okay. Just be still. I'm here.' I was so glad she was alive, but God ...

"When the accident happened, Paul flew right out the window in his baby carrier and landed on a strip of grass. Totally unharmed, like all of Marion's family. There Paul was -- all wrapped up in the basket!" Al exclaimed, as if reliving a miracle, like finding Moses in the bulrushes.

"They took me next to two-year-old Ted. He was all bandaged up. They fixed him up pretty good, but there's still a mark on his forehead where it got smashed in. You can hardly see it now, but that's where his scar came from. When you meet him, you'll see.

"Then they walked me over to Davey's bed. His head was all bandaged up, too. He was about seven, I guess." Al's voice began to quiver. "Know what he said when he saw me?"

"No," I murmured, emotionally caught up in his story.

"He said, 'Here's my dad! He'll fix everything.' Ya know what that feels like, to have your little boy believe in you that much? That I could make everything all right ..." He wiped his eyes. At that moment I felt very close to him.

Al paused and the story rested there, in the air between us. Then I spoke. "It must be painful to recall that story, Al. It makes me feel vulnerable. Something like that could happen to anyone, even a pregnant woman. A lightning strike that alters your life in a flash."

Al twisted a silver ring on his finger. He couldn't speak, but sat in sad contemplation. Now I really felt sorry for him. He looked pitiful, like a child who didn't want to be comforted, as he tucked his fingers under his arm pits.

"Thanks for showing me that side of you. I really appreciate your story." Our talk continued. "You know, this was the deepest I've ever gone into the subject of parenting and I'm grateful for your experience and insight. I know you believe I'm pregnant and it's beginning to rub off on me. I'm beginning to wonder if I might be!"

In those few days of waiting and wondering what-if, I saw how much I wanted a husband who cared for children like Al did, who knew the awful possibilities and wonderful rewards. But I was definitely not into forcing a man into a role he did not want.

The big "It" was quite late, but eventually made a bitter-sweet arrival, and Al stopped mentioning parenthood. I had tasted the tender possibility of a wanted pregnancy, but was spared the ultimate test.

Thirty-nine

DRIVING IN CIRCLES

We were making good time on the Beltway. Mom was flying in from San Francisco and needed to be picked up at the Charlotte Airport. I hadn't asked for his help, but as soon as he heard that my mother was visiting, Al volunteered his services, which I took as a very good sign! As we headed toward the airport, the sky was bright, the sun making the foliage appear translucent, an iridescent North Carolina April day that made you squint. Al rolled down the window, resting his elbow on the frame.

"Ever hear of an actor called Lloyd Nolan?" Al asked.

"Wasn't he the star of *The Caine Mutiny Court Martial*?"

"Yeh, he had the lead role in a play on Broadway. *One More River*. It all takes place on a ship. My part, the character's name was Columbus, wasn't very big, but I played the hell out of it and Lloyd liked me." Then he mumbled, "He was such a gentleman. Rarely in the theater do you meet a man like Lloyd Nolan. He told me that if I moved to Hollywood he'd get me an agent. Can you believe that? I told Marge about it, but we both wondered if it was bullshit. Lots of people say things they don't really mean."

"Yeh, I've been there, Al."

"Well, we kept putting off the decision to move to Los Angeles. I had an agent in New York. What if Lloyd didn't really mean it? When we did move to L.A. because of *The Munsters*, Lloyd got hold of me and kept his promise." Al's face scrunched up with that recollection and a lone tear rolled down his cheek. His voice wavered. "He handed me a piece of paper with his agent's name on it. 'I told him all about you, Al.' That's what Lloyd said. 'Call him up. He's waiting for you.' How many stars would do that?"

Al appeared to be holding back his emotions. "Smooth ride, don't you think. I got the same model at home. Mercury Marquis." He seamlessly changed the subject, making that awkward feeling disappear.

I saw the airport sign and directed Al to turn off the highway, toward short-term parking.

"Is that your mother?" he asked. I spotted her coming out of the gate beaming. We ran to each other and hugged.

"So this is Mom!" He grabbed her and literally lifted her right out of her shoes.

114

On the ride home, my mother and I were so involved chatting that we missed an exit and Al had to circle back. He was clearly miffed. Karen, the navigator, had fallen behind in her duties.

"Where the heck are we going? Geez! We passed this store already!"

"No we didn't," I whispered in a calming way.

"Are you sure? Where the hell are we? We missed the turnoff! This friggin' Beltway! Are you looking at that map? Or are you just foolin' around!?" Al had his head back bellowing like a bull!

Mom, her eyes darting all over the scenery, psychically removed herself from the conversation. Then she anxiously flashed me an entreating look that said, Is he alright, or has he lost his mind?

We eventually got back to the actors' complex, and once we'd unloaded her baggage into my room and Al had retreated to his apartment, she asked, "Is he always like that?"

"No, Mom. He just can't stand being lost." I was too proud to admit it to my mother, but I didn't like the yelling either.

My mother attended *California Suite* that evening and every other performance while she was in Charlotte. My own loyal fan (yes, blindly devoted), she praised my work to the skies, but was also staggeringly awed by what Al was achieving on stage, "and at his age," as she put it. When I wasn't acting, we cooked or cozied up to talk, mother and daughter style, with tea and coffee in hand. Mom imbibed with her hot beverage the latest tidbits of my affair with Al, acknowledging that it was in the throes of defining itself, in its fragile unfolding. My mother reminded me that Al and I had a long way to go, and gently warned me that fame had an important place in my relationship.

"He's on a different level in his career. He has different obligations, Karen."

"Yes, Mom, it is a bit overwhelming, but he's such an interesting guy."

"Interesting? Don't you mean challenging! Oh, you Aries. You love a challenge." Her smile told me how happy she was that I was involved with a good man, and one who could handle her quirky daughter. Yet, the conversation always seemed to return to our burning question: Would this love last?

On the third day of her visit, my mother observed, "Al's disappeared. Is my presence keeping him away? Ask him to lunch. On me!"

Al was delighted. "You think she really wants to? Or are

you makin' it up?" he teased.

Al discovered my mother had a fine sense of humor and couldn't resist making her chuckle. "You're lots of fun, Mom!"

"He's older than me and he calls me Mom!" She laughed until she cried, and poked my thigh in delight. Watching these two interact filled me with joy. I liked to imagine that Al was serious about me, and his performance at lunch indicated that he was. "When a man wants to meet your mother ...?"

After Charlotte, Mom planned to fly north to visit with my Grandma Mayme in Pennsylvania. Again, Al volunteered to drive her to the airport. This time, no yelling. Al was getting used to the Beltway. And my mom was getting used to Al.

"Did you enjoy meeting my mother?"

"Oh, yeah, she's a laugher."

"Isn't she!"

"But you're both a little backward." He looked totally serious then burst out laughing, in cascading volleys.

Forty

NASHVILLE SPATS

SAVE, TOSS, GIVE AWAY

Here's our old audio cassette player. I press "play" and the mournful sound of Hank Williams sails out into the room. Perhaps ole Hank can help me through another cleanup decision. On the floor by the guest bed lays a cache of Grand Ole Opry selections that Al had collected, dozens of them, housed in slotted wooden trays. Roy Acuff, Dolly Parton, Johnny Cash, Minnie Pearl, Patsy Cline ... These too remind me of a part of my life with Al. Save. As Hank sings, 'I'm so lonesome I could cry.'

Al was on the phone to L.A. and he was excited. "Okay. Okay. I like it. Yeah. Send me the revised script. Yeah, to the theater address.

116

Call me back." He plopped the phone into its cradle in his usual fashion, without saying goodbye. "Hey, Karen, that was my agent, Ruth, calling. She lined up a gig in Nashville."

"Congratulations!" I enthused.

"It's called *Big Al's Doggs*," he answered. "About an old-time agent who pulls his career out of the mud by taking a chance on some unknown, musically talented kids."

"When?" I asked, excited for Al.

"Don't know. I have to wait until it's in the bag." Al paced back and forth across his living room, rubbing his forehead until the phone rang again. There was much lively back-and-forth about the salary and start date. I was amazed at how he handled his business. Al pulled no punches and told his agent exactly what he wanted. Navigating business deals usually left me ruffled. When my agent called, I simply said yes. No matter what!

Al hung up the phone and yelled, "She signed the deal!"

"Let's celebrate!"

"Good idea! Come on, let's go eat," Al added without missing a beat.

At a late-night truck stop we ordered a snack. "They're shooting the pilot at The Grand Ole Opry. Hey, you ever been to Nashville?" Al asked.

"Sure. Didn't you know I'm a country western singer?"

"You could be. But you need bigger hair!" Al laughed. "Do you want to come with me while I film the pilot?"

"Oh, not really."

"What's the problem?"

"I have an acting job coming up. I feel nervous about traveling. And I'm on a very tight budget."

"What are you nervous about?"

"How do I get there? Where will I stay? I want to take responsibility for my own personal business. I mean, who will owe what to whom if I said yes?"

"Geez. Why can't you just say thank you?"

"Because I don't take those things for granted. I'm proud of the fact that I always pay my way." I had to protect myself and tell the truth. Al was less than thrilled with my mature response.

"Can't you just welcome the opportunity, meet new people, and see how the world works?" Al questioned with irritation in his voice. "What are you so scared about?" What do you say to Professor Henry Higgins when he thinks he's found his Eliza Doolittle in you?

I said ... "What am I so scared about? Getting stuck on a plane with a cigar-chomping lunatic!" He laughed and tapped his ashes.

"Yes, sure, I'd like to go with you," I said, "I just want to know what's involved. What's wrong with wanting to know what it's all about? Am I supposed to let a generous friend pick up the tab and wonder what I owed him later?"

"You worry too much!"

"I just don't like hidden agendas."

Al screwed his face up in an annoyed expression and blew out a plume of smoke. "Geez, what a worry wart," he grumbled.

"Thanks for inviting me to Nashville, Al."

He looked irritated. "Well, it took you long enough."

"I haven't accepted yet. I'm just thanking you for inviting me. I have plans of my own that I have to consider, like going back to California via Los Angeles, where I can stay with friends and check out some leads. Oh yeah, and I have an acting job, *Three Men on a Horse,* lined up in late spring in Berkeley."

For a brief microsecond, he actually seemed to reveal some vulnerability. His face said, "You don't need me, do you?!" Maybe one layer just peeled off the old onion. Then I said, "I'll let you know."

Al pulled the car into the Charlotte Airport parking lot. After we parked he charged ahead, apparently fully expecting me to keep pace. I bellowed in my race track announcer voice, "Aaaaaaand he's off!" This was the Dick Gregory Experience revisited. I should have learned by now to pack my track shoes.

I struggled up the aisle of the DC 10, looking for Al and/or my assigned spot, my carry-ons banging against the seats. Where was he? I think that's my seat but someone's sitting in it. A smiling flight attendant approached me asking my name. "Are you Karen Ingen ...?" I nodded. "Right this way, Miss. Mr. Lewis is looking for you!" What?

"Where is he?" I asked, totally confused.

"Oh, celebrity upgrade!" she beamed, herding me toward First Class. I saw a crowd was gathered around someone in a seat. I wonder who that could be. It was a little difficult getting to my seat because I had to make my way through the adoring horde. Al waved me in with a big smile. "Whadda ya think?" I knew he was hoping to impress me with his upgrade maneuver. I was impressed, but it wasn't the gift that I really wanted. If instead he had given me an explanation of his behavior or a clue about his feelings, I would have happily sat in coach with a bag of peanuts.

But, I sat in First Class for the first time in my life! Thanks to Al's fame, we had the best seats in the house, and they came with a floor show, The Al Lewis Shmoozerama. Al immediately adlibbed up the aisle, leaving me to stow the carry-ons. When The Star finally joked his way back to his seat, he stretched out his long legs and commented on the spaciousness in the front of the plane. I managed to say, "Thank you, Al, for giving me the opportunity to share your good fortune."

"Don't be silly," he proudly stated as he stuffed the up-graded tickets into his pocket.

"Al, I'd love to clear something up," I said politely.

"Yeah, sure." Then he paused a moment taking in the luxury around him and added, "Just a second." Al stood up and straightened his clothes, tucking in his shirt. "Be right back." I watched as he headed toward the restroom and I shook my head. I quietly waved to the flight attendant and ordered a glass of wine. If I was going to clear things up, I needed a little more courage. As I waited in my window seat, I heard laughter behind me. From the slaps and pats, I knew Al was shaking hands with passengers seated behind us. Then I heard the old familiar tease that I mouthed along with Al, "Did you have to put your stinky feet in my face every night?!" and I counted the usual one-and-half seconds for the inevitable guffaws.

The wine goblet landed in the little hole on my serving tray just as Al planted himself in the seat next to mine. He was still glowing from the ego strokes and the rave reviews he'd just garnered. I tried again. "Al, I want to clear something up with you. It's important." The flight attendant nervously fluttered over Al while serving him his first course and her attention was far too encouraging to resist. "Isn't that a Waldorf Salad?" Al asked.

"Yessir!" she giggled.

"That reminds me of the time Fred Gwynne and I were in New York for the Macy's Thanksgiving Day Parade." With the mention of Fred's name, another flight attendant cocked his head from the galley and the folks on the other side of the aisle turned to listen. Al had them hooked. "So Universal puts me up at the Waldorf Hotel. Nice. I had this gorgeous suite. Huge. I decide to invite all my friends over from my old neighborhood and they're excited. Hell. None of 'em's ever set foot in that hotel." Al suppressed his laughter. I watched as two more flight attendants in aprons peered from the galley, sending Al's volume up a notch. "There must've been twenty-five of us. So I call room service and start ordering up all kinds of dishes. For my friends! It's going on my tab. The one Universal's picking up, see? Hundreds of dollars. So I just keep ordering more and more stuff. My friends have never seen anything like this. Guys in mufti carrying in tray after tray. We're all sitting around with our jackets off, sleeves rolled up, enjoying the hell out of all this wonderful food."

I took a good sized slug from my wine glass and jumped into the brief silence, "Al, can we talk ...?"

"Funny story, huh?! Wait'll you hear what happens next. When I get back to Universal, I know what's going to happen. Oh, yeah. So I'm sittin' in the chair with my wonderful makeup man, Perc Westmore." Eyeing the fluttery flight attendant who was now twisted around the galley curtain hoping to get an earful, Al eagerly plunged ahead. "I tell him the whole Waldorf story. He loves it. In comes this little guy in shirt sleeves. He's got little slips of paper in his hand. Someone from Accounting's sent this poor schmuck over to in-vest-i-gate the room service tab. I see his body language. Head down. That's when I start with Perc. 'Oh, I have such a pain.' I hold my head. 'It's this scene. I just can't get the lines!' The guy takes a step toward me, holding out the little slips. Then stops. So I start in again. 'Perc, what am I gonna do?' I get louder. 'Oy vey. The lines! They're all over the place. My head!' And sure enough the guy's backing out slowly. Then he quietly pulls the door closed as he leaves. Perc laughed! God, how he laughed."

"Al? I need to talk to you right now."

"Yeh. What's on your mind, Karen?"

"Ladies and gentlemen, welcome to Nashville!" The head flight attendant drawled out the news.

"We're here, Karen, we're here!"

"Al, you've got perfect timing. Friggin' impeccable." I shook my head in surrender and frustration as our plane came in for a bumpy landing.

A sleek black limo met us at the airport. This was the legendary red carpet treatment of novels and theater stories, rolled out for Al Lewis. The car moved through Nashville like a shark, forcing everything out of its trajectory, gliding toward its destination. Sitting back in the deep luxury of the interior, Al chatted up the driver, eliciting a tour-guide description of the rich Tennessee scenery as we passed through it. Engine idling at the VIP entrance to the The Grand Ole Opry Hotel, I gasped. "It's beautiful! It looks like Scarlett O'Hara's Tara!" Al grinned. He'd been here before and was enjoying knocking my socks off. Well, that was no compensation for Al hiding his feelings and motives, but I had to admit it was pretty spectacular.

"Wait'll you see the brunch!" Al teased, wiping his lips over this mouthwatering memory of rooms of food. Everything about our stay was First Class, Deluxe, Luxurious, and Top-of-the-Line: the food, the interiors, the guests, and the staff. But he still hasn't told me who's paying for all of this wining and dining or what my obligations are, financial and otherwise. And I can't squeeze it out of him.

Right next door was the Grand Ole Opry Theme Park, adopted by the film company, and transformed into a film and sound stage for *Big Al's Doggs*. An intense spotlight that glowed as brightly as Las Vegas, everything in this part of Tennessee paid homage to Country Western Music. It was garish and big like Al. It was Southern and sweet. Except for bringing my makeup kit, I'd arrived unprepared. Al had come here to work. He was already revving up, strategizing, and positioning himself to grab his share of that Grand Ole Opry limelight. He had a checklist, people to meet and impress, lines to learn, and appointments with designers, actors, and producers. Where was my checklist? Well, if I had one it would have read: smile, keep smiling, and find some Tylenol for the stress headache caused by all that fake smiling.

I met the friendly cast, most of them teenaged dancers and singers who fell upon Al in ecstatic, groupie-eyed bliss. Relegated to the "audience" section during filming, I sat among theme park visitors who ohh'ed and ahhh'd in excitement. One fellow elbowed me and said, "Don't you wish you knew that Al Lewis personally?!" I said, "Yes I do. Wouldn't that be great?"

We were fed and entertained whenever there was a break in the filming. Producer Jim Owen cynically tallied the number of fans who approached our table for Al's autograph, a hedged bet on the success of his pilot. Music filled the air day and night, but Al was too busy or exhausted to hear it. Witnessing the strenuous nature of this film schedule, I became worried. Was I helping Al, or in his way? As usual, he wasn't giving me any feedback.

Outwardly, things went well in Nashville. And finally *Big Al's Doggs* was ready for editing. This had been Al's gig and I'd watched agog as he turned an ordinary job into something extraordinary, his ordinary practice. All the best this remarkable town had to offer had been handed to Al and me as his guest, and it had been wonderful. But all that excitement and luxury was merely a momentary distraction from the rumbling in my inner landscape.

Without my own agenda, a functional plan for myself, I felt like an outsider, oddly redundant, useless, and uncomfortable. Ever since *California Suite* had closed and my employment as an actor was terminated, I was on "someone else's trip." And that trip was Al's. I want to cast myself in his life, but I can't get him to agree to what my role really is.

Even though our Nashville excitement was behind us, and we boarded a non-stop flight to Los Angeles, I still wanted answers to my questions, but I'd given up trying to get them from him. I sat in a First Class seat for only the second time in my life. Out came the silver service, the linen napkins, and the wine goblets. Our food came in volleys of banter from the staff, accompanied by that now familiar star-struck gaze, and heartfelt desire to please Grandpa Munster. I imagined them excitingly sharing these exchanges with their loved ones. "Guess who I spent the day with, honey!" Repeating every word the Old Munster uttered.

I looked down at my less-than-first-class attire: hand-me-down polyester blouse, skirt from Penny's, same old blue boots. I tried to head off a blossoming feeling of inferiority. All around me people were brandishing obvious tokens of wealth: gold chains, chunky rings, designer shoes, silk shirts and blouses, and three-piece suits. What did they think of this Berkeley waif seated next to Al Lewis? Al seemed to ignore ... I mean, adore that waif.

Once again, the flight attendants tripped all over themselves to speak to Mr. Lewis, who was already in full swing, teasing them until they were bubbling with laughter, their First Class decorum falling away. His playful, professional comic tennis serve whizzed forth so naturally that he took each attendant by surprise, acing them all, much to their delight. Soon the galley was atwitter, and sure enough, the Captain emerged for a brief greeting, grinning from ear to ear, stretching out his hand to shake Al's. "Sir, you've entertained my crew and me for years. Welcome aboard!" Interesting how Al could disarm anybody without even trying, but he couldn't be disarmed himself. Damn. How does he do that?

Al's plan was that his friend, Al Smith, would meet our plane when it landed in L.A. and drive me to the Hollywood home of my friend, screenwriter, Philip Gerson. Then Al Smith would take Al Lewis home to Encino.

After our meal, Al took a meaningful breath then ... "In California my kids come first." An alarm went off in my head.

"Yes, of course, but ..."

"No. I mean they come first. I won't have time for anything else." I looked at him in startled confusion. The tone. Did someone die?

"What are you telling me?"

"Just what I said. It's just me and my kids." A lumpy pause ensued as Al silently followed the trajectory of my confusion until it dropped like a ball into a slot. Large, round tears danced on my lower lids. I felt like I'd swallowed a grapefruit, now stuck just above my

122

collarbone. Turning toward the window, I wrestled tissues from my purse and dabbed my eyes, looking at the clouds marbling the windowpane. I pushed down the emotions that threatened to climb up out of my chest. How could I speak my mind here in First Class, a breath away from a galley full of *Munster* fans? What a dirty trick! To tell me this privately in public! I couldn't discuss it with him. During the rest of the flight, I could think of nothing to say that wasn't about my feelings. So I said nothing. And anyway, my voice was clogged with compressed tears. The agonizing silence was broken only by the continuing giddy squeals of the female flight attendants, alighting next to Al to share a few quips - their voices as irritating as adolescent girls encountering their teen idol. If they only knew the man behind the *Munster* mask. The man who had smacked me with his non-negotiable decision without softening the blow. And it stung. All I wanted now was to get off this damn plane and I considered going up to the cockpit to encourage the pilot to step on it.

On the ground in Los Angeles, I glued a smile to my lips as we said farewell to the crew. They'd prepared an impromptu gift for their special guest to present to him as we debarked: a bottle of champagne wrapped in an airline napkin and zipped into a company flight bag. Al laughed, thanked, hugged, and pinched cheeks, praising them to the skies. My stomach felt like a washer in an out-of-balance spin cycle, but just to save face, I pushed back my shoulders like a runway model and made a fuss over the captain.

At the gate, Al Smith, a giant of a man radiating warm humor, goodwill and buddy-love, grabbed his friend and nearly swung him off his feet in a happy lumberjack's hug. Then turning to me, he smiled and embraced me, too. "Al has told me so many wonderful things about you, Karen! You gave Al here a new lease on life." He had a Paul Bunyan stride and large rolling vowels like a radio announcer's that filled the waiting room. He wedged his way through the milling flocks, protecting Al from any adoring *Munster* fans that might impede our exit out of LAX. Al Lewis never said a word as Al Smith launched into the-wonders-of-Karen as told to him by his closest friend, Mr. Lewis. Thank you, Al Smith. At least now I know that it wasn't just a one-way street. I glanced at Al, half-hoping he'd be uncomfortable with this praise. Still, I felt the curtain coming down on what had been the most exciting and challenging love affair of my life.

Forty-one

DUMPED

Al Smith's big car pulled into the driveway of Philip's Hollywood home. Alone in the back seat, I caught Al Lewis shooting a secret conspiratorial wink to Al Smith. Then in perfect sync, they emerged from the front seat. What was up? Al Smith opened the door for me and held it like an attentive chauffeur. I sat frozen for a minute. Hold on. I've got to think clearly. What's wrong with this picture? The Brown Belt inside me barked a karate command, "*Chumbe!*" *Attention.* Hyperawareness. I jumped out and surged past Al Lewis toward the rear of the car for my baggage. Al Smith in one motion deftly grabbed my new suitcase and placed it on the front step.

Philip quickly answered the door. "Hello Mr. Lewis, I'm a big fan of yours!"

"Hey, that's great. This is my friend Al Smith," Al said. "We just brought Karen from the airport. Have a nice day," and he quickly backed out to the car bowing. I didn't even have a chance to say good-bye. I had just been deposited at Philip's house like a stray kitten dropped on someone's front porch.

This was not the arrival I'd imagined at all, where energized by Al's love, I'd share my happiness with Philip. I planned to quickly contact old friends and meet up with Al in a few days. Instead, blindsided, I was shaken to the core and couldn't understand what to do with my feelings. Fetal position. That was perfect. Maybe some truffles? Did that airline gift champagne end up in my luggage? Philip listened like a true friend, as I speculated on this sudden turn of events. Was this a swift triage, Al cutting me out of his life before arrival on his turf? Was there something I didn't get? I planned to cry my eyes out at the first available moment.

The next few days passed in a blizzard of wet Kleenex. Eventually I reached for the phone. "Maybe I should come home, Mom," I moaned.

"Why don't you follow up on all those good L.A. contacts? You'd be upset if you came back here before you really explored things down there."

"You're right, Mom. I'm not going to let Al jerk me around."

"No, you're in L.A. to see if there is theatrical work for you."

"I'm not here to be an Al Lewis groupie."

"That's right, honey. Go directly to Hollywood and Vine!"

"Schwab's Drug Store, here I come!"

Forty-two

CASTING DOUBT

Hollywood. On the surface, a glitzy fantasy world. But underneath? The Desert. As I trudged through this arid wasteland, my resources were quickly drying up. There had to be relief here somewhere. Then it appeared. A mirage? No, the real thing! An oasis.

Someone actually returned my call. It was Seth Freeman, an old classmate from U.C. Berkeley, who ten years later, was now a staff writer on the esteemed *Lou Grant Show*. He showed me around his humble office in Studio City and introduced me to his friendly co-workers: scriptwriter Michelle Gallery and casting director Fran

Bascome. Seth and I recalled all the outrageous projects we'd worked on together, our improv group, numerous plays, and even a short film, most of which Seth had written. What a delightful reunion. Then he dropped a bomb. "Well, perhaps you'd like to audition. With your resume ...?" I was so stunned I could hardly speak, but I managed, "Yes!"

"Could you work up a scene for a producers' audition?" Fran asked. "There's one scheduled in a couple of weeks, at lunch time, so lots of casting people will be there." I didn't know then I'd have to pay $200 to be auditioned. And then I had to audition to be able to pay the fee to audition! Catch 22. Just like New York. Hooray for Hollywood!

"Karen! Our casting people liked your scene very much!" enthused Michelle Gallery. We have our eye on you for some upcoming parts. No schedule yet. Everything changes around here. Constantly!"

They couldn't commit to telling me any more than that. Business Hollywood-style, a small taste of the L.A. tap dance I'd heard so much about.

In another stroke of good luck, friends I'd met in a 1978 production of *You Can't Take It With You,* Stefan Fischer and Gwen Lee, were looking for a roommate for their Hollywood home. I gratefully moved in with them at once. It was a great relief to find a hospitable place to live with supportive friends. When I revealed my broken heart, they extended themselves even more. "Well, let's see how this all turns out," advised Gwen as she hugged me. "The Universe is one tough teacher!"

"Karen! Everything okay?" said Al, "I got your number from Philip."

"Yes, I'm fine. How're you?" I asked flatly, not at all sure how I felt at that moment.

"Hangin' in there."

"Had a call back to see an agent. Things are opening up." I was keeping it businesslike.

"That's gooood! Take care." Click.

"Nice talkin' to you, too, Al," I said to the dial tone.

I got one of those hit 'n run calls every few days. Although it hurt to hear Al's voice and not really converse as we had before, I convinced myself to accept whatever token concern he was offering. Anyway, controlling my emotions was an occupational necessity. I couldn't show up red-eyed to every audition.

As time went on, Al began to talk longer, even though he never revealed his feelings. "Hey, Karen, can you talk to my son, Paul? He thinks Chuck Norris is a good karate teacher. You tell 'im. The Japanese guy the neighbors brought over from the old country's far better. Here he is. Pauli? It's Karen." I was happily surprised that his kid knew about me.

"Hey, Paul, you're looking for a karate teacher? Chuck Norris is okay, but in my experience those quiet, neighborhood guys are the real thing. Yeh, my school's a collective and my Master's just like that, humble and dedicated. Sure! You're welcome!" That Paul was such a live wire, I found him irresistible. Was Al actually trying to build a bridge here and create a real friendship, or was he just stringing me along and showing off for his kids? My heart still ached.

One day Al phoned, bubbling with excitement about two guys who'd kept calling him, Robert Zemekis and Bob Gale.

"They got this script. Hell, I don't know what to make of it. It's called *Used Cars*. What a premise! It could be very funny."

"What's your part? Crooked salesman?" I asked.

"Ah ha ha! No, a hanging judge."

"Perfect!" I shot back.

"What a character! I'll be leaving for Arizona to film it and I don't know when I'll be back." His leaving town made me think about where I was stuck. I just didn't resonate with L.A., but his phone call suddenly made me realize that it had been grounding for me to know that Al was nearby. I had to face how I would feel when he was far away.

Forty-three

THE CITY OF "ANGLES"

Los Angeles

      the loneliness was palpable

from the sleet gray of the morning to the pink gray of the sunset

I felt I was stepping in oatmeal lifting my feet slowly

      because they stuck

glued like the hairy mammoth's in the La Brea Tar Pits

stuck and lonely even as friends smiled and I met new loving

      exciting ones

as brilliant and kind as found anywhere

they had purpose

I couldn't find it in the elusive mirage of Hollywood

my own illusive dance with love

the vegetation shimmered around me

a lush hot verdant landscape known round the world

> *That's Hollywood!*

palm trees pools convertibles strawed tall drinks and lots of skin

> *what was I doing here?*

the gynecologist's office hidden within a labyrinth of buildings through a maze of corridors past a series of doors and checkpoints

> *what was this? top secret?*

> *I was just here for an exam!*

then the upholstery!

silver frost mauve stripy taupe and meticulously planned

> *steely mirrored*

I only needed a check-up not a ride through Architectural Digest the office was as lavishly appointed as any modern hotel I'd ever visited

> *and twice as cold*

once the doctor finished poking me I was released to the
> *loneliness of the street*

back to The Desert

wasn't the desert a place where you go for long spiritual tests?
> *forty days and forty nights and all that*

I drove dressed for success from auditions

> *to readings*

> *to performances*

> *to classes*

warbling along to revealing songs blaring from my car radio
my love for you is a sinking ship and my heart's out on that ship
> *out in the ocean*
> *I wailed with the McGarrigal Sisters*

endless hours locked in a wheeled metal box

gliding down ribboned freeways reeking of exhaust

even as the fecund scenery played on my eyeballs like a film

or was it the film of smog on my eyes that burned so badly

I listened to air pollution warnings on the news

whipped off with the cheeriness of a birthday announcement

that sent my feeble heart into sci-fi movie terror

kids and folks with respiratory problems should stay inside!

no reference as to where it came from The Smog

L.A. a dazzling shimmering stinking lure

yes smog smells

like flaked iron like burnt tennis shoes like sidewalks hacked

> *with a pickax*

the color of it hanging off the sky the tint of an insult or a sin

> *misty muck*

> > *the shade of a guilty inmate's aura*

> > *shit + fog = smog*

> > > *the color of a culture gone wrong*

> > *smog ate away at my soul*

Forty-four

CALL WAITING

    Days passed, each one looking and feeling exactly like the last. As they sank slowly into gorgeous, Western smog enhanced sunsets, I realized that spending time like this was not for me, and I vowed to transform my daily existence and weave a fresh new life for myself.

For years I'd wanted to take acting classes from Paul Richards when he was teaching in the Bay Area. A veteran of the Actors' Studio, Paul had a reputation for helping actors develop. He demanded an atmosphere of respect for positive encouragement and growth, with zero tolerance for empty criticism and backbiting. Fortunately, there was a spot open and I got in. As the months passed, I felt a rare sense of liberation and support as classmates commented on my lively theatrical instincts, humor and depth which built up my confidence. I, in turn, helped to build up theirs. I found myself once again joyfully in the midst of other scruffy actors struggling to better themselves and find work.

During that time, I taught karate classes. Paul Richards' wife, Barbara, promised to get me a few more karate students if I'd agree to teach her and their young son, Robbie. Perfect. That was also a great opportunity for me to practice for my Black Belt test, which my Berkeley mentors, Black Belt Erica Stone and Master Jim Larson, applauded. My new students were thrilled to have a woman teacher of this male dominated martial art. Otherwise, many of them would never have explored karate. I enjoyed helping people stretch their boundaries, which in turn, encouraged me to test my own.

The woman sitting next to me at a funky Hollywood café was eyeing the book I was reading. "You're interested in Carl Jung?" Judith Richardson told me she had just written an article on how important artists are to the world – visionaries who dream the direction of society.

"You're interested in Jung, too?" Her message was exactly what I needed to hear now, just when I felt like I was being commodified by Hollywood and losing my artist's soul.

"Meet me on Sunday at the Gnostic Center," Judith recommended. "I'll introduce you to Stephan Hoeller and perhaps he'll give you a Tarot reading. He knows all about archetypes!"

"This card is The Fool," Reverend Hoeller explained; his melodious voice and Hungarian accent engaging me. "A symbol for new beginnings and the indomitable spirit of inventiveness and spontaneity." The image on the card looked just like me, a happy hobo about to walk off a cliff! And a new beginning? I sure needed one. "People underestimate the Fool," Reverend Hoeller said. "They believe the Fool's a clown and can be easily dismissed. No. This card must be taken seriously. Here, it's a sign of how to proceed. Joyfully!"

"Considering the depressing days I've lived through since arriving in L.A., this is welcome advice!" I responded.

"What about this card?" I was struck by the majestic card in front of me.

"That's the Magician, a powerful card, indeed."

"What does it signify?"

"Ah, the ability to utilize every resource we have available to us." That sounded familiar. Where had I heard that before? *Use what you got to get what you need.* "The Magician is in control of his own thoughts and that is why he appears to be powerful. That is personal power." That description fit Al. But Reverend Hoeller had something else in mind. He directed me to find this power inside myself.

"This is you here. The Priestess," he continued.

"What about The Fool?" I questioned.

"The Fool is how you proceed. With joy. But The Priestess represents your powerful intuition. That's what she's all about. But I must warn you of her negative aspects: emotional insecurity and the dangerous temptation to use emotional blackmail." He smiled sweetly as if to say he knew I would never engage in that.

I kept attending meetings and lectures at the Center. Bit by bit, by trusting my intuition, I began to birth clearer self-images of my roles as an artist and a woman. I liked this new Karen a lot.

Mom sent a card plumped out with photos she snapped in Charlotte. There were several of Al and me that instantly took me back to our time together. Part of me felt warm and mushy inside, recollecting how Al had driven me to karate class each week, encouraging me to be strong, not just to pass my Black Belt test, but to be a more powerful person.

Looking at those photos made me feel nostalgic for Al. Selective memory kept my thoughts on all the mentoring he'd given me. What a great excuse to call him and possibly catalyze a nice deep conversation with him.

"Hi, Al, I was thinking about you!"

"Yeh! Why?"

"Well, you really helped to clear some things up for me."

"Yeh? That's good. Now why are you really calling?" And he cheerfully laughed.

"Well, I miss you," I admitted, and hearing my own sad, lonesome whine, added, "And ... I want to thank you for helping me transform my life good-bye." I hung up quickly, embarrassed, suddenly deciding I could and would handle the loneliness myself. God, I just sounded like my mother.

Forty-five

SIMON SAYS ...

The Public Library called. *The Sunshine Boys* script I'd requested had been returned and was ready for pick-up. I was determined to learn more about popular theater. As part of my self-improvement scheme, I started reading every Neil Simon play on the shelves, and now this special one was in my hands. I have to admit, my ulterior motive was to check up on Al's claims of having a character based on himself. I opened the Samuel French edition, and yup, there it was: *Al Lewis* on the list of characters. Neil Simon, the King of Broadway, had put Al in his script! My hands were shaking. So I brewed a pot of tea, then found just the right spot in my sunny bedroom to ritually, carefully absorb the play and see what insight it gave me about Al.

Al was telling me the truth. Neil Simon did use his name, his style of comedy, and his actual routines to tell the bittersweet story of two old vaudeville comics. Al had tried to tell me what it meant to him, but it took reading this play for me to truly understand how huge a thing it was. It made me think about an entire era of physical comedy, meticulously studied and performed, revered by audiences everywhere, its popularity eventually fading and dying as the lives of those comics drifted into the mists of time, forgotten.

Through this play, I entered Albie's secret place, where his personal history bonded with theater history. God, it touched me, just as those two Neil Simon characters, so frustrating and so funny, touched me. My heart was stirred. I heard Al's voice in every word his character uttered. He even poked his comedy partner with his finger! The play made me fall in love with him all over again and I wanted to express it. I was crying as I dialed Al's number, but of course, I got the answering service. I hung up. I didn't want to leave a message! I wanted to commune with Albie. That rascally, bristly bastard, that artichoke, that prickly pear, that fuckin' cactus. Why do I still care so much about him?

People can put you through a lot of frustrating and aggravating scenes, yet sometimes you see something in them that others may not see. Something that makes you fall in love with them.

Reading the play, I saw what Al had offered the world and the price of that offering. Obviously, Neil Simon saw it too.

It's Love that allows you to accept your lover's clay feet and to keep smiling. It's easy because they are his feet. Are there words for the light in a person's eye, for the happy circus of his soul, for the melancholy, the autumns and winters which pass through his expression, for the tenderness underneath all the bluster and iron? Any words for the fury I feel standing outside his circus tent being told it's "Rained Out"?

Forty-six

DESPERATELY SEEKING SELF

After a year of struggling, I was making just enough money to cover basics by taking on jobs I hadn't done since high school, babysitting anything from kids to flowerpots, and delivering casting breakdowns to agents. At age 35 I had a paper route. Maybe I could do better.

I pulled down one of the thousands of flyers that were posted everywhere in Hollywood. "Are you nervous at auditions? Are you sabotaging yourself? WE CAN HELP!!" There were hundreds of gurus at the ready offering classes, seminars, and workshops targeting Hollywood wannabes.

To my credit and my mother's urging, I had started watching more television and assuming a more professional attitude at my commercial auditions. I thought I should supplement my efforts with the latest motivational techniques. I embarked on a journey of career-directed enlightenment: Dream Actualization and Professional Outcomes Visualization, Acting Actualization Action, Goal Targeting, and Wealth Visualization and Show Business Actualization, a seminar called "Improving your Circles of Influence through Networking." A weekend workshop in self-hypnosis was also embraced as an essential prescription for change. But weeks later, after nightly trips down my inner staircase, and counting backwards, ten, nine, eight ... I had an amazing breakthrough. I finally saw myself clearly ... shelling out good money for bad advice.

So I moved on to what comforted me, and I held intractably, idealistically, to my belief in the creative purity of the actor's impulses

133

on stage. In other words, I auditioned for as much Live Theater as I could, and promptly got cast on the popular television show *Lou Grant*!

Forty-seven

TAKEN FOR GRANTED

SAVE, TOSS, GIVE AWAY

Newspapers and old magazines. If I sift through all these, it'll take hours. Work on one box for a whole day and still have more to do? No, OUT! No more paper piles. Wait. What's this? A TV Guide from 1980.

"We want you for the role of the Librarian," chirped the secretary from the *Lou Grant Show*. "Bring in whatever outfits you have for a fitting tomorrow and we'll give you the shooting schedule." That felt ... well, amazing! I went through my closet like a whirlwind, looking for librarian clothes, and piled them into my car.

Very early on the morning of the *Lou Grant* shoot, I fired up Sweet Pea, my '64 Ford Mustang, which I'd recently purchased complete with rear-end dent and bad muffler, and zoomed toward the set. I was so euphoric that I didn't care about the brown smog of Hollywood. In fact, I rolled down my windows, sucking it in. I turned up the radio and sang along with Carole King at the top of my lungs, serenading my trusty Sweet Pea, *"You are the wind beneath my wiiiiiiiings!"* As I pulled up I saw the trailers, the "honey wagon" catering truck and technical crews waking up in the chilly morning air. I was playing a librarian who took a stand against censorship in a California town that was burning books. I guess all my years of protesting were finally paying off?

"You're playing Miss Teel, the Librarian? I'm Bob Walden."

"I know. I watch you all the time. I'm Karen."

A warm, giving actor, Bob was eager to go over our scenes together. It felt like rehearsing in a supportive theater company, but soon the major studio Standards & Practices was implemented. I was pulled aside by the dialogue coach who wanted to be sure I hadn't substituted my words for those in the script. As Bob and I finally started in, we were interrupted by the writer, then by the producer, each with script in hand, double checking our readiness to sell their "product". I thought I was prepared for this. I'd been in films before, but they were low-budget spectaculars. This was the world Al described to me, where making money took precedence over the artistic values I'd been trained to hold dear. I was a commodity. My hands and feet got cold.

My hairstyle was changed several times in an effort to more sharply differentiate my character from another one. I was spun around in the makeup chair like a top. We shot only one scene before I was pulled aside. Huge problem. My bra was clearly visible through my soft mauve sweater. They had to find me a slip. My clothes were furiously pulled off, and the layering started afresh. I felt like a Barbie doll, or worse, a store manikin. Dressed, undressed, checked and rechecked. All this was taking time, and on the set time was money.

I knew I was supposed to adore this doting, royal treatment, but after years of legitimate theater where I managed these things myself, I didn't enjoy being fawned over at all and it made me feel helpless and stupid. I found it difficult to relax, even as I assured these professionals that I was fine, that the interruptions had not affected my scene. I knew they could be penalized for destroying "the creative mood," and I did not want them to think I was going to register a complaint against them for ... for what? Not noticing the "unseemly" outline of my bra before we began filming! This miserable pecking order that ensured psychological insecurity in the land of easy-erase angered me. It reminded me of plantation politics.

When my scenes were in the can, they moved on to the next and I was whisked out of the way and soon forgotten. I hope my friends of two days ago will still remember me on the way down. That's Hollywood.

The Five Stages of an Actor's Career:

1) "Who the hell is Karen Ingenthron?"
2) "Get me Karen Ingenthron."
3) "Get me a Karen Ingenthron type."
4) "Get me a young Karen Ingenthron."
5) "Who the hell is Karen Ingenthron??"

Despite my feelings about the big studios, I was proud to be on *Lou Grant* because it <u>was</u> different. Its leading actor, Ed Asner, was twice the Screen Actors Guild President and he set the tone for production standards. His popular program had industry clout, a great reputation, and a staff which was extremely sensitive to labor issues. I was shown tremendous respect and given possibly the best experience a TV actor in those years could have had.

Forty-eight

ON CLOUD...7 ½

Unexpectedly, and at the last possible minute, Al invited me to dinner with his kids. I was excited! Then I got nervous. Then I got annoyed. Why was he doing this? Every time I'd met with him before, he'd been alone. What was his motive for introducing me to his family? I drove to the Valley to the appointed spot where Al was waiting in his car with his two younger boys, Ted and Paul. Then a motorcycle pulled up, straddled by Al's oldest son, Dave.

"This is Karen. She was in the play with me in North Carolina," Al enthusiastically exclaimed. They warmly acknowledged me as we headed into the Pizza Hut for a casual Sunday meal. The boys were loud and full of spunk, and like their dad, looked comfortable in their own skins. I found myself feeling totally at home at this table. We talked about karate, *Diet for a Small Planet*, Dungeons and Dragons, 13-year-old Paul's passion of the moment, and *Dr. Who*. The engaging conversation and banter bounced back and forth, distracting me from focusing on Al's hidden agenda. I was comfortable with everyone -- except Al. Why did he invite me here?

"Alright, everybody. In the car. We're goin' for ice cream!" An excited cacophony of "yeahs" ensued as the sons raced each other to their dad's car, leaving Al and me to bring up the rear. Will Al use this minute alone for some personal expression? He simply opened the passenger door for me which caused some speculative elbowing from the boys in the back. They were clearly checking me out.

"So, are we going to Carvel's?" I asked.

"You know about Carvel's!?" Ted yelled.

"Sure. You like it, too?"

"Yeah, it's only the best ice cream you've ever eaten, right!?" said Dave, and turning toward his brothers, awarded me a bold thumbs-up. I felt like I'd finally got my foot in the door with this bunch. Is Al noticing? Is this trip a test to see how well I interact with his kids? Paul leaned forward, his chin in the indentation between the two front seats, and assailed us with esoteric information. "Did you know that both Einstein and Charlie Chaplin played their violins left-handed?"

"Wow. Do you know what famous artist never sold a painting while he was alive?" I quizzed. In unison, the answer came back: "Van Gogh!"

"You fellas sure know a lot!" I raved from the front seat. What a wonderfully creative, playful family, I thought, and really felt like I was beginning to fit in, which made me feel very nervous, waiting for the other shoe to drop. As soon as the car stopped, the boys leaped out, racing, tackling and plowing into each other, fraternal ebullience personified. Al looked as if he was in heaven, a cigar tucked between his teeth, surveying them like a mama bear enjoying her cubs. We ordered ice cream, devoured our cones, then piling once again into the Mercury, headed back. Watching Al with his kids, I felt a warm blanket of love descend over me, but the closer I got to my car, the more I felt that old cold familiar about-to-be-dumped-again feeling.

"Well, here's your car. Nice having dinner with you," Al said. Plop. There went the other shoe. As I got out of the car, Al sat with his hands on the wheel as his sons called out overlapping goodbyes and thank you's.

"It's been great ..." I said, as the door slammed shut with a dull thud. "Up until now," I mumbled. I beamed at the kids as I opened the door of my Mustang. "G'night, everyone!" I called cheerily, my best acting job of the day. Al pulled away as waves and smiles assailed me from his back seat.

Sweet Pea took me back to Hollywood alone and had to listen to my rant about letting myself get emotionally sucked into those joyful, comforting familial feelings that surrounded me this evening. And I had to promise myself to accept the unchangeable reality of Al's statement, "In California, it's just me and my kids." That was Al's family, not mine. I was on my own. And I'm probably better off.

"Page A-71 ... Top left column ... Monday, 10 PM!"

"Hi, Mom."

"The TV Guide. You're in it! Oh, I can't believe it. I'm so proud of you."

"I'm in the TV Guide?"

"You're going to watch your show, aren't you?"

"What show do you mean?"

"*Lou Grant*, of course!"

"That old thing. Yeah, I guess so. But, I'll have to borrow a TV set!"

"Ohh. You are so anti-establishment! I give up. But I'm still proud of you!"

I did put together a little TV party to watch Karen's episode of *Lou Grant*. Of course, my friends enjoyed all the excitement, and because of the controversial subject matter it got lots of play in the L.A. papers.

My proud father back home in Albany, California, had set up one of his photographic experiments in my honor. "Hi, kid. You were great. I documented some of it. Right from the TV!"

A few days later, after grocery shopping at the Griffith Park Albertson's, an actress who'd auditioned for the same role hailed me in the parking lot. "Hi! You got the part on *Lou Grant*! Good goin'. Who did you sleep with to get cast?" she asked matter-of-factly.

"Excuse me? You're kidding, aren't you?"

"Come on, now. We all know what you have to do to get a juicy character role like that one." I stood there dumbfounded as she continued. "It's all T & A around here. Parts like that are rare as hens' teeth. I don't blame you if you don't want to give me the skinny. I probably wouldn't either. Yeh, well, break a leg. No, I really mean it. Break a leg, bitch. No, I'm kidding." Even if she had stuck around to hear my side of it, I didn't want to disillusion her by telling her the truth. It was even easier than sleeping with somebody. It was a simple matter of 14 years of legitimate acting, dinner theater performances, film roles, Shakespearean productions and hundreds of grueling auditions to get that part. I couldn't wait to tell my roommates that I'd attained that level of enviable achievement when another actor is jealous enough to insult you. In my days living with Al, we'd have laughed about this for hours. No doubt he would have said, "Now you know, Prudence Pennywhistle. Hollywood can be a very vicious place."

My life was changing and I was growing. But in the cracks – falling asleep, parking the car, doing my laundry - when I was least aware, a longing for Al rose up like an ancient mist fogging my brain. The breakup with Al echoed early childhood abandonment experiences and increased my need to be cherished. My parents had divorced when I was almost five and my brother and I went to live with our father, a rare phenomenon in those years. As a child, I looked longingly out my bedroom window each time my mother flew away after a visit, and waited for a sign of her return. Al's departure from my life stirred up that wound and feeling of loss, turning my situation into both a mine field of self-doubt and a gold mine of self-discovery.

Forty-nine

PEDAL TO THE METTLE

Legitimate theater in La La Land? Director Henry Hoffman cast me in *Transformations,* a play built around the poems of Anne Sexton and starring Salome Jens in an all-female ensemble at the Westwood Playhouse.

Al called to congratulate me for the great coverage for the play. "Waaah Wow! A whole page in the Los Angeles Times! Not bad, Pru, not bad. Yeh, I know Salome. From New York."

"Really? I'd never have guessed."

Al continued unfazed. "What a spectacular run in *The Balcony,* the Jean Genet script. Did you know Salome was JFK's secret lover in those years? What a knockout!"

"She's still a raving beauty, Al. Why don't you come and see the show? You can say hello to Salome." Oh shit, did I really just invite Al? What was I thinking?

It was opening night, and the audience response was strong. I felt good about it and I was hopeful that I'd get a positive review from Al. After the show, we stood together in the theater parking lot. I looked at him expectantly. "Well, what do you think, Al?"

"Too static, too long, and you look frozen in your part." It took several seconds to process that statement.

"That's a good one, Al, but now what do you *really* think?"

"I just told you."

He shrugged his shoulders and pressed my face with his palms. "I love you! See you later." Then he rushed off to his car. I yelled after him, "Up yours, Al! This ain't a Neil Simon play, this is real life! And you've never been funny. Or nice. Hack!" Well, that felt good. Did I just say that? Then I burst out laughing. I suddenly felt free, and that feeling made me smile. I did a happy karate dance across the parking lot, chopping through two kinds of hot air.

One sunny morning, the Hollywood sky was unusually clear of smog, rendering visible the mountains to the West, and I was filled with the beauty of the day. I felt completely whole, a silky landing into centered grace. Everything appeared to be as it should, just like the Cat Stevens song: "Morning has broken, like the first dawning ..."

Driving north up Route 5 with Sweet Pea, my dented green Mustang, I watched as each bit of scenery came into view then faded into my rear view mirror: brown winter hills, cows mooing by the slaughterhouse, smells of dung and death. But there were also lovely things -- like rest stops, Anderson's Pea Soup Restaurant, cars driving into the horizon and disappearing like the clouds on a Japanese scroll painting. This endless highway seemed to be telling me to let it go. Let it go. Wasn't a romance with Al Lewis a treasure? Yes, it was. But it's a lost treasure. Let it go.

The Five Stages of a Hollywood Romance:

1) "Who the hell is Al Lewis?"
2) "Get me Al Lewis."
3) "Get me a nicer Al Lewis."
4) "Get me away from Al Lewis."
5) "Who the hell is Al Lewis??"

I had stayed connected to my old Berkeley dojo, practicing for my Black Belt test. Finally, as if in a hokey martial arts film, I'd been 'summoned by the Master.' I was excited and scared. It was time for my Black Belt test back home!

Fifty

TOUGH ENOUGH

For one month back in Berkeley, I worked out for long hours every day, practicing karate forms, breaking boards, studying self-defense and sparring techniques. After that I went to the gym. I was also required to learn basic Tae Kwon Do history, theory and philosophy. There were days when I felt like I was fulfilling an ancient rite of passage and I wondered what kind of person I'd be at the end of this relentless trial. Hell, I was being melted down, poured into a new mold. Maybe I'd be re-conformed into a 14-year-old boy!

During the test, the pressure was on. But I kept breathing and stayed focused, passing through obstacle after obstacle.

After my last bow, images from my long karate journey flashed before my eyes. Total exhaustion, sore muscles, worry, doubt, and terror, sweating and sparring, the scores of broken boards and swollen knuckles, the dozens of tubes of arnica gel, the trips to the ER for sprains and cracks, the rainbow of previous belts striven for and earned, the kindness of my karate mates. The blood, sweat and tears of committed study.

The Master approached me and paused for an eternity, his face a blank slate. I kept my swollen fingers crossed. He finally handed me a carefully folded Tae Kwon Do Black Belt.

As I took in the faces of the students standing at attention, I realized that they were smiling. I'd done it! No, it wasn't easy at all. It was a test calculated to press my limits and I passed it.

"Come on! Hurry up!" the Master commanded. "Let's celebrate!" We rushed to change clothes, and then the whole school went out drinking!

I was a little drunk after the party and wanted to call someone to celebrate. Unfortunately, I dialed a number by habit. "Al? Al? I'm a Black Belt! Yeh, I passed the test!"

"That's wonderful. That's just wonderful."

"Wonderful? Oh, you know that word, Al? Why didn't you ever use it about my acting?" I blurted.

"Theater is a bullshit medium. In karate, either you break the boards or you don't! You busted four. With your foot!!" I slammed down the receiver, but I had to smile because I knew then I'd always have to be Gracie Allen to his George Burns. Thanks, Al. I'll consider that a pat on the back.

A day later. Total surprise. Bay Area director Doug Johnson, known for his brilliant comedies, called me. He was directing a show in San Francisco and needed a replacement for Diz White, a seasoned comedienne with a Drama Desk Award under her belt. "Would you like to audition for the backstage comedy, *Footlight Frenzy!*?" Would I? Would I! Like in a Buster Keaton film, I got there before he hung up the phone. The auditions were tests of comedic daring with numerous callbacks, and I squeaked through and got the part. Hollywood was finally behind me now.

Fifty-one

LOVE THE ONE YOU'RE WITH

"Oh, thank heavens I finally found you!" said Jack Hallett. "I want you for another play I'm directing." Fortunately, he'd been able to track me down through all my moves. "How about going back to North Carolina to perform in *Murder at the Howard Johnson*? It's a three-character comedy." Jay Thomas, who'd become popular as Robin Williams' friend in *Mork and Mindy,* would head the cast. The other character was to be played by George Peter Ryan, known best for his hilarious national commercials. My American Tourister was packed in a flash.

My memories of North Carolina duly noted, I was determined to create a fresh start, and feeling Al would always be a part of me, hoped for his brand of continued, close friendship. But that romantic root? I pulled it out like an unwanted weed. Yet there were those root filaments that simply would not come up, no matter how hard I yanked. I let them linger there, so far below the surface that I hoped that they would die off.

The play went off without a hitch. George Peter Ryan urged me to try New York again and promised to help find me an agent if I moved there. A few weeks after the play closed, I was living on Manhattan's East Side, sharing a third floor walkup with an old Berkeley friend, Noka Zador. Al was in Los Angeles with his kids, of course. I gave or received the occasional call from him, the man who had moved me more than any other, and moved away from me just as much.

"You've gotta figure out what motivates you," said George as I complained about being without a mate. "You can't keep asking other people to save you. It's time to do it for yourself. I mean you're a Black Belt!" He hugged his head in disbelief that a Black Belt could be singing "Some Day my Prince Will Come." Al's prescriptions for confidence building were working in every area of my life except one: romance. I realized that I had always wanted men, and that included Al, to rescue me from my own insecurities and bad habits. To love me when I didn't love myself, to anchor me. It was time to provide for myself what I had always hoped a man would give me.

I had an idea about something that would center me and draw all of the desired elements together. I went to see Ken and Jessica, my former roommates who'd moved to Brooklyn. I announced, "I need to marry myself."

"We'll help you," they happily agreed in unison.

"I want a wedding celebration to unite my male and female sides. I believe that I can become whole this way."

"Okay," said Ken. "Let's do it right now!" They flew around their apartment gathering props: a coat rack stand-in for Mr. Right, a guitar (my mate will be musical), Balinese masks (he must have many facets), and some incense to purify the ceremony. Willie Nelson's voice rang from the record player representing, according to Ken, "the best part of your male half." My friend was right. Willie was taking me home: "All of me, why not take all of me ...." I wanted to bring all of me into the act of committed love! When Willie's next song came on, "Mammas Don't Let Your Babies Grow Up To Be Cowboys," we laughed at the absurdity of this music popping up at my wedding. But curiously the song called to me with its symbolic lyrics, "cowboys ain't easy to love and harder to hold, they'd rather give you a song than diamonds or gold." I *knew* he was talking about my outsider ways, my creative spirit that I no longer wanted to fight, but to embrace. And weren't those "cowboy" boyfriends, like Al, who never wanted to commit to a relationship, really already a part of me? Wow. This seemed so right!

Our service, hilarious and deep, was completed when I placed a gold ring on my left hand, integrating my inner lovers. I was surprised that this improvisation could move me the way it did. With its potential to trump power, love was such a mighty force, that I already felt a revolution fomenting inside me. Surely my inner marriage will actually work. I felt happier than ever, and my friends noticed a joyful gravitas in me, something akin to (take it, Willie) "Amazin' Grace."

Fifty-two

WHAT FOOLS THESE MORTALS BE

Starting in February 1983, four pillars in my life fell, just months apart. The slide into a period of darkness, of mourning profound, began with the death of my maternal grandmother, Mayme. Three months later my day job employer, the great musicologist and philanthropist Carleton Smith, passed away. Soon after that my great-aunt Marie, who was responsible for lots of my cultural education as a child, also passed on. Then Michael Liebert, the founder and Artistic Director of The Berkeley Repertory Theatre, died in October, 1984. These losses marked the movement into my middle years and a burgeoning awareness of how tenuous our hold on life is.

Solemn and reflective months went by before I was able to plan another trip to California to line up lots of industry-related activities directed at getting more work. Since I planned to be in Los Angeles first, I thought it might be good to see Al again. It would surely be an opportunity to see if any shred of our friendship still existed. It would also be a chance to test my mettle. I knew I could do it. I was a Black Belt and the marriage to myself was strong.

"I'll be in L.A. next week, Al. Would you like to have lunch?"

"Sure. I can tell you about the kids. Call when you get in."

We met at Fromin's Deli and had a long, talky lunch. With all those recent deaths still on my mind, I had to ask Al something. "Will you contact me if you ever need me?"

"Ahh, nothin's gonna happen to me. I'm made of stainless steel, remember?!" I knew he was trying to cheer me up, but, damn, it was frustrating not to get through to him.

"Come on, Al, I care about you. What if you get sick?"

"Was the lunch that bad?! Heh, heh, heh."

Frustrated, I grabbed his lapels and said, "Look at me, Al. I'm telling you I care about you."

"Come on! We're going for ice cream."

"I give up! Again!"

Surprise! Al's youngest son, Paul, was standing behind the counter at Baskin Robbins, ready to serve us. I hardly recognized him, as he'd grown from a scrawny teen into a handsome young man. He hugged me, and appeared to be as delighted to see me as I him. Wow. I remembered him playing Dungeons and Dragons, and now he was picking out colleges and working out at the gym. He looked fantastic.

As Al tilted his head up to read flavors from the extensive menu, I seized the moment and whipped out a business card, handing it to Paul. I said, "Would you do something for me? If ... anything happens to your dad, would you let me know?" Paul looked directly into my eyes, read my concern and nodded.

Noticing a crowd gathering, Al, ever the performer, started ordering hilarious, make believe flavors. He called out to his son, "Gimme a double scoop of Bubble Gum-On-Yer-Shoe. Wait, make that Almond Roca Joka. Oh, you're out of that one? Then make it Peanut Butter Honey Pretzel Chocolate Lava Drip. No? Okay (resigned), a single vanilla in a cup." He soon had the other patrons in stitches. Over cascades of laughter, Paul scooped, and we lapped our delicious treats.

Afterward we stood outside in the December sun finishing up our talk, not quite ready to say good-bye. He put his arms around me, clearly happy for the visit.

"You look spectacular, "Al said. "How do you do that?"

"It's Max Factor!" Al laughed and took my face in his hands. "It's seeing you, Al. Even though you're a big pain in the ass, I still think you're wonderful."

"Karen, I'm old. I'm going to be 74."

"When you gave me this speech last year, it was 71." Al chuckled.

"Anyway, I got aches and pains." His eyes were the same as always, deep and penetrating. He kissed me gently on the mouth. He looked, well, piteous. "Who can put up with a broken-down old wagon like me?"

"A broken-down wagon?" That's so unlike Al. Was this a sympathy ploy?

"Who knows how much time I got left?"

"As usual, you're not telling me your feelings, Albie, but I'll tell you mine. I can't control your circumstances, but whatever happens, I want you to remember, I'm always there for you." Al nodded, quietly taking that in. I nodded, too. "There. I said it, I meant it, and you'll have to deal with it." I turned on my heel and walked toward my car. "Good," I whispered to myself, "Karen, you stayed grounded and you stuck to your truth." I felt my skin tingle. I was certain that Al had really heard me, and with that thought, any nagging expectations about our future together mercifully slipped away. That sense of liberation was so tangible that I danced a karate-meets-Isadora salsa before opening the car door. I would have given anything to see the look on his face as I drove off! I adjusted the rearview and I couldn't see his expression, but I could see mine. And I was smiling.

My trip continued when I flew to Northern California to spend Christmas with my parents, and to check out some theatrical leads.

"How was Al?" my mother asked as soon as I came through her front door. "Any chance he's back?" I gave her the wrist, flicking her off with my now polished Al Lewis gesture of dismissal.

"You never know!" Mom chirped. "Look what I saved for

you!" She held up a crossword puzzle from the Oakland Tribune. Sure enough, another Al Lewis clue. It read, "____ 54 Where Are You?"

"Know why he's always in the crosswords, Mom? Because he always has a cross word and he's a puzzle."

"Karen, you're still culturally deprived!" She looked like an imp as she scurried away to stir her holiday gravy.

Although they'd been divorced for 35 years, my parents shared holidays. At the dinner table, my dad slumped in his chair, clearly suffering from Parkinson's symptoms. But he shakily raised his glass in a Christmas toast. I could see he was trying hard to rise to the occasion.

A few months later I was back in New York, very busy taking care of my late great-aunt's possessions. When the phone rang in my walkup on Forty-ninth and First, I was sure it was the Rent-A-Truck outfit calling me back.

"Hello?"

"Karen, hello. This is Paul Lewis, Al Lewis's son." My heart turned to lead. Emergency. My inner voice alerted me, is this one of *those* phone calls? "You asked me to call if anything ever happened to Pop." Oh God No! "He's in the hospital." There was a pain behind my ears that dragged me toward the floor. I slid down the wall and sat, knees bent, on the carpet. "He had a nosebleed that wouldn't stop. But these wonderful doctors got it under control. Pop's right here. I'll put him on." I knew I should be relieved that Al was alive but ... it was too late. Terror-adrenaline was coursing through me. I had to catch my breath.

"Hello? Hello! Boy, Karen, you should've seen what happened to me! I was sitting on the couch watching the boys pack for college. Then I get a nosebleed. It wouldn't stop. The kids had to take me to the hospital." Al was rolling through the tale of his crisis like a bullet train. "Finally, this young doctor stuffed my nose with cocaine. Yeah, can you believe it? I was high as a kite. Still am. Thought that would do the trick, but no. They ended up putting a gallon jug of water on my chest with tubes up my nose. Pressure. That's what did it, thank God." My own adrenaline rush started to abate as I realized that the storyteller was back and Al would be okay.

"Jug of water on your chest? Cocaine? What kind of hospital is that?" I laughed nervously.

"Doctor told me I coulda been spared a stroke. That nosebleed took the pressure off my brain."

"Thanks for letting me know, Al. I'm so relieved that you're alright. Take care. God bless you ... Albie."

After that, I kept in touch with Al and often sent him a card or a letter wishing him well, not expecting anything in return. I found acting work through friends from Berkeley who were spread out around the country. I was moving from one show to the next and in each note to Al described where I was and what role I was playing. I signed them, "Love, Pru," then kept on trucking, absorbed by my string of jobs and wondering if Mr. Right would ever make his entrance.

Fifty-three

CODA

February 12, 1985. My father died unexpectedly at age 67. This loss silenced me. I went for days without uttering a word. I hid under my bedsheets and cried. I had lost my anchor and I ached. I called Al in Los Angeles to give him the sorry news of my father's passing. Solemn and plain, he offered his sincere sympathy to me and my family. "Karen, your father was a good man. I'm glad I had the chance to meet him. My condolences to you, your mother, and your brother. Take care, Pru."

To settle my father's modest estate, I flew back to the Bay Area, stayed with Mom, and worked with my brother to clear out Dad's house, our childhood home. Together we sorted souvenirs from our past, emptying the physical contents of Dad's life into our own lives or into the trash or into Goodwill bags. Yeah. Save. Toss. Give Away.

Fifty-four

SNAKE OIL ANYONE?

September 1985. Dad's house was sold, and my life was finally in order. I'd start rehearsals soon for a play in San Jose. Everything was going smoothly and then my mother's phone rang.

She covered the receiver and, eyes popping, mouthed to me, "It's Al Lewis!"

Even from two feet away I could hear his voice. "Hey, Mom, I'd love to visit. Whadda ya say!"

"What! When?!"

"How about this weekend?"

"Well ... please come! Where are you, Al?"

"Los Angeles. An hour flight." My mother and I were stunned. I was a little scared. What was he up to? I'd only seen Al four or five times in as many years. What was going on here?

Mom said, "Well, it's just for two days. What could happen? He's probably scouting basketball players, or checking out a job. Anyway, it doesn't matter, he's coming." Mom was on fire and I hadn't seen her so animated in a long time. I was excited too, but guarded. I had a hundred questions running through my mind. Why is he coming? Why did he invite himself? He didn't ask to talk to me about it. Why did Mom accept? What does Al want? Heck, what does Mom want? Guess I better brush up on my self- defense moves.

"How about a salmon platter? He'd like that, wouldn't he?" Mom asked, excitedly fingering through her recipe file box.

"Well, if he insists on coming, we might as well show him a nice time." I scanned the entertainment section for things he might like to do or see. Then I tidied up the guest room.

When we picked Al up at the Oakland Airport, he was sporting a thin mustache, and bubbling with good cheer. My mother asked him why he had made the trip, and he answered, "I just came to visit you!" He did appear to be delighted to see us, but I still had grave doubts about his hidden agenda. You never knew what The Trickster had up his sleeve.

It wasn't bad seeing Al again, especially on my turf. We spent the two days visiting interesting Bay Area restaurants and night spots. During Mom's wonderful salmon dinner, she made a point of inviting him again. "Now, Al. Anytime you want to visit, you know where we are," my mother stated solemnly. I shook my head "no" at her behind Al's back. Then I shook my head with resignation. Mom seemed to have a not- too-well hidden agenda of her own. After dessert, I drove Al back to the airport, and walked him to his departure gate where he scooped me into his arms and hugged me until I was gasping.

"I had a wonderful time. Thank you, Karen. And you thank your mother. You hear?" As we waved goodbye I realized that during this short visit I'd felt calmer with Al than ever before, like really close platonic friends. Back at Mom's we looked questioningly at each other. He breezed in and he breezed out. What was that all about?

Mom was baffled. I was too, but also happily taking pleasure in the relative closeness I'd felt in one weekend. Well, we both agreed that we enjoyed his company, but he certainly could stir things up. In any case, this wasn't just another Saturday night Bingo game for Mom. Al had stepped out of her Crosswords into her living room.

Al took my mother at her word, and some weeks later came to visit again! Did he know that she was taking her annual vacation to see Grandma in Pennsylvania, and would be gone for six weeks, leaving me alone in the house? Probably. Seeing Al was pleasant enough, but on the other hand, I was definitely on my guard. I drew protective lines in the sand. "You're in the guest room, Al."

"Sure!" and he plopped his overnighter on the bedside chair. Al went to his room at night. I went to mine.

My room was where I quietly took counsel with my heart. Al had won my mother over, that was pretty clear! I'm sure his plot was: "Get the Mom on your side and you're in." She'd opened the door for him, and he looked totally at home and comfortable. A familiar feeling, for it had been like that in North Carolina, too. While I was drawn to that comfort, I knew I had to test him. How often had I'd thought we were good for each other, two equal and opposite forces, with just enough creative friction to produce sparks, only to have those sparks turned into a destructive blaze. It was so obvious to me that we were probably better together than apart. But, I needed to examine my dreams of togetherness within the context of real life with Al. So I kept my cool, with the intention of engaging in honest, open curiosity about who we were as a couple. Sensible, huh?

I wasn't in rehearsal yet, just preparing for my next play which would start in about a month or so. I treated Al like a friendly guest. When I drove him to San Francisco to see the sights, and we passed through North Beach, Al pointed out the famous nightclub for female impersonations, Finocchio's. "I worked there!" Al announced. That astonished me and also cracked me up.

"Of course you did, Al. I should've guessed. You'd be one ugly-gorgeous babe. Who did you impersonate, Marjorie Main? Sophie Tucker?

"You guessed it. Sophie Tucker."

"That was just a wild ..."

"Can you imagine me singing 'Some of These Days' in a sequined gown?"

"No way! Well ... actually, yeah!"

"Thanks, Karen, such a quick wit." Al shook his head to tease me. "Just like the fellas in the cast. I have great memories of matching wits with those crazy, colorful performers. Nobody can dish badinage like those guys," Al gushed with nostalgic admiration.

We parked the car and walked to City Lights Bookstore. "Here's where I met Dash. Yeh, right here."

"You mean ..." We said it at the same time, "Dashiell Hammet."

"Come on, Al, slow down. I'm trying to keep score here. I got a notebook full of famous people that you knew. It would be easier to keep track of the ones you don't know."

"I don't know what possessed me. Time on my hands, I guess. I love Mysteries, so I signed up for his writing class. At his place on Post Street."

"You? You never write. One postcard in all the time I've known you!" I teased.

"Only one?" Al look confused, like he wished he'd written more. But it was a fleeting thought and he quickly returned to Hammet. "That was one tough class. I agreed with Dash. I'd be a better criminal lawyer than a writer!"

"Yes, I've experienced your cross examinations!"

"All that Yeshiva training," Al said, as if it couldn't entirely be his fault that his mind was a steel trap.

"Yeshiva," I said, "you could get a nun to confess." Al's eyes flashed. He liked my spunk, maybe it was because he was catching on that I had gotten a handle on his brand of brashness.

"Today you're a tourist, Al. How about Fisherman's Wharf?"

"Yeah! Let's eat at DiMaggio's."

"Wait. Don't tell me, Al. Let me guess." Sure enough, at the front door we were met by Joltin' Joe himself. I just shook my head.

"Oh, it's Grandpa Munster," he laughed, "the original Bat Boy!" DiMaggio seated us in a private booth.

"Al, tell me how many more lives you've led that I don't know about."

"Guess."

"Astronaut?" He shook his head.

"Deep sea diver?" He shook his head again.

"Snake charmer?"

"Bingo!"

"Get outta here, Al. Just get outta here."

"No. Amateur herpetologist! I spent a zillion weekends at the Bronx Zoo looking in reptile cages. Crocodiles, whatta stink. I like snakes best."

"You would. You love everything that scares the rest of us to death."

150

"You're right. I love 'em! I took a ball python on Johnny Carson. They hired me to spritz him. I was on a ton of times. One time I went on the show with a baby orangutan."

As Al and I chatted, I was surprised to find myself so content. He had caused me such grief over the years. But now I had to admit that I kind of adored this guy, clay feet and all. Maybe it was because I was being entertained and not dumped.

More sight seeing. There were physical signs of his former affection: an arm suddenly on my shoulder, grabbing my hand when we stepped into a busy intersection, sneaking in kisses. They seemed innocent enough. I was being a friend. Period. Even though I felt that ole familiar feeling, the tingling, and desire, I wasn't budging.

One morning over breakfast, he looked up over his newspaper and zapped me.

"Wanna get married?"

I was stunned. "No!" I snapped. I wanted him to think about what I'd endured when he broke up with me. Besides, I was a feminist and had objections to traditional marriage! He gave me an implacable smile and let my response go.

I was surprised when several of my friends were suspicious about Al and wanted to know why he was still visiting. They quickly reminded me of the fact that Al's rejection had turned me inside out, and I'd recently gone through heavy mourning. Perhaps I'd been too tenderhearted and forgiving, they lovingly scolded. And perhaps I needed to brush up on my survival skills? They were my friends, my protectors, so I promised to guard my heart like a Rottweiler guards his bone. But, truthfully, once I got over the shock of it, Al's proposal started to seem attractive. Of course that was a secret. I was still holding the line, reminding myself that I was in mourning, and vulnerable.

Fifty-five

GETTING GRILLED

I promised to take Al out for a great, cheap lunch. We pulled into the parking lot of my favorite burger eatery, just above College Avenue on Ashby. If you looked east up the hill, there she was, Berkeley's majestic Claremont Hotel. This tiny unpretentious joint was like a poor cousin, sitting at her feet. It was a spunky little place with delicious food that I had wanted to share with Al for some time. As I turned off the engine, Al snapped, "What you got against marriage?"

"What? What are you talking about? Is this a joke?" Blindsided again by that slapstick of his.

"How long did yours last?"

"Okay, so this isn't a joke. Do you really need to pick a fight right now?"

"That former husband of yours. Why'd you stay with him if he was such a louse?"

"Why are you attacking him? Why are you making me defend him? What's this all about? Yes, he was a louse and he was other things, too."

"Other things?" he sneered. I had to keep my balance.

"Al, if this is so important to you, yes, he was a wonderful teacher and actor. And a mind, like a library. Besides, he accepted my life in the theater because he loved the theater too. Okay? Now can we eat?"

"I never would have put up with his nonsense. His eye for the ladies."

"Oh, come on. What are you trying to prove? You were married, too, Al," I reminded him, trying to figure out his purpose for this attack.

"Yeh."

"And divorced."

"Yeh."

"I'm sure you learned a lot from your marriage. I know I did." Al became quiet, taking in what I said. His mind seemed to toss the thoughts around and then it settled. From his expression I guessed that he had reached some accord with me. Maybe he saw his former marriage as I saw mine: a boot camp that built character and compassion. Would he concede this point?

"You don't have any confidence," he stated, a total non-sequitur out of nowhere.

"Al, are you nuts? What's this new topic have to do with our meaningful marriage discussion?" I thrust a stop-BS-ing glare at him.

"Maybe everything. Maybe nothing. But you got no confidence." He looked through the windshield toward the sky.

"What game are you playing now?!"

He shook his head and said, "No confidence."

"If I don't have it, maybe you know where I can get it? Are you selling it? Doctor Al's Confidence Elixer?"

"Nah, you gotta build it. That's what's wrong with you. No confidence."

"I'm not on your basketball team, Al. You're looking at a person whose life is at its lowest ebb to date. I lost my father and five other people close to me. But, guess what? I *am* confident. I've accomplished a whole lot on my own since we were together six years ago. Want the list, Coach?"

"Oh, so you got a list."

"This is a waste of time. I can't do this."

"Do what? Talk?"

"Be raked over the coals for no reason."

"Raked over the coals?! With you I gotta walk on egg shells."

"Deep breath … Al, knock it off. Just shut up and listen. You don't owe me anything, but you have to offer me some empathy. I'm grieving right now, in case you hadn't heard." Mourning was the pits. I felt tears pressing behind my eyeballs, ready to tumble. The flood gates were opened. I reached for the glove compartment, right by his knees, for my little packet of tissues.

"Look, Al, I don't care what you call it. Lack of confidence, not being able to sell myself. I can't take your bullying me. I can't. All things considered, I'm doing great. But I miss my dad. It's going to take a while. So, if you can't accept me as I am right now … go home." He suddenly looked dazed and stunned. "I think the best thing is for you to go back to L.A." A very long moment of silence ensued as Al seemed uncharacteristically at a loss for words. But then he came back with, "Will you come to my funeral?"

"What did you say? Will I what?"

"Will you come to my funeral?"

"Sure, Al," I said with mock cheerfulness. "Let me get out my datebook. When is it? I'll pencil you in." I threw the purse and my pencil into the back seat in frustration, turned the key, revved the engine, jammed Mom's Chevy into reverse, and peeled out into traffic, tires screeching. "Thanks for the lunch, Al. It would have been great."

I watched him take inventory: There'd be no lunch. I'm in Karen's car and the woman I'd just spent an hour insulting is driving. And she isn't too happy. Where is she taking me?

It was a long, silent ride to Alameda.

What did this man really want? How much of this aggravation did he expect me to put up with? I pulled the car sharply to the curb in front of several Park Street motels. "Take your pick, Albie.

Everything in Alameda's close to the airport."

"I'm not sleeping in no motel. I'm going home with you," he declared.

"I don't think so, Al. Unless you tell me the truth, you're gone. You have no respect for my grieving soul and you're not even coming clean about why you're here. In Alameda. 'Visiting' me."

"You've got a lot to learn, young lady!" He boomed, like a decree from Pharoah. I inhaled slowly before I spoke.

"And you're the only one who can clue me in ... Albie." He sighed. He looked out the window, bit his lower lip and said, "Let's go some place where we can talk." Sensing that the odds were pretty good, say, one out of ten that he would open up, I drove a short distance to the strip of beach front facing San Francisco Bay and stopped the car. The view was breathtaking. A blanket of fog rolled in over the City as the autumn wind lifted gulls and terns in whirling configurations above us. I wondered if I'd forever link this stunning sight with the day I kicked Al Lewis out of my life.

"Tell me what you're feeling, Al. No stories. No jokes. No wisecracks. No bullshit."

"It killed me. Perc Westmore's funeral."

I started the car. "That's it, liar! Pick a motel!"

"No, no, no. This ain't a story. I'm trying to be honest. Hear me out. Perc Westmore. Famous as all hell. When he died, it was the sorriest funeral I ever saw. Maybe four people showed up. Karen, I don't want to end up like that. I got millions of fans, too. But do I have one friend?" He looked at me with sad, longing eyes. "I came here to audition for the part of loving husband. You are the light of my life, Karen, but given my track record ..." He shrugged. "So I joke. I tell stories." There was a short pause as he cleared his throat. "So. Here's the truth. I love you, Karen. Along with my kids, you are the best thing that ever happened to me."

"What's all this funeral business?"

"It's not about a funeral. It's about needing that one-in-a-million friend which is you."

Al's admission really touched me. For the first time in a long time, I believed him. Almost. "Al, I need to know what you have in mind. I need to know your intentions. And I need to have a promise from you that you're not going to yank the rug out from under me, jerk me around, or do your vanishing act."

"Look, I'm starting over, Karen, as a new man. I swear on my kids that I'm going to do my level best to share my life with you, as a loving partner. On my honor, I'll do ..."

"Okay, okay, don't gild the lily, Albie!" With that I opened my arms and this crazy, relieved man flew into them.

Fifty-six

POUNDING THE PAVEMENT

We drove round and round, Al's lap was covered with the street map, and I looked out the side window at the house numbers. Every day we followed up on a few leads – from the local paper, a friend, a real estate ad. Al was happy. I was a bit anxious. I had a job coming up and we needed to settle into a place of our own. Soon.

He loved the rhythm of it: the newspaper, the route, the car ride, the ringing of door buzzers, shaking hands with strangers, the invitation to view what they owned, to check out their stuff. He was a snoop. It was as if he was writing detective novels and needed to research where and how things could be hidden or saved. He enjoyed the search for a home so much, psyching out the home owners, that I wondered if he'd ever stop looking and help me find one to live in!

Finally, we found a nice apartment right in Alameda, convenient to everywhere we had to be. Close to Mom, San Francisco, and San Jose. Calling up all the film and theater contacts I had, we made appointments for Al to connect with agents. They were thrilled to meet Al Lewis, but acknowledged that they might not have much to offer a Hollywood star of his caliber, or his era. They asked him if he would mind flying back to Los Angeles for interviews, ironically, just after he moved from L.A., which seemed to be a common phenomenon for actors.

My mother gushed when I asked her to drive Al to appointments in San Francisco. "Oh, I don't mind!" she cooed. "He doesn't know his way around The City." Since she'd recently begun a second career acting in walk-on and extra parts, she now suddenly knew all the basics of travel and protocols for actors. "I'm taking him to meet my agent! Why not?! And he can't use that old headshot. That was okay for *California Suite*, but he's changed since then. Oh, you have to keep current. I'm going to take him to my photographer, the place where I go." Mom, the new authority on all things theatrical, took his career in hand. Al was amused and flattered, quite happy with his new "agent."

Mom's Headshot

Fifty-seven

PACI-FIST!

"What's so great about karate? A bunch of bowing." Al shrugged his shoulders as if to dismiss the whole discipline.

"What's great about it? It's physical, psychological, spiritual, and artistic, as in martial *art*. I've spent years practicing karate, getting my Black Belt. It's a huge part of my life. I love going to class, what? Three, sometimes four or five times a week, not only for the blessing of the workout, but for the camaraderie. I often get a chance to teach. Yes, there's a lot of bowing. But it's to honor the spirit, humanity, and essence of the other person we are bowing to!"

"I hate bowing," Al griped. "Hierarchies. Who's on top. Who sets the agenda. Who obeys. Or else. Yeah, I don't like those ideas one bit," said Al, almost sweetly.

"Bowing is beautiful. I honor the life force in my opponent. You know when you bow, there's that meditative moment, Al, when you have a second to change course on pulverizing. I could get pulverized, too! I have to consider that."

"And by the way, I thought you said you were a Pacifist."

"Yes, that issue bothered me – from my very first class. But my intention was never really to pulverize anybody. I was learning self defense. And the cardio workout *is* excellent." I grinned.

"I think it's all a power trip," muttered my partner, "all the lower ranks kissing up to the leaders."

"Yeh, so what? It's also about women becoming powerful. I thought you were in favor of empowering woman."

"I hate to see women bowing down, their eyes averted. They don't need any more trembling in fear."

"We're not trembling in fear because we know we can castrate an attacker with one well placed KICK!" I thrust my foot at Al carefully and intentionally missing his vital parts by an inch before he could jam his knees together. Then I executed a perfect bow.

His eyes got huge and he laughed a fake/scared laugh and said, "Don't get excited. I just want you to be aware of the politics you're involved in. I love you just the way you are."

NYC Tae Kwon Do Class

Geez. It was hard enough to do karate without having to think about politics. Still, I held onto my idealism and kept going to class, even as my toes were stomped on, my knuckles were smashed, and arnica became my ankles' best friend.

Fifty-eight

STICKING TO IT

In 1985 pre-nuptial agreements were in the news just about every night. Maybe having one would help Al and me.

"I ain't negotiating nuttin'!" Al barked.

"Why not? We're building a partnership! Why not commit to it? Talking about a pre-nup is a good way for us to open up a dialogue about what we want out of our relationship."

"Dialogue? What is that? Berkeley bullshit?"

"Yeh, same as Brooklyn bullshit, only it smells a lot better." Al had to chuckle. "So, dear? What if this pre-nup had a clause that said you could kidnap me in Nashville and dump me at somebody's house at will? Then would you sign it?"

"I got a regular Joan Rivers over here."

"It's a way to look at our future."

"Karen. This is us. I love you. You love me. It's not up for negotiation."

"But you're a trickster, Al. How do I know I can trust you?"

"Karen. When Marge and I were getting divorced ..."

I broke in. "That's right. The perfect time for a long story."

"I'm goin' somewhere with this. Right there in the courtroom, the judge wanted to negotiate visitation rights. Negotiate visitation rights!? No way. I went right up to him, right into his face, and said, Your Honor, they're my kids! I'll visit them any time I want to! You know what he said? 'Of course, Mr. Lewis.' Heh, heh. Don't know what he thought. Is that Al Lewis nuts or what? But he saw my passion and that was it. I visit my kids whenever I want."

"So, nothing in writing then?"

"It's our relationship! It's just like making spaghetti. Boil it. Throw it up against the wall. If it sticks, it's done!"

So unBerkeley and politically incorrect, yet honest and direct! "But still you know you've got a poor record in the sticking department. You didn't stick with me in L.A."

"Yeah, you got me there. But this here's Alameda, Karen, and I got a good feeling about us." Al pulled me close and kissed me, then danced me around our Alameda kitchen, masterfully negotiating around the spaghetti pot handles protruding from the stove. And around the unresolved pre-nup issue.

"Danny Kaye ... you know him? The big star? We were friends from high school in Brownsville, Brooklyn," Al said, wiping his hands on his apron. "Danny took Chinese cooking very seriously. Even had a stove brought over from China and everything."

"What are you making, Hon?"

"A conflagration of opposites!" he yelled. "Chinese style. Sweet and sour, hot and cold. I learned this when I studied in New York with a Chinese Master Chef, Madame Wong."

"Right, Al. And I studied acting in Russia with Stanislavsky."

158

"You don't believe me, ask Marge. I cooked for my kids when they were young. They'd invite their friends over because they liked my cooking! When I was home, I probably cooked eighty percent of our meals."

"Well, you can cook eighty percent of our meals!" I joked affectionately as the steam poured out of his pots.

It was so nice to have someone feed me while I was rehearsing *Passion* at San Jose Rep. My work took up so much time.

"Ah," I said, wiping my lips with my napkin, after a truly delicious feast. "Every actor needs a wife!"

"That's me!" Al boomed, laughing his head off. I looked at the wall and noticed that the spaghetti was still sticking.

Fifty-nine

NEXT!

The alarm rang at 6 a.m. It was that same young man calling again, involving Al in his hilarious, off-colorful on-air radio interviews in which Al thwacked out the powerhouse over-the-fence humor homers. He happily rose very early to take these calls and "stir it up," his name for these drive-time improvisations. During the commercials, this young radio host would thank Al profusely for helping him re-launch his career.

"I don't get it," said Al, shaking his head. "Why do people want to listen to that crap? There are so many real problems in this world. Oh, well. He's a nice guy, that ... What's his name?"

"Howard Stern."

"Oh, yeah. Howard Stern."

My actor friend of twenty years, Thomas Lynch, biked to Alameda from Berkeley for a visit. He liked Al and wanted to spend a few hours with him talking show business. I was sick with the flu and was fading into the couch, curling up next to a tissue box. We sat around the living room catching up when Al dropped The Bomb. "Do you believe in yourself?" Uh-oh, here we go. In the silence that followed, Thomas looked at me and I croaked, "Do you really want to do this? I'm too tired to defend you. If you want to get into this with Al, you're on your own." He looked at me questioningly and then declared, "I'm capable of defending myself."

I felt my stomach twist as Al commenced to take Thomas where he'd taken me that infamous North Carolina day, to the Al Lewis Spanish Inquisition hot seat. I faded in and out, their voices sounding like a verbal tennis match. Then the volley seemed to come to an end and I awoke to hear Thomas saying good-night. I saw in his face, written in a drooping font, "Who am I anyway?" Oh, shit, Al did it again. My heart sank. I was certain that I'd never see Thomas again.

I questioned Al about it and he said, "Aw, go on. You're over reacting." Still my heart was heavy. A few days passed. The phone rang and I picked up the receiver. I heard a sober male voice that was seriously grounded. Thomas was calling to thank Al for the journey he'd put him on. "It was kinda ugly," he admitted, "but I'm better for it now." Al directed a meaningful nod at me. "You see? Not everyone walks on eggshells like you," he teased. "That Tom, he knows his ass from a hole in the ground." Al laughed, "But you? Your poor father sent you to U.C. Berkeley. Look what happened! You know, I gotta go over there ... and get his money back!" He roared into a belly laugh. I playfully pounded on him. Then, just like Alice on the *The Honeymooners*, I shook my fist at him. "One of these days. One of these days ... to the moon, Al Lewis!"

Sixty

TWO OLD FIENDS

SAVE, TOSS, GIVE AWAY

Gee, Karen, you've already dragged boxes of books to the thrift store and there are still more! It's endless. Well, this time, don't look at them. Just pack them up or you'll want to keep them all. What's this one? Oh, Fred Gwynne's book of illustrations. And he autographed it. How can I let that go? Save.

By the time my show in San Jose closed in early 1986, Al and I were packing up to vacate our Alameda home. I was signed for two more plays, *A Flea in Her Ear* and *USA*, in Springfield, Massachusetts. Our plan was to drive to New York and get Al settled into my old East Forty-Ninth Street apartment before my next acting contract began.

Al placed a call to Fred Gwynne, his old friend and *Munsters* co-star, opening the channels for a visit. I could hear from their conversation that Fred was excited about Al's return to New York. Following a few animated minutes of chatter, Al said, "Hey, Fred this is Karen," and suddenly handed me the phone. Oh, God. This was actually the same Fred Gwynne I saw on stage in *Ty Cobb* in New York! Just jump in, I urged myself.

"Hello! Yes, I'm Karen." There it was, the light sweet sound of the voice I knew from his stage performance. "How are you, Fred? Al misses you. He was telling me just the other day how you loved to go to hockey games together in L.A."

Fred laughed, "That's right! He insisted that I go. I was certain I'd hate it. But I didn't. In fact, I became a rabid hockey aficionado! Thanks for making Al so happy, Karen."

"You mean he actually told you that?" We both laughed.

"It'll be a pleasure to meet you. And please, you're welcome to stay with Debby and me for as long as you like. We finally closed on our loft on Bleecker Street. It's been quite a battle," he hummed.

"We're anxious to see it, Fred. Can't wait to meet you."

We put almost all of our possessions in storage, saving just the bare essentials for our cross-country trip. Al made sure that the Chevy Citation, which I inherited from my dad, was thoroughly serviced. Saying goodbye to my mother and my brother's family, we rolled south, sharing the driving. Al was great behind the wheel, especially loving the challenges of endless stretches of road.

In Tarzana, we stopped to say farewell to David and Pepper, Al's oldest son and his wife. Welcoming me with a warm hug, Dave said, "It's great to see you again, Karen! How long has it been? Six years?" We stayed overnight and then reluctantly had to push on as there were two more sons to say good-bye to.

It took us a day and a half to get to the University of New Mexico in Albuquerque where Ted and Paul were studying on basketball management scholarships. Invited to share a meal with the team and coaches, Al grabbed some food and then made the rounds as I sat talking with Ted and Paul until the players dispersed to study hall and evening practice.

Seeing how busy the boys were with studies and basketball

161

duties, we decided to head out. We drove through state after state, sticking to the southern route to avoid inclement winter weather.

Traveling with Al was ... surprisingly easy!

We took a sharp left turn in Arkansas, driving northward, and sped along the open road heading toward our future: New York City and Fred Gwynne's Greenwich Village apartment. Arriving there late in the day, it suddenly hit me. I was about to meet Fred for the first time and didn't know what to expect. He answered the doorbell and rushed down to meet us on the ground floor.

The door opened, and I had to rear back to take in all of Fred. He was tall! This 6' 7" tree of a man, in Ivy League khakis and a button-down shirt, smiled down at us. "Al! My friend." He took Al into his arms, laughing with joy, as tears filled his eyes. Then turning to me, he smiled again. "Didn't mean to ignore *you*!" He shook my hand and delicately flecked a kiss onto my cheek which made me feel included and welcome. "Right this way. Let's get those bags upstairs." Fred's attitude warmed my heart. Dragging our luggage, Fred escorted us to the elevator which opened inside the foyer of his apartment. "Put your things in the parlor and I'll give you the tour. This loft is a work in progress."

The apartment filled the entire floor. In one room, rows of duck decoys, hand-carved by Fred himself, seemed to waddle across the floor in formation. In another room, black and white sketches filled the walls. Throughout the loft were paintings and illustrations by Fred on walls and shelves and hanging from the ceiling. Al stopped when he saw a copy of *Easy to See Why,* his most beloved Fred Gwynne book, written and illustrated for "children of all ages." In it, dogs and their owners look hilariously similar. Soon Debby arrived and we were introduced. "I've organized a little dinner at Fred's favorite bistro, just two blocks away."

"How exciting!"

Marching along, following Debby's lead, Fred seemed like a very tall teddy bear, clearly happy to have his energetic wife managing the details. At the restaurant, under her careful direction, the maître'd seated us at Fred's usual table. Although Fred and Al were cut from very different cloth, and their obvious dissimilarities made their connection appear on the surface to be impossible, they clearly adored each other.

"I gotta get this over with, Fred. Butch is trying to set up a *Munsters* celebrity gig," said Al. He was acting as Butch Patrick's messenger, hoping to enroll the whole horror family in a fan event.

"I told you, Al," Fred's voice struck like a ball peen hammer, "I don't want anything to do with *The Munsters*. I refuse to be type cast. It's hard enough at my height to get good parts. I don't need agents thinking of me as Herman for the rest of my life. In fact, I'm surprised that you don't stop doing *Munsters'* appearances. The show'll haunt you forever if you let it."

"Well, the fans gave me my celebrity, Fred. They got me where I am today. That's how I feel about it." Al's loyalty to his public touched me.

"Have you had any other kinds of roles recently? Other than vampires?" Fred questioned skeptically.

"I haven't had any roles ... period." And Al guffawed at his own misery.

"Maybe that's why."

"Who knows. I ain't independently wealthy like you, Fred! I gotta go where the work is!" Al merrily raised his glass to his friend.

Al's working class background in contrast to Fred's upper class pedigree was unexpected fodder for humor and enjoyment, as each man reached over the invisible barrier between them. Fred ordered more drinks, then lifted his glass to Al. "Nobody taught me as much about acting as this man sitting right here. He's a master teacher. Without his guidance on the set, I would have been lost, Karen. He knows everything there is to know about telling the truth on stage."

"Yeah, on *stage*," I cracked.

Al laughed and muttered, "Yeah, yeah," rebuffing both Fred's compliments and my remark.

Debby cut in. "Fred talks about you all the time, Al. Every time he takes on a new role he thinks about what you taught him during *The Munsters*." I instantly recalled the uncomfortable scenes on the set of *California Suite* where the cast rebelled against Al's insistence on doing things his way. They voted unanimously with one abstention, me: "There's only one director, Al, and it's not you." But here, at Fred Gwynne's table, Al's talents were honored and respected. Fred seemed to have eagerly enrolled in Al's Truth or Consequences Acting School, but our cast from the past had not bought it. Different strokes for different folks? Or had the adamant *California Suite* cast, including me, missed a once-in-a-lifetime opportunity? I may never know.

"Have you spoken with Pat, Karen?" Fred asked.

"You mean Pat Priest, the second Marilyn on *The Munsters*?"

"Yes, she'll tell you about this fellow!" Then to Al, he said, "She knows what a remarkable man you are. You supported her through the whole transition, when Beverly Owen left to get married and she took over the part. And remember, Al, when Yvonne was acting the Diva?"

"How can I forget? She had all the big credits. Yvonne De Carlo was a Hollywood Star, a beauty! None of us had been in big movies like she had."

"That's right. But her attitude was terrible. She made everybody wait all the time."

"You had that suit to wear, Fred, and the big headpiece that made you so hot. Those killer boots." And to rest of us, Al explained, "Sweat! God, they had to squirt water down his back to cool him off, and still she made us wait."

"She could have ruined the happy chemistry."

"Yeah, Fred, as a kind loving family." Al turned to me. "That's what was so incredible about *The Munsters*. We looked weird, but we were really a normal family. We cared about each other. But behind the scenes ..."

Fred continued, "Can you imagine where we would have been if you hadn't talked to her?"

"Yvonne was aging," Al said. "In Hollywood that was the kiss of death. At forty she looked spectacular in *Munster* monster makeup. She was a comical, scary housewife, but deep down, Yvonne was afraid that her career was over. By demanding special treatment, mainly by keeping everybody waiting, she was trying to prove she was still a star."

"You know that one Friday, Al, when we were hoping to finish up on time so we could get home to our families for the weekend? The cast and crew were forced to wait for hours for her. But no one, including the director, had the guts to call this diva to task." Fred turned to Debby and me. "Finally, Al took it upon himself to speak to Yvonne. What did you tell her, Al?" Fred asked, admitting he'd been waiting years to find out. I too was dying to hear Al's response.

"The truth! I went to her dressing room. Knocked politely. She took forever to open the door. I said, 'Yvonne, you're a big star, far bigger than anyone else on the show, but you have no right to waste everyone's time. Get out here. Now!' One second later she walked out of her dressing room onto the set."

Fred pointed his finger at Al. "Only you could pull that off!"

Al continued, "After that, she was like a pussycat. Kind, respectful, everything. We became friends, remember? Got to meet her husband. Nice guy. A stuntman."

More drinks arrived and soon Al and I were begging off the invitations to further imbibe. After our late supper, the four of us hunched against the frigid, February night and hurried back to our hosts' apartment. Fred was several sheets to the wind with Debby holding fast to his arm, like a grumpy police woman with her flasher blinking. We said goodnight and shuffled off to our room.

"You've known Fred a long time," I said with admiration.

"Yeah. Fred had four kids with his first wife, Foxy. One of 'em, Kieran, was disabled. God, I loved him." Al's face softened as his memory took him back. "When we were filming *The Munsters*, Fred and I took our families to Hawaii for the hiatus," the traditional Hollywood break between television seasons. "It was beautiful. We flew to Maui and stayed at a gorgeous beach hotel. Go down for breakfast and there'd be tables and tables of cut fruit. I loved the papaya! Heh, heh. I never saw that in Brooklyn."

"You Brownsville fruitarian!" I smiled.

"Ethelle went with us too, right after Teddy was born. She took care of the kids for us during those years. David was having fun playing in the water with Kieran and the other kids staying at the hotel. Suddenly Marge and I hear Ethelle screaming. She's looking out the window onto the beach. Davey's down there with Kieran and he's drowning. We run down as fast as we can. My God. Kieran's lips turned blue. Ever see that?" Al shuddered, trying to shake the image from his mind. "The lifeguard applied mouth-to-mouth and called an ambulance. When it arrived, you know what Fred said? He looked at me and said, 'Should I get in?'"

"Should I get in?!" Al reiterated those unthinkable words. "I said, 'Get in or I'll punch you in the mouth!'" Now years after the event, Al, his hand pulled back into a fist, shook his head in disbelief. "My mother, may she rest in peace, would have threatened to poke his eye out with a fork. That's how she thought. That's how I was raised."

"How can you still be friends!"

"He's my best friend. I love him. I can't help what soil he grew up in." I inhaled this information, realizing perhaps for the first time, that like our relationship, Al also "threw spaghetti on the wall" to test all his friendships. It appeared that Fred's noodles were still firmly stuck to the wall.

"What happened with Kieran?"

"They saved him, thank God. Yeah, they saved him." Al sat quietly for a second. "You know, Marge and I wanted to adopt him ... later, when Fred told me they were sending him to a special home for the retarded, or whatever the hell he was. Kieran could have come to live with us. But what could we do? You can't go around adopting your friends' kids."

God, I loved Al when he talked that way. He stuck with the people he cared for, and I was beginning to trust that he would never leave me behind. As far as I could tell, our spaghetti was still hugging the wallpaper.

Sixty-one

PUBLIC AFFAIRS

My old New York apartment was a simple European-style, third story walkup with a view from the window of the iron fence surrounding the United Nations. It was situated in the fanciest neighborhood in Manhattan, where mansions co-mingled with old tenements that had been commissioned by the rich to house their workforce during the late 1800s. You could tell it was that old because the shower was in the kitchen, and the toilet, literally a WC, was in the living room. Unlike me, Al accepted all that at face value, never once remarking on the difficulties of such an arrangement, even the three flights of stairs he had to climb. He seemed to revert to the kind of behavior of his youth in poverty stricken Brownsville. In fact, he turned into Leo Gorcey of the Bowery Boys, much more interested in what was happening in the streets than what was happening in our home. If he forgot something on the way out, he'd yell up to me in the window and I'd throw it down to him. I think he did that on purpose, just so he could yell.

As we moved into February of 1986, I relocated to Springfield, Massachusetts, to perform at StageWest, while Al held the fort in Manhattan to work on his projects and go to auditions.

On my weekly day off, Al visited me. He would hop the Peter Pan Bus Line that left the Port Authority terminal and ride four hours into Springfield. Loaded down with reading material, he used the time to dig into his favorite newspapers, magazines and murder mysteries. "I don't mind the trip," he said. "I relax and get my reading in!"

The day before one of Al's planned visits, the United States bombed Libya and it was all over the news. I admit I was still tender and sore about losing my father the year before, and my emotions were just below the surface. I thought my experience in Berkeley prepared me for whatever might happen in world politics, but this was something new. And I just couldn't understand why the U.S. attacked Libyan citizens in retaliation for a terrorist bombing of a military barracks in West Berlin. It seemed now like anything could happen. I got into bed, grabbed the phone, and hid under the covers. Then I dialed for help.

"Al," I cried, "I've never been so scared in all my life."

"Scared? What's wrong?"

"The U.S. bombed Libyan civilians. I heard they killed Qaddafi's daughter."

"Yes, Karen. That's what the U.S. does."

"But send 66 jets to attack innocent women and children in Tripoli? That's horrible! What happened to diplomacy?"

"We're so powerful we can get away with it." Al stated simply, trying to calm me down, but not doing very well.

"If I was a Libyan citizen right now, I'd want to bomb the United States!"

"Maybe they do want to, but they can't. It'd be suicide. We have all the military might."

"How can individual countries bomb anything or anyone they just don't like? Are we becoming a rogue state?"

"We don't call it that in the United States."

"I see. Might makes right," I answered in despair. "Oh, God, Albie, I'm overwrought, I guess. I'm afraid I might drop out of rehearsals."

"You can't let that happen. You've got to fight back. Stick up for yourself and what you believe in. I'm coming up tomorrow. You'll be okay, Karen, my love. You'll be fine." His voice consoled me. "And, don't forget your public!" he chirped.

When Al arrived, he dropped his bags and put his arms around me. We crawled into bed, and holding me tight, he pulled the covers up and rocked me. Feeling Al's belly against mine immediately shifted my anxiety, as the warmth of his body magically drew the terror right out of me.

Sixty-two

FACE VALUE

"I know. I know. Springfield is famous for what? The Basketball Hall of Fame. Ta Dah! But I still don't want to go," Al

167

declared.

"Why not?! I'm eager to see it and I don't even follow basketball."

"I know what it'll be like. A whole lotta hype. That's not for me. I got into basketball for the raw, honest game I remember from my childhood."

"Well, I'm going. I'm performing here and I want to know more about this town."

Reluctantly lagging behind me, Al grabbed his winter coat, and grumbled. "There's too much money in it now. When I'm bird-dogging, flushing 'em out of the bushes, scouting for talent, I look for a player's genuine desire to play the unencumbered game."

Well, Al did go and, of course, the staff at the basketball museum was delighted to see him, and he was high-fived by everyone from the ticket-taker to the curator, creating an opening for him to show off his expertise and ask about the local high school talent. He actually jotted a few names down in his ever-present basketball notebook. I shot him a smile and nod, an I-told-you-so look, just to rub it in. He waved me off with a fake frown. A whole lotta hype, indeed!

Back at my Springfield loft, Al started to connect with basketball teams by phone, using his newly gathered references. He really wanted to see a game! He made his way to a high school and caught some hoop action, after which he boarded the bus back to the Big Apple.

He phoned to tell me that he arrived safely, and he was laughing.

"Never guess what happened to me."

"No. What?"

"Got to Port Authority. Thought I'll walk home. It's a straight shot across town on Forty-Second Street and then up First Avenue. I get to Bryant Park and decide to go in."

"What? Why?"

"To find a place to smoke my last cigar. Can't smoke on the bus. So I light up, find a nice bench and sit down. I swear Karen, it hadn't been 30 seconds, when out of the corner of my eye, I see three guys coming right toward me."

"Oh, my God!"

"My street smarts tell me to stand up. You don't want to get caught lower than your assailant! But before I could get on my feet, there they were. Holy shit." And Al started sweat-laughing.

"What happened? What happened? What happened?"

"I know they're either dealers or junkies by their body language. I hope they're dealers! Then maybe I'll have a chance to out-palaver them. But three! Geez."

"Albie! Why did you go in there?! Even I know Bryant Park is a jungle after dark!"

"So I say, 'Good evening. How are you?' Like this is normal. I put out my hand which gives me a chance to stand up. That threw 'em a bit. Then one guy looks close at my face cuz it's dark in there, and he says, 'You ain't Grampa, are you!' Yeah, that's me! Then the second one says, 'Wow, it's nice to meet you,' and the third one says, 'Grampa, what chu doin' in here at night? I knew that was you, cuz of the cigar. This ain't no place for you. Let's escort you outta here, Grampa. If you're with us, you'll be safe.' So they walk me across the park and I come out right by the library. The one with the big lions? I say goodbye and walk home!"

"Oh, Sweetheart, you idiot," I said, sighing in relief.

"Fans have helped me more times ..."

"Even the drug dealing fans. But I'm so glad you're home safe. Didn't your mother ever tell you to stay out of that park at night?"

"She was watching out for me, that's for sure! When I was a kid, it was safe!" He paused and I heard the sucking sound of Al lighting a cigar. I guess he never finished the one he started in the park. "I been thinking," he muttered.

"Umm. About what?"

"Looks like I got fans out here," he began, meaning New York. "Maybe more than I realize if my trip to Bryant Park means anything!" We both laughed. "I got a call from a coupla investors who are interested in developing a restaurant. You know, like we saw driving across the country. Loretta Lynn's? Other stars have 'em too. Theme restaurants are really big now. They want to exploit my name. In the positive sense, exploit. Know what they want to call it?"

"Tell me! What?"

"Grampa's. What else would they call it!" Merriment flooded the phone lines. "I can't spell it the real way. Universal would never let me use it. We'll spell it just the way kids say it. G-r-a-m-p-a. Gotta meet the suits in the morning. G'night, my beautiful Karen."

"Goodnight, Albie. Thanks for letting me in on that done deal. Be sure to let me know when your restaurant's up and running."

"For you, an engraved invitation."

Sixty-three

ANOTHER HELPING OF LOVE

SAVE, TOSS, GIVE AWAY

More stacks to sift through and another file box marked "Grampa's Bella Gente." The first object I touch is oversized and pink. Pulling it out of the box I see it's Al's face in black caricature strokes; shiny, pink and black. The restaurant menu: Fred Gwynne's drawing of Grandpa Munster. Instant emotion. I plant a kiss right on his nose ... Save.

"Can't come up to see you until next week, Karen. We got about three or four places to look at. One's up in the Bronx. Not crazy about the location. I want one with lots of foot traffic!"

"Oh, right, the famous restaurant."

"Yeah, they want to build on my name recognition. I keep tellin' 'em, I have no desire to have a restaurant where people visit once to see me, and never come again. I want the food to be so good that people will come first to see me and come back again to eat. I don't want no celebrity truck stop."

It's annoying, but I can't get too bent out of shape about his autonomous decisions.

When I returned to Manhattan after my three-month engagement at StageWest in Springfield, plans were moving forward on Grampa's Bella Gente. This restaurant would be the way for Al to make his presence known in New York, and hopefully to acquire acting jobs. When a spot was identified on Bleecker Street right off Carmine, blueprints were drawn up in preparation for a total rehab of the existing space. After exploring several options, all agreed that Grampa's should be bright, cheery, inviting, and noisy!

I was eventually invited into the project as a consultant. We fussed over color combinations and style, calculated to make families feel warm and fuzzy as if they'd entered the world's most wonderful ice cream parlor. Pink! Plus mauve and burgundy to integrate the design components.

"Hey, Karen, get your camera. I want some pictures of an iron railing I spotted when I was walking the neighborhood." We walked down First Avenue to take a closer look at it. It was the gate in front of the U.N.

"Yeh, I like it. Get a good shot of that!"

The winter of 1986-87 was so cold it was hostile. Workers huddled over a table in the dust and dirt of reconstruction at 252 Bleecker Street. The mini concrete mixer made a low grinding groan. Bundled up and still freezing, Al and I moved closer to the mega space heater, plugged in for the construction crew studying the blueprints. The entrance was in the center of the space, with elevated areas to the left and right, separated from the central dining area by

railings patterned after ... Aha! those in my snapshot at the U.N.

Permits and other pre-opening requirements were a New York nightmare. Al and I finally worked as a team attending special goodwill meetings negotiating with commissioners. Al was a unique emissary, entertaining while promoting in his inimitable, humorous, in-your-face manner, building relationships wherever he went. One result was lots of media buzz as word of the new establishment spread. Al was masterfully clever at hilarious interviews and irresistible photos:

Al stabbing food, balancing pizzas, wearing a chef's hat and apron, providing an inordinate amount of splash and excitement. People were talking!

"Karen? This is your mother."

"I do recognize your voice, you know."

"Oh, be quiet. You know what I mean." She sounded just like Lucille Ball. "Now listen to this." I could hear her lick her finger and turn pages. "Eight across. Right at the top of the puzzle! Munster Restauranteur! I know, I know, it's resta-rah-teur. Geez, no one says it that way. This time it's five letters, so it's just the last name. L-E-W-I-S! Oh, Karen, isn't it wonderful!"

"I think Al's press agent is writing those crosswords. But, yeah, Mom, it's exciting. People are talking." It was gigantic butterflies-in-my-stomach exciting. But I wasn't copping to that.

As confident as Al seemed to be, he was really climbing out on a limb. He hadn't lived in New York in over 30 years, and he was starting over because of me and our relationship. Since I thought he was 76, I tried to help him as much as I could. When I found out he was only 64, I still tried to help him.

So, in April 1987, Grampa's Bella Gente (Grampa's Beautiful People), was born. The menu, with a caricature by Fred Gwynne, featured a host of delicious Italian dishes including designer pizzas, all at reasonable prices. I was the official taster, a job I happily created for myself. I got to try everything on the menu. My personal favorite was Gamberi Alla Grampa: shrimps rolled in prosciutto, dipped in egg batter and cognac sauce. "Can you get me another plate of the Gamberi? I just want to make sure my palette registered the subtle nuances."

"But that's your third plate!"

"Yeah, elusive nuances!"

In preparation for the first public seating, Al scheduled two rehearsals, giving the wait staff, the kitchen crew and the cashier a chance to work out the kinks. The first rehearsal was for family and friends, including Mom, who flew out for the event all aflutter. The second rehearsal was a restaurant opening party with some of *The Munsters'* cast celebrating Al's transition to restaurateur. Beverly Owen, the first "Marilyn," arrived. Seeing her with her grown children brought tears to Al's eyes. Co-star and artist, Fred Gwynne arrived with his family in tow. And Butch Patrick, Eddy Munster, joined in the festivities. It was clear that they had enjoyed working together and had a lot of catching up to do. In addition to the Munster cast, lots of City officials were present.

Opening night, people lined up for blocks hoping to get in and be greeted by Grandpa Munster. They were eager to enjoy the lively, inviting atmosphere. As the patrons left the establishment, they gave Al spontaneous rave reviews for his food and fun. Grampa's Bella Gente was considered by everyone to be a roaring success.

Even after the opening the lines were long. There were queues of hungry diners waiting to be served and queues of wannabe waiters and busboys begging to get on the waiting list for future employment. Word of the restaurant's success spread quickly and attendance never let up. Al could have just gone home and let the restaurant run itself, but of course that was not his way. He happily stood outside every evening welcoming his guests, Joe DiMaggio style. In inclement weather, he sat at the front as maître d' of the establishment greeting folks, generations of Al Lewis and *Munster* fans, as they arrived. Lots of his old film and theater friends found him there. Eddie Albert teased Al when he brought his grandson to the restaurant for a birthday treat. He humorously complained, "I wanna take the kid out for his birthday, and he wants to eat with you!"

As time went on and the restaurant flourished, Al got more involved with his clientele and I really loved watching him in action, taking photo after photo with smiling customers. Al's favorite trick never failed to incite raucous guffaws. "Sit right here in front of Grampa," Al urged an eager kid, "and we'll take a snapshot." Then, just as the shutter clicked, he'd stretch the kid's ears out, creating a hilarious keepsake. Al never stopped challenging himself to find ways to make every guest's visit with him memorable. He told jokes, hugged wives, tickled kids, and made faces, humoring the diners until the room was ringing with laughter.

You'd think all of that would be enough for old Al, but he kept working at it. "Every day I tell myself, there's got to be more I can do to make the restaurant successful and fun for people," he told me, burning with purpose. He was that dedicated.

After pounding the pavement, looking for acting work all week, I'd tell Al on most Fridays, "I'm coming down for dinner."

"What'll you have? I'll put the order in for you and sit with you if I can."

"What else? Gamberi Alla Grampa!"

"Sorry, Karen, we ran out," he kidded. "My official taster ate it all."

When Al's middle son, Ted, graduated from the University of New Mexico, he joined the staff at Grampa's, backing up his dad as maitre d'. When the crowded restaurant had a long waiting list for seating, Al and Ted worked in tandem, smoothly moving the line along, keeping those waiting happily in the loop. It was at Grampa's that Ted met Andrea, the woman he would soon marry. She was a brilliant and beautiful student at Cardoso Law School, who had come by to test the restaurant.

"Guess who's comin' by the restaurant tomorrow. Circus clowns! Yep. Barnum and Bailey's in town," Al announced at home the night before.

"That sounds like fun!" But Al had his head down. Something was wrong.

"Lou Jacobs? The Auguste clown?"

"He's been on all their posters for years."

"Yeh, he said they should pay their respects to a great clown ... Al Lewis." Al looked at his toes, twisted his shoe, then looked up at me. For Al, this was better than any Academy Award. And for me, this rare humble moment stirred my heart.

"See if you can come to lunch, too, Karen. You can meet 'em. A guy called me. I think he's a clown. I don't know him. A Ted Ferlo. He organized the visit."

That luncheon was a delightful affair with long tables arranged in the center section of the restaurant peopled with circus performers, folks Al loved and respected. He walked among them, cigar securely clenched between his teeth, shaking their hands, listening to their stories, all the while following up on their orders.

Al motioned me over. "This here's Ted Ferlo, and his pretty fiancée, Mary Beth. She swings on ropes and rides elephants." Al made a terrified face, and when the couple laughed at Al's backhanded compliment I knew I'd get along with them. In fact, we became fast friends. Ted arranged a clown visit to Grampa's every time the circus played New York City. And in 1991, we even attended the Ferlos' wedding in Troy, New York.

By establishing this restaurant, Al had created his own version of "Facebook" years before the Internet and social networking came into being. The opening of Grampa's Bella Gente blew in a flurry of news coverage that Al then built on, using this interest to land acting roles: the pawnbroker on the soap, *As the World Turns*, a commercial for The Connecticut Lottery, a series of short cartoons called *Grandpa's Silly Scaries*, the host of *Super Scary Saturdays* for Ted Turner in Atlanta, the lead in the New Zealand children's film *Moonrise (My Grandpa is a Vampire!)*, and calls from Director Jonathan Demme to discuss a part in *Married to the Mob*. It seemed that all those endless hours Al had poured into the restaurant business were ultimately worth it.

And what was this successful and adventuresome couple doing besides growing this grand enterprise? Buying snazzy hats to wear to the track, sharpening horse race intuition, and marking up racing sheets. There were plenty of tracks in the Tri-State area and we celebrated at all of them.

During this period, I poured out to Al my frustrations with the Theater. Telling statistics corroborated the fact that I and other actresses over 40 were getting roles less frequently than we had before we hit mid-life. "I think the Theater is suffering an identity crisis!" I wailed.

"God knows you paid your dues in the theater, Karen, but there aren't that many parts written for *mature* women," Al consoled. "You gotta rethink the whole picture. Redefine yourself. Don't let anyone dictate who you are. Hey, you're always writing," Al enthusiastically observed. "All those performance pieces and one-acts. Why don't you write about what you know?" The Henny Penny sky was still falling, but I listened.

By volunteering to write public letters for Council on Economic Priorities, a corporate watchdog, I got a zesty taste for the writer's life, although it wasn't fiction, but hard facts.

Excited about the prospect of truly expressing myself on paper, I signed up for screenwriting and playwriting courses at Hunter College. Following this passion, my life expanded into teaching playmaking for the Police Athletic League's hallowed theater program, The 52nd Street Project, and for Main Street Theatre and Dance Alliance. The sky seemed less threatening now.

In a theater history class, I saw my struggle in the theater as part of something larger than myself and realized that I wasn't alone. It was documented: hundreds of middle-aged actors were leaving the American repertory system because as they aged, without sufficient acting jobs available, survival became difficult if not impossible.

My study of history led to a growth spurt and my sky became sunnier.

I answered an ad to act as personal secretary to Eastside socialite Gloria W. Milliken. During my interview, she warned, "You have to be a self-starter and write a lot." That was intriguing. "I've just founded my seventh non-profit housing organization. Are you the one I need to make it a success?" When she learned I was a Black Belt, she hired me on the spot. With that, Mrs. Milliken opened the door for me onto what would become a 20-year commitment to the Tenants' Rights Movement in NYC. Through Gloria's mentoring, I was eventually groomed to succeed her as Executive Director of Eviction Intervention Services when she retired.

Thousands of New York tenants, at risk of losing their apartments, were saved from homelessness by that feisty not-for-profit. With our band of guerrilla fighters, attorneys and advocates, we took on landlords and improved the lives of their suffering tenants. That magical nerve center was not much to look at, nothing more than a roomful of tables, phones and computers; a storefront operation. Something out of nothing. This work resonated with my soul. And "Brookyn Al" loved the scrappy feel of this ongoing David v. Goliath battle.

Al admired my conviction and reveled in my development. "Karen, I just read one of your grant proposals. It's a knockout! See, I knew you were a fighter all along."

"No, sorry, Al," I smiled, "still a lover."

Sixty-four

ALL'S FARE IN LOVE ...

Al and I had just climbed into the back of a cab in front of our apartment building at 49th Street and First Avenue. Al leaned forward to give the driver instructions, then turned to look at me with an oddly blank expression. Something was up. Al fumbled in his pocket for something which he then placed in my hand. I curled my fingers around a small square box. I opened the tiny fuzzy container and was startled by the contents. A gold ring!

"Read it," Al said softly, embellishing his words with a shy smile. Around the circumference, engraved, were the words *Vous et Nul Autre.* (You and none other.) He took it from me very carefully as we bounced along, cautious not to drop it. He slid it on my finger. He knew to place it on my right hand, because my left ring finger was occupied by a ring with tiny rubies symbolizing my 1981 marriage to myself. This was no problem for Al. He knew that's where it belonged and it was a perfect fit.

"I mean it, Karen. No one but you," Al said as the cab bumped over a New York City pothole. His brown eyes blazed his intention. "We're married."

"By what authority?" I blurted, bemused.

"Mine. If I say I'm married, that's what I am."I guess you're not going to ask me to marry you, are you?"

"No!" He smiled.

"I guess this is as close as you're going to get to a real proposal?"

"Yup!" He grinned.

"So there's not gonna be a proposal."

"Nope."

"If you're asking me to take you as my lawfully wedded husband, in sickness and in health, nod your head." He burst out laughing. I did too, and threw my arms around him and held tight as the cab bounced and careened.

"Looks like I just got married in a cab going up First Avenue!" I remarked. "Not exactly what I dreamed of as a ten-year-old."

"I love you, Karen."

"So, Albie, on your authority, if you say you're loved by me, then that's what you are. Got that? Drat, I had my heart set on getting married in Vegas by an Elvis impersonator."

Sixty-five

AL-A-PALOOZA

Al's days became more and more fruitful, exciting and creative, and he returned home each day happy to see me. He would rest his palm on the side of my face and gaze lovingly into my eyes. I gazed back, so happy to see him thriving. I carefully watched him rebuild his life and career and saw how I benefitted from his example, not only from observing his progress, but also by feeling his desire to please me and create a loving home.

"I'm doing this for you, Karen. For us." At first it made me feel oddly unsettled to have someone his age working so hard for our future.

"You don't have to work so hard, Al. Take Social Security. Have that extra padding."

"I want to work for my money. That padding ... I don't like it." Al got energy out of facing the challenge of supporting us. "We are a couple, Karen. We help each other!" He radiated love and I was beginning to understand that we were a team. Lewis and Lewis on the road again.

Private Parties feature Al Lewis as special guest in Connecticut, New Jersey and New York ... Worthy causes want Lewis' face, autograph, titillating humor to raise awareness and funds, Meals-on-Wheels, Bide-A-Wee, The Red Cross, Police Athletic League, The Leukemia Foundation, The Shriners... *Car 54*'s second coming. It films in Toronto ... New cigar shops discovered and smokes ordered from fancy catalogs ... The kids come to visit; Mrs. Lewis makes family dinners. They visit the kids; the kids make family dinners. Wonderful grandbabies are born. More family dinners ... The friendship circle widens, as the Lewises meet new people in government, business, education, the non-profit world, the arts ... *Moonrise* (*My Grandpa is a Vampire*) is featured at film festivals where Al is feted and celebrated in Seattle and London for his contribution to children's entertainment ... Grandpa Munster flies to Minneapolis to host Trout Air, a gigantic outdoor Halloween Hayride fest at White Bear ... *Deadtime Stories* rides the tails of Grandpa's tuxedo, by making Mr. Lewis their spokesman ... The Little People's Symphony chooses Grandpa to narrate "The Sorcerer's Apprentice" at Lincoln Center for hundreds of children. Al schmoozes and signs autographs for privileged and under-privileged kids alike ... He marches in protest against Apartheid ... WBAI radio becomes their second home as the Lewises co-produce a talk show called *Al Lewis Live!*

The world was Al's oyster and mine as well.

During that time I had a few little hobbies of my own: secretary, butler, concierge, housekeeper, cook, accountant, travel agent, costume designer, and escort. I was still honing my theatrical craft, studying and teaching, and aiding tenants. Did we have any time for ourselves alone? Sure, when we were sleeping.

Sixty-six

ROCKIN' THE SHOCK JOCK

All week Al was riding me. "He's going to rip you up! Are you ready for this?" As quickly as I could assure myself that I would survive an interview with Howard Stern, Al would start in again. "Have you really listened to him? He's going to ream you! Or at least he's gonna try!"

It was a few minutes before 5 a.m. and I pulled on the costume I'd chosen for my role as Al Lewis's "hot" wife. I wanted to look my best. Even though I might be painting a target on my chest, I picked out a fuzzy red V-neck cashmere sweater and the tightest jeans in the closet. Who cares, I thought, this is radio. But I wanted to help Al shock Howard.

After several years of setting up gigs with Al, Howard's staff noticed that frequently a woman answered the phone. Who was she anyway? As a result of their curiosity, I'd been invited to *The Howard Stern Show*, so they could pry into the "curmudgeonly old geezer's" sex life. I knew the patter and expected the inevitable slide into sleaze. Could I surf through it? I figured I had a chance. Fifty-fifty?

Al and I walked along Forty-Ninth Street in the early morning light. "I'm telling you, Karen, Howard's gonna try to slash you to ribbons! You don't hafta go, you know. I'm not saying not to go. No. No. It's just...do you know what you're in for?!"

"Yes, I do, and I've got a few lines ready, just in case." We descended into silence until we hit Second Avenue, where Al hailed a cab and <u>had</u> to tell the driver where we were going. Our turbaned cabbie adjusted the nob on his radio and yelled, "Dispatchah? Guess who's riding vit me? Grandpa! Destination, Howard Stern!"

At the studio, Gary, Howard's infamous assistant at the time, was serving up Chinese chicken for everyone to try. Even though it was only 5:30 a.m., he and Al started slinging one liners and stuffing chicken morsels into their mouths between laughs. I had no appetite.

"Show time! I'll get you right in," Gary announced, like a pushy dentist's receptionist. I prayed I wasn't about to get drilled without anesthesia.

Howard, helmeted with headphones, his black curly hair surging out around the equipment, was grinning from ear to ear.

"Oh, my God, here's Grandpa Al with this gorgeous babe! Al, Al! Who is this? THIS isn't your lady! You couldn't score this in a million years!" Al paused for only a microsecond, and then sprang from the high dive.

"What's the matter, Howard? Can't believe she's wit me? Huh? Huh? Oh, yeh. I may be old, but I ain't dead!" With that he launched into his signature laughter symphony, crowing and suggestive. "I'm a sexy old dude and she likes me fine." The engineers, previously half asleep, woke up and squealed, "Oh that Grandpa, he's outrageous!" Revved up, they thumped each other on the back, celebrating his audacity.

I leaped into the fray, backing up Al's claims and holding my own. "Aged to perfection, Howard! That's what Al is! I love a man with experience!"

"She's too good for you, Al! How much are you paying her to play your wife?" I enjoyed the spontaneity, the delightful, flattering way I was let off the hook, and the surprising underlying sweetness of this sleaze slinger, Howard Stern. Al appeared to have a bubble of love protection placed around him by the players in the room, the tech staff and the talent. And sure enough, when listeners called in to speak with Howard, they took Grandpa Al's side and smothered him with admiration. Howard simply played off of all the energy generated by this crazy, funny, wild guest. And the jabs at me were softer than I expected.

The next segment featured a man in a dress who was to replace us at the mic, and Howard signaled us to the side. He wanted us to stay for the entire show. The guest who crossed in front of us was, at closer inspection, comporting bits and pieces of clothing suitable for either sex, clearly an easy target for Stern's attack-dog humor. Howard did go on the attack, but seeing shock wrinkle across my face, covered his mic to whisper, "I love this guy," and scrunched up his nose to reinforce the fact that taking this guest to the cleaners was part of his job.

So, this was all about acting. On Howard's part and on Al's. That's how Al was able to handle all this sexist nonsense, by acting! I suddenly got it. Performing in this studio was tantamount to an acting class improvisation assignment, creating a character for a morning shock-jock who was himself creating a character. Al had spent his life perfecting his White Clown persona by building on his "type" from Burlesque, Vaudeville, Circus, and even Commedia. But the White Clown always needs a partner and now I had my chance. I would play The Sweet Young Thing type! I was beginning to enjoy this.

Fifteen minutes passed and Al and I were eagerly back at it. Howard's sidekick, Robin, wanted to know if we were in love, and pressed us to tell all.

We talked about how we met performing Neil Simon's *California Suite*. I described our scene in the bed and Al ran with it, colorfully filling in the blanks, pelting the airwaves with hilarious metaphors and double entendres. Al then seemed to turn into a ten-year-old boy, taunting Howard, "Do the words *Danish Pastry* mean anything to ya, Howard? Huh!? Huh? You can eat your heart out, Howard. I got something better to eat. I don't go to no bak-er-yyy, Howard! I got all the dessert at home I want. All that sweet creamy filling. Whenever I want it. Danish Pastry, Howard. Soo delicious." Then he burst out singing the Danny Kaye song, "Wonderful, Wonderful Copenhagen!"

When we rose to say goodbye, Howard grabbed me. "We've gotta have you on more often!" Al pulled me away from him with a tug. "Get away from her, Howard! Get away! She's the best thing that ever happened to me. And you can't have her!" Al strutted like he'd been crowned Mr. Universe.

It was nine o'clock in the morning but Al and I felt like we'd already had our day. We walked out into New York City's bustle, hand in hand, our feet barely touching the pavement, attempting to ground ourselves, get our bearings, after flying through the radio wires for several hours.

"Yeh.Well, uh. I have to admit. I. Well. I gotta tell ya. Heh. Heh. Yeah. You were very ... good, Karen." His words floored me. After years of refusing to praise me or even comment on my work, I was stunned.

"How do you think I did?" he added.

What else could I say but, "Oh, how did you do? Al, you gotta learn to believe in yourself, get some confidence, or you'll never get anywhere in Show Business!" He clown-punched me for that one.

In April of 1987, not long after my debut on the *Howard Stern Show*, Al received an urgent call from Howard himself. He was in trouble with the FCC and planned to counter this assault with a huge Anti-Censorship Rally at United Nations Plaza, only a few blocks from our apartment. He begged Al to make a speech supporting him. Al was eager to play his part, to stand up against censorship, even as he grumbled about having to get to the Plaza on a celebrity bus instead of walking around the corner.

On the day of the big rally, Al left home at the crack of dawn. I had an assignment for my new class at Hunter College and stayed home to work. When Al got back, he bounced through the front door, high on the experience he'd had.

"Whoa, you shoulda seen what I just did. Heh, heh, heh."

"What happened?"

"Oh, I knocked it right out of the ball park!"

"What! What did you do?"

"Howard called me to the podium, see? And I was ready! I said, 'First of all, I am so happy that we're all here together. That's beautiful.' The crowd liked that. That made 'em feel like they were in on something important. Then I said, 'We all have a purpose being here. And that purpose is to say ... Fuck the FCC!!' The staff pulled me off of the podium - with some difficulty, I might add. You know, to shut me up! Howard grabbed the mic right out of my hand and boy did that jock look shocked!" Al laughed and danced all over the kitchen, a kind of touchdown victory dance. But I was stunned.

"Al, what have you done? You'll never work in radio again!"

"Are you crazy? You don't understand anything. You don't know how things work." He looked disappointed and walked away.

Sure enough, by the time I left for class at 6 p.m., Al had been featured on every local channel, his four-letter word bleeped out. Judging from the reporting, Al's antics didn't have the effect I had been expecting. He was clearly still a folk legend and a working man's hero with no apparent damage to his reputation. In fact, it seemed to have improved. He had understood that his satiric attack would directly point out how censorship worked - and make people laugh. Al knew what he was doing.

Sixty-seven

HOT PANTS

SAVE, TOSS, GIVE AWAY

Stashed on the top shelf of my walk-in closet, a pink eyelet dress, squashed into a 12" by 12" block, bound by a satin sash. A raspberry party dress from 1984. Still with me in case I needed it ... Is there a theater company somewhere performing Hairspray? Give away.

Al sat slumped in his favorite spot on the couch. "Jonathan

Demme called me at the restaurant."

"Wow, well, you don't sound very happy."

"*He* called *me*. Why didn't my agent call me!"

"Well? What did Demme say?!"

"Oh, he wants me to do a cameo in his new movie, *Married to the Mob*," Al mumbled softly.

"That's great!"

"No it's not. I want a real part."

"What do you mean? Aren't you listed in the script?"

"Don't you see? I'm doing my agent's work. He should be lookin' out for me." Al was frustrated.

"You're right, Al."

"A few lines … like a token performance by an old icon … One tiny scene," he groaned, "I don't know why I was even cast."

Al moped around for a few days, but I noticed that he was studying his part, changing his physicality in preparation for this cameo performance as "Uncle Joe Russo."

On the day he was scheduled to film, he was pumped up and in character. Al only got a day's work on the film. But Jonathan was so pleased with everything Al did on the picture that he wanted to add him to the trailer, featuring Debbie Harry singing "Liar Liar" to a chorus of hardened Mafia types including Al's Uncle Joe.

The movie wrapped a few weeks later and then work began immediately on the trailer, which was to be filmed in an abandoned Brooklyn warehouse. "I hope we don't freeze to death," he grumbled. I tried to cheer him up, handing him a heavy scarf and gloves. "Better take these. Your own hot air won't be enough to keep you warm."

"Score one for the Danish Pastry."

It took a couple of days to complete, but Al didn't say much about it, making me think he wasn't very happy with it or it wasn't very good. It was not until months later that I finally got a chance to see the trailer.

It was filmed in evocative sepia tones, satirizing Mafia-movie images. It wasn't just funny, it was very funny, not only because of Al's awesome dance, but because of the comic thrust of this short clip. Especially, Al's pull-out-all-the-stops terpsichorean turn. All the performances were great and of course Debbie Harry was a knockout.

The wrap celebration was held on a party boat that circled the southern tip of Manhattan, floated up to Roosevelt Island and cruised back to Our Lady of the Harbor. I wasn't sure what to wear to a cast party of this caliber and settled on a dress I found in my closet, a raspberry parfait party frock, in eyelet. As soon as we crossed the gangway, I was shocked with embarrassment. I was met with a sea of Godiva Chocolate, a huge box full of seriously succulent Hollywood stars in their finest couture. Uh-oh. And me in a spun pink cotton candy mistake, and with turquoise fishnet stockings yet. I could almost hear the horrified reactions of the glitterati around me. "Is that Grandpa Lewis's maid or did he adopt an exchange student from Romania? It's his wife? Is she performing in *Hairspray*? Maybe it's graduation day at Clown College."

Stop it, Karen! What are you doing, comparing yourself to these people? I'm not just another party guest. I am Al Lewis's better half, damn it, even though I do wish I was better costumed for the part! Oh God, this is a bad Hollywood flashback. Here comes all the old insecurity flooding back in. And to top it all off, I feel the green-eyed monster creeping up on me. Why is Al so damned interested in Debbie Harry, drop-dead gorgeous in her sleek black dress?

Al pulled an Al and darted away from me. He quickly jumped into the ship's elevator, leaving me in his wake. I tried to follow him, but the doors closed so quickly that I had to jump back to save my nose. What was Mr. Lewis up to? Was Dick Gregory here tonight? I eventually found the floor that Al was on, and when I stepped out of the elevator, he was already edging toward Debbie Harry, who was talking to a man in a bright Hawaiian shirt. Al was homing in on her, almost stalking her, until she finally turned and glared at him. I watched him stop in his tracks, pause, and do a near-military about-face like in a Daffy Duck cartoon. I caught myself giggling. I had to admit, watching Al get rebuffed was a rare, delicious sight. But still, my jealousy hadn't gone away or even diminished. If anybody was Al's dream date, it was his former wife or Debbie Harry, both handsome blondes with bodies and talent. And Debbie was the only one of them here. I slumped away. Jealousy is such an ugly emotion, especially at festive occasions!

I really didn't want to question Al and make a scene but I wanted to ask him: Can you tell me honestly that you're not after Debbie Harry? Was he the Liar-Liar-Pants-on-Fire aboard our party boat? When he found me a few minutes later, I pretended that I was looking at the skyline and had missed the incident. Of course, I wondered if her angry eyes were really for public benefit, because the green-eyed monster had viciously bitten all the way through my raspberry party frock and turquoise tights and sunk its teeth into my butt.

Al came up behind me suddenly at the ship's railing, as the

harbor breeze blew into my stylish coiffure. I took a deep breath and asked, "Isn't this romantic?" I acted purposefully, trying to steer my own boat straight, staring dramatically into the sky at the setting sun.

"Yeah!" Al gave me a peck on the cheek and called to me as he left, "I'm going to say hello to the people we know." Okay, that's it. I don't belong here. I don't have the guts, or pretentions, or wardrobe to break through to this crowd! Or to impress my husband. And Debbie's got the tight black sheath dress that's burning into my retina. Why don't I just take off my pink eyelet outfit and toss it overboard? Why don't I toss it overboard with me in it? Then the ghost of Stanislavsky spoke to me: "You may not have on the right costume, but you can behave as if you do!" Right. I'll just imagine that my shabby pink thrift store dress is hotter than Debbie's. With renewed self-confidence, I set off to find Al.

The production staff had placed numerous TV screens all over the boat, looping the trailer featuring Debbie Harry and her boys, including Al, who was, of course, dynamite, singing and dancing to "Liar Liar." The song had tickled me for decades with its silly lyrics. "Liar, liar, pants on fire, Nose is longer than a telephone wire. Make a little effort, try to be true, I'll be happy, not so blue."

I found Al in a small crowd of champagne drinkers, toasting the film and watching the clip on a monitor. I approached him and quietly asked, "Was Debbie the reason why your performance was so fantastic? You couldn't let that blonde beauty down?"

"Huh!" Al seemed momentarily startled. "Yeah, that's me. A lady killah!" He seemed to be flattered by what he thought was playful jealousy. He winked and turned away from me to enter a conversation with a group of celebrity friends including Judge Jerry Crispino and Harry Guardino. Oh, that went well.

I turned around and recognized a group of politicians from The New York City Council that I knew from my job at Eviction Intervention Services. I'll go talk to them. Pink dress and all? Yeah, why not? I shook hands and made political small talk and found myself sliding easily into the conversation. One of them politely handed me a drink. That's when I saw Al, who'd been holding court, turn his head my way and watch me from a distance. Was that admiration shining in his eyes? Maybe just a little jealousy? Hee hee. It looked for a moment like he might join me, but it didn't matter any more because my evening was now going very well indeed!

When my group broke up and moved on, Al called out to me, "I want to introduce you to some of my friends from the film." I met the director, Jonathan Demme, who greeted me with respect and kind words about Al's work, and many of the actors including Dean

Stockwell, Mercedes Ruehl, and Michelle Pfeiffer. As tiny as a button, Pfeiffer warmly embraced us both. It was during our schmoozing with Dean that I learned that Debbie Harry's boyfriend was very jealous and all males were warned to keep their distance! Maybe I should thank Ms. Harry's "stink eye" for keeping Al out of the hospital!

When we got home later, I decided that I didn't like myself very much when I was wrapped in jealousy. I slipped the raspberry concoction off my shoulders, and ceremoniously folded it into a neat package. I took the sash and carefully tied it around the dress like a present. Then I stuffed that pile of pink fluff into the garbage. I opened my diary and wrote, "It's not what you're wearing, Karen, it's what you can pull out of yourself." Then I placed my little diary squarely on a narrow shelf in my closet. That party dress knew my story, so I dug through the old newspapers and soda bottles to hoist the raspberry lump back out of the bin. I wanted it to remind me - whenever I needed reminding - about what really counts.

When *Married to the Mob* opened in New York City, Al quietly refused to attend the gala premiere, maintaining he had work to do at the restaurant. With just one scene to claim, I believe Al felt embarrassed at the possibility that he had been handed token consideration for his celebrity. In stark contrast, as soon as it moved to local cinemas, I heard that audiences were standing up and cheering when Al appeared on the screen.

About a week later, failing to drag Al with me, I went to a movie house on the East Side to view the film for the first time. The picture was a clever, comic coup that the audience enjoyed immensely. Their responses rolled in as white-water waves of laughter. More like an event than a movie night out, it was often hard to follow the dialogue through the noisy cheers.

When Al dominated the screen mid-movie as Uncle Joe Russo, a surge of recognition rose from the floor, as the audience jumped out of their seats, screaming "Grandpa! Grandpa!" Ironically, their spontaneous stomps and claps obscured his brief on-screen moment in the sun. When the applause and cheers subsided, I sat hugging myself in the dark. It was true. Al was garnering standing ovations in movie theaters everywhere. Melding with the crowd, savoring my anonymity, exiting the auditorium, I had a luscious secret bursting in my heart: I'm in love and married to Al Lewis. In my book, he'd won the People's Academy Award, and when I got home, the Awardee got the full report.

"Yeah?" he questioned. "You're telling the truth, right?"

"Umm," I responded, looking fiercely serious. Al bobbed his head side to side, as a cloud lifted. "So nobody's been bullshitting me? Heh! I gotta call some people we know to go see it!"

"Why don't you start with Debbie Harry. She could be your date."

"Get over here you day-old pastry!"

Sixty-eight

CROSS STITCHED

In 1989, Roosevelt Island, a tiny residential island in the East River, became our home. It was Al who decided to redecorate, full of confidence born from reading home improvement magazines for months. "We got to make our new home ours!" he crowed. We tossed out the odd collection of furniture we'd gathered, saving only a few items that we cherished. At Al's insistence we went furniture shopping. We searched through various stores and tested demo beds, bouncing on them like kids, to the mock chagrin of all the sales people who had recognized "Grandpa." Finally, giddy from all the bouncing, we purchased a bedroom set in cherry wood. The lines were clean and the wood was full of colors and light. "It's a Scandinavian delight for my Danish pastry!" Al said, with a twinkle in his eye.

Our first night together in the bed was a celebration of a new beginning. We snuggled and giggled over our purchases and ended up making love in the heavenly bed, toasting it royally. Then Al pulled the new sheet up over our heads and softly tucked it in. "Our cocoon." Barely able to see, we held each other close, our hands wide, embracing, my feet resting on the tops of his. "Like we're in one skin," Al whispered, pressing me to him again. "That's what union's all about, Albie," I whispered back, contentment whirring through me. "We're two peas in a pod."

Al went faithfully to the synagogue one day a year, on Yom Kippur, in honor of his mother. "I told my mother I'd always say Yizkor for her. I'm "small r" religious, but I made a promise. There's a little shul I can go to over in the garment district. I'll walk."

"Why go there? We've got synagogues right around the corner."

"Those big synagogues sell tickets for the service."

"So, we'll buy one!"

"Karen, it's wrong. People shouldn't have to pay for that!"

"Just like Jesus throwing the usurers out of the temple," I responded.

"When I was a kid, nobody paid to go to shul to pray. If you had the money, you could give. But admission tickets!" Al was outraged. "Sure, I can afford it now. But I just don't like it. I'm gonna walk. I don't mind walking, my mother did. We walked everywhere. She was tough. Sold apples from a pushcart. Never had a vacation in her life, my mother. Didn't know what a vacation was!" Al put his head down and rested it in his open hand, letting his own words sink in – no vacation. Ever. When his head came back up, he continued. "In addition to working in the Garment District, she'd sell apples on the street corner. Right in the middle of everything, where there'd be plenty of foot traffic. People'd buy one for a couple of pennies. When the cops'd come by to evict her from the sidewalk for peddling, she'd yell, 'Vat? You got nuttin' better to do! Go chase a robber, not a poor woman trying to make a living!' She was so loud, my mother, they'd leave! The cops'd leave!"

Al shook his head, as he smeared tears away carelessly, with the heel of each hand, his voice a squeaky blur. "She was my best friend." After a few stifled sniffs, his visage settled, but I noticed he was hugging himself. I patted his shoulder.

"I love your mother, Al. Would you say a prayer for me?"

"Yeh, I will. Now where are my sneakers?" He put them on and grabbed a yarmulke, stuffing it into his pocket. "See you after. I'm walking to the Garment District to say Yizkor for my mother."

Sixty-nine

THE NAKED TRUTH

Al was watching Midnight Blue on cable TV just as Al Goldstein, the host of this late-night porno pitching show, leaned toward the camera. "Do you want that knock on your door? Spies looking into your bedroom? The American people have rights! Just read the First and Fourth Amendments." Goldstein was on fire, a force to be reckoned with.

I said, "Is that Screw Magazine guy talking about the

Constitution?"

"That's right, Karen. Nobody's just one thing. That's why I don't like putting anybody in a box."

"So he's serious about keeping the government out of his own bedroom too?"

"Yeah, he's an interesting guy. I remember him when he was a cab driver, before he launched Screw Magazine!" Al yelled over Goldstein's TV tirade. "Gotta lot of different sides!"

A few days later, Al excitedly announced, "Guess what? We've been invited to Sunday brunch. Guess where?"

"Nathan's Hot Dogs?"

"No, Al Goldstein's!" Al grinned.

"Oh my God," I gasped. "What do we wear?"

Al playfully chuckled and pinched my butt. "Yeh, well, whatta you think, it's the Pornographers' Ball." I laughed with Al, but quickly went deadpan wondering if he was serious. "It's at Mulholland Drive, that popular brunch hangout on Second Avenue. He's invited about 20 people."

"No, Al, I mean it. What do I wear, a G-string and pasties?"

"Nah, nah. You got the wrong idea."

When Al and I walked into the restaurant at noon, we were wearing clothes. Clothes that the average American might wear to church – Al in a jacket and fancy tie with matching handkerchief in his breast pocket, and I in an up-scale green silk suit.

The place seemed filled with families with kids and grandparents, elderly couples in elegant Eastside attire, the occasional single treating himself to a special meal, and wannabes who'd taken their jewelry to brunch. There was no evidence of any obvious pornographers in attendance. Someone was waving from the back of the establishment. It was Goldstein. He had a beauty at his side and several suits flanking him. We walked towards him. Al Lewis was prepared for this encounter, his side burns bristling, ready to ad lib and sling it.

"Al Lewis, oy vey, and with his beautiful wife. How can you put up with him, Karen, that *alta kaka*? You've got to come live with me."

"Ten rounds in The Garden," my Al joked, winding up a fake punch, "winner take all."

"Oh, God, Albie, is this going to be another Howard Stern encounter?" I asked. But, all my fears evaporated when this benign overfed lap cat welcomed us. "Let me introduce you both to Michael Baden, the City Coroner, and his lovely lady." Turning to an exotic woman on his other side, he announced, "This is Cleopatra, a

190

dominatrix. She has her own business downtown, on the Lower East Side. Give them your card, Cleo. This is my brilliant son, Jordan, and his mother, my former wife, Gina. Isn't she beautiful? You can't say I don't have good taste in women!" Gina glared at Goldstein as her mellow companion, Chuck, patted her thigh to calm her down. He knew it was all *spritz* chez Goldstein. I then understood it was Goldstein's specialty to assemble this disparate group just to sit back and watch the fireworks. I relaxed a little, calling up something I learned from my morning shock jock experience: to take this seriously would be a frustrating mistake.

More guests filtered in through the grazing patrons to find the big table in the back, and kissed their host before finding their place with the aid of Goldstein's secretary of the moment and her magical seating plan.

Soon the conversation heated up and bubbled over. Chuck wanted to know how I felt about astrology, especially Saturn Returns, and Al Lewis grabbed Michael Baden's attention for his take on the Jeffrey Dahmer case. Also present were a watchmaker, a filmmaker, a chef, Goldstein's cleaning lady, whom he declared he was going to marry, and the man he claimed was his psychiatrist, Dr. Ted Ruben, and his wife, Ellie. Everyone was carefully seated, to ensure lively conversation. The Coroner was positioned next to a prostitute, and so on. We were carefully seated between a porno star and a stripper.

The atmosphere was electric, as these disparate elements of New York society scrapped in search of high ground or common ground. Bad-boy Goldstein was in heaven, where he could foment controversy and ignite ideas. From time to time he dominated his guests with a question, planted as a happy challenge for the pugilists at the table. They took it up or hurled it back onto his plate. Periodically, I checked to see what my Al was up to. He was on a roll, working the room. Waving to porno star Ron Jeremy, he called out, "Hey, if you ever need a stunt double, here's my card!"

Grappling with my ambivalent feelings about our luncheon host, I found a crystal clear sounding board in Dr. Ruben, the psychiatrist, who suggested that Goldstein was loveable, but psychologically sick. Chuckling, he told me that our host was never really his patient. He had only attended a psychiatric session or two before he bailed. The conversation shifted to fat farms since Goldstein, many pounds overweight, was about to make a sojourn to North Carolina to, "lock himself in for three weeks of starvation."

"Why do I bother?" Goldstein beamed. But the prospect of the trip and discovering this new method of weight reduction seemed to feed his curiosity, even if his commitment lagged miles behind. Dr. Ruben shook his head. "He knows he's going to quit, so why is he bothering to go?"

We lingered briefly over dessert and coffee. Then, having spent 90 minutes with us, our host rose. Goldstein thanked us all profusely for sharing time with him. He clearly respected our Sunday scheduling constraints and excused us with love. We shared goodbyes and began to disperse, leaving with a small group walking south toward the Roosevelt Island tram.

"Before you go home, come and meet my pig. He's so cute!" We followed our host down the few steps into his Eastside townhouse. Once inside, we discovered that this was a very elaborate warehouse of sorts. The living room, looking out over a garden, was functional and beautifully appointed, but everywhere else storage boxes, labeled and stacked, rose to the high ceilings. Al explained that the other three stories were just the same, storage for all the gadgets he'd reviewed and tested. He casually claimed to be addicted to gadgetry and was considered an expert. He had written hundreds of articles evaluating them. As Goldstein pulled out the latest in trendy wine bottle openers to demonstrate, the cleaning lady, who *was* apparently also his latest fiancée, arrived with the chubby darling, a Vietnamese Pot Belly Pig, the latest hula hoop of pets. As he squealed and scooted around the guests' legs, we excused ourselves and headed for the door, where we thanked him for the wonderful invitation, the provocative conversations and his friendship. "I bet you two really love each other," Goldstein murmured in mock derision. And looking down at our intertwined fingers, he added with apparent envy, "Oh, God, you even hold hands."

"G'bye, Al. Have a good trip to North Carolina."

As Al and I walked to the tram, he groaned, "Poor pig. I give him a week."

"It's really sad what happens when new owners wake up to the reality of their animal's special needs."

"Of course, Goldstein would be into a trendy high maintenance pet. But he'll get tired of his latest obsession pretty quick."

"And another exotic animal goes homeless."

Walking down First Avenue, we felt closer than we had in a long while. Al Goldstein's obvious inability to commit to a mate made our own commitment stand out in bold relief. We grabbed each other's hands tightly, and as I snuggled into Al's side, we picked up our pace, skipping, delighting in each other. I tried to make sense of what had transpired at this demimonde'ish lunch. I'd had fun! But I'd learned something more about life. To quote a famous blowhard, "People gotta lot of different sides."

Al Lewis and Al Goldstein sharing a smoke

Seventy

NO UNSOLICTED MANUSCRIPTS

Al was frequently and enthusiastically asked to write a book about his life, and always responded with the same answer: "I'm not interested! I'm a performer, not a writer!" But Al's stories about Roikja, his small, tough, uneducated genius of a mother, made me want to write about her. My job was to encourage and convince him that writing that book with my help would be a good idea.

My mother, brother and I were going on a Caribbean cruise and Al didn't want to go. He had too many bad memories of being on the water during his stint in the Merchant Marines, he said. So I gathered my notes and a new thick notebook for the trip because I wanted to surprise Al when I got back. The cruise was fantastic, with just enough at-sea time for me to write in the ship's library for a few hours every day.

When I returned home, I had my completed summary for the Roikja book. I knew I had to make a strong presentation to Al, proving I'd thought about and researched the subject, and then let him decide if it was worth pursuing.

First, I shared my book proposal with my trusted Aussie friend and neighbor, Dr. Heather Canning. At the local oasis, The Green Kitchen, we pored over my outline for *I Remember Mamala, Aging Gracefully in an Ageist Society*. My aim was to approach a serious problem in a humorous manner. The idea was that Al would draw from his deep well of experience, focusing on the lessons learned from his mother. We would render advice about the traps inherent in growing older, such as stereotyping and ageism. His in-your-face style, I felt, would be refreshing for anyone feeling vulnerable. I had a tentative Table of Contents and several sample chapters finished.

"Well, what do you think, Heather? Will it fly?" Heather knocked back her last sip of coffee. "You spent hours outlining it. I think it's pretty clear, Karen. You did a great job. It looks like a winner. Let me know what happens when Al reviews your presentation!" She kissed me and wished me good luck.

Dr. Heather Canning and me

194

Back at the apartment, Al was reading in his favorite spot - my dad's old leather armchair. I decided the surprise would be better if I didn't tell him I wrote what I was about to give him. "I'm not interrupting you, am I?" I asked, giddy with anticipation. "Do you mind looking at something I have for you?"

"Sure," he cheerfully agreed. He looked at the title with the word *aging* in it and sneered, then flipped to the Table of Contents, rustled through the notebook, and read aloud, "My mother came to America when she was sixteen."

"Who the hell wrote this?!" As my mouth opened to answer, he hurled the notebook across the room, where it crashed against the sofa. Crushed, I turned on my heels and sought asylum in our office and, an hour later, I was huddled with Heather, too numb to cry.

"You know how he can be, Karen. Try again later," Heather advised.

"I'm not sure I want to," I said. "I don't know why Al reacted the way he did, but I've had enough. Heather, seven years ago when Al and I lived together in California, he made me promise something. He said, 'Karen, if ever it's over for you, please, pack my bag and put it outside the front door. I mean it. You promise?' It had sounded so serious and final at the time that I asked him why would I do that? And he said, 'Because you didn't want to live with me anymore.' He held my hands tightly and made me promise. I said, 'Okay,' and wondered under what circumstances I would ever do such a thing. Heather, maybe this is just such a time."

"Take your time and think about it. You can't bluff Al."

For the next few days, The California Suitcase Promise circled my consciousness as I weighed the probable outcome of packing his bag and placing it outside our apartment door. Again and again, I ran the scene through my head. I realized that if I did reject him, he would take me at my word, and out of pride would never look back. Heather was right, there could be no bluffing. He would be gone.

I decided to keep my own counsel until I really knew what I could accept. In the process, my usual enthusiasm for life disappeared. I felt sucked into myself and numb. Al didn't know what to do or say and walked on egg shells. He knew he was wrong, damn it, and awkwardly tiptoed around me. Al didn't do apologies.

Several days later, the light went on in my head. In the early hours of the morning, swimming out of sleep, I realized there would be no second chance if I told Al to leave. I can't live with that, I thought. I just want better communication not banishment. As if he heard my thoughts, Al came to me and took my hands in his. "Karen, sometimes I'm a bull in a china shop. Whenever it happens with you, I die inside. I'm ... well, I'm ... sorry." I was stunned. This was a first. He said the "S" word!!!

"I love you and your honesty, but sometimes you hurt my feelings so much."

"I know. That's not what I ever want to do."

"Good."

"Will you give me another chance?" Al implored.

"Okay," I agreed, "but what was that word you said? I don't recognize it. That 'S' word. *Sorry*? Is that Yiddish?"

"I meant it." He was serious. Even so, I silently put him on probation.

"How can you stand it when he does dumb things like that?" my mother asked during our weekly phone conversation.

"Most of the dumb things roll right off me. They just don't bother me."

"Oh, you always forgive him."

"I know, Mom, because he makes me laugh. He's a pig-headed buffoon. But he's just like Jackie Gleason on *The Honeymooners*."

"Oh, God," my mother moaned, and then laughed her head off, recognizing my comparison. "*Pow, right in the kisser*," she quoted.

"Should I have divorced him, Mom?"

"Don't be silly. You two are in love. You can see it a mile away!"

DEAR DIARY:

That was a close one. I almost called it quits, I was so hurt. But I stood my ground and Al eventually said he was sorry. Can you believe it, the "S" word? I wonder what it took for Al to come out with that?

We're happy kids again. The clouds are gone from our sky. Why? Al lifted his size 11 D off my enthusiasm and played fair. And apologized!!

Seventy-one

LOVING WITH NEW ZEAL

SAVE, TOSS, GIVE AWAY

Al's Maori green stone, carved in the traditional shape of a wavy
fish hook. It was his farewell gift from the New Zealand producers
of "My Grandpa Is a Vampire." I hold it up to the light: a
translucent curl, a jade sea wave. No question. Save.

Roosevelt Island, 1991. The phone rings.
"I'm in Auckland!"
"Oh, that's wonderful, Al. I was worried. You arrived okay!"
"Yeh. Guess what? In New Zealand you can smell the air! I mean, it smells like real air, like air smelled when I was a kid."
"Al, Al, you already love that country."
"And, get this. The producer, Murray Newey, picked me up at the airport himself! Everyone I meet is so friendly. The Regent of Auckland is out of this world! You've gotta see this room, Karen. It's like a suite, but it wraps around the whole side of the building!" I was hearing the voice of Al, the lovable little boy, excited about discovering the world.
Al had wanted this part with a passion. After weeks of back-and-forth with the Screen Actors Guild, working out kinks in his international contract, he was finally starting 12 weeks on *Moonrise*, later renamed *My Grandpa is a Vampire*.
"Guess what part I'm playing?"
"I'm gonna take a wild guess. Vampire?"
"Bingo! But this one's different. He's retired from the trade!"
"That is a stretch!"
"Oh, and I negotiated a plane ticket for you, Beautiful!"
I was dumbstruck, then touched, then excited. "New Zealand! Thank you, Al."
"I love you, Karen. Can't wait till you get here."

I boarded my Air New Zealand flight armed with books about the country. Two highly touted novels about Maoris, *Bone People* and

Once Were Warriors, were in my carry-on bag, along with a travel guidebook. I was looking forward to immersing myself in the Maori culture during my long flight.

As we circled Auckland Airport preparing to land, the view was breathtaking. The shimmering blue of the Hauraki Gulf was framed by jagged beaches. When the aircraft door opened, I smelled that air! Fresh, clean and infinitely breathable, just as Al had promised.

Al and Producer Murray Newey were waiting for me. It had been nearly three months since I'd seen my husband and I was so happy to lay eyes on him that I leaped into his welcoming arms. He hugged me tightly, crushing all of that fresh New Zealand air out of my lungs. He was so excited that words exploded out of him. "Karen! You're here! I kept checking with the airlines! Isn't it gorgeous? Oh you look beautiful! Was it a long flight? Are you okay? Did you get enough to eat? I'm fine! Oh you're here!" He finally introduced me to his producer, and I noticed astonishment in Murray's face. Was he expecting someone else? It was March, and with winter on the way, I was wearing a long wool tunic over leather trousers and a colorful scarf flew around my neck. As I bent down to pick up my carry-on, my long auburn hair fell in my face. Murray was still gawking at me when he grabbed my bag and we bumped knuckles.

"So happy you arrived safely! Welcome to Auckland. I thought you'd be, well ... different!"

"Older?"

"Well, heh, heh. Old Al here is full of surprises!" I think Murray envisioned a mature Jayne Mansfield or Jane Russell.

Al, by now of course, knew everyone at the Auckland Regent on a first name basis, including the bellhops. As we got settled in our room, my husband said nervously, "I gotta confession to make, Karen." He shifted his weight from one foot to the other. "I finished shooting, got back early, and had a bite in the hotel restaurant. After dinner I decide to have a smoke. I can get cigars at the smoke shop. Beautiful. They let me pick out what I want in the humidor. Geez, huge. World class. So I get four nice cigars. Nothin' fancy. Just really good Cubans. I tell them to put it on my tab, which I pay every week. I sit in the smoking section in the lobby, talk to a few people, and go up to bed. Well, Karen, yesterday I get the bill. I look at it and there's this item. Bar expense: $320? Good grief! I don't drink. I'm thinking, what the hell is this? I musta got someone else's bill! I go down to the purser to get this straightened out. When I get there, the lady, oh really polite and sweet, she says, 'Mr. Lewis, this is for four cigars.' Yikes. That's me! I bought 'em. Eighty bucks a pop? Boy. Then I find out it's mostly tax, but it all goes to support universal health care here in New Zealand. So how do you like that? I'm ruinin' my health and helping other people to be healthy! But I feel bad about spending our money on smokes, Karen."

"Did you enjoy them?"

"Yeh! I did!"

"Well, then?"

"I love you, Karen!"

Later, I met all the incredibly generous and friendly people working on Al's picture, including co-producer Judith Trye. Al's colleagues were down to earth, kind and open, and made it a priority to ensure that our stay was memorable.

We received a special invitation to visit Auckland's Maori Museum accompanied by excited, follow-up whispers that this was a do-not-miss opportunity.

As we stepped inside the museum's halls we were pulled into another reality. We were struck by the beautifully and intricately carved walls, longhouses, huge totem poles, longboats, fearsome masks, weaponry, and ceremonial totems created by master carvers who respected nature and especially the sea. The objects they created expertly imparted the dignity and mystery of this indigenous people.

Along with a small group of other guests, we were invited to a special presentation in a ceremonial space within the museum, full of Maori images and symbols. This was the kind of event that Al routinely ducked out of, fearing a stiff tourguide style, politically correct "official" presentation. But this day he stayed the course.

Maoris dressed in native kilts sang, lifting us with their intricate harmonies and engaging storytelling. Forming a circle, we now represented the first Pakeha, or white people, to arrive in Aotearoa, the indigenous name for New Zealand. A warrior drew a worried looking Al from the crowd to represent the Pakeha leader. Then several men armed with spears began their fierce dance, punctuated by pounding feet and frighteningly extended tongues. Al looked pale. The leader abruptly thrust his spear into the floor within inches of Al's feet, challenging friendship. *Friendship!* Al extended a shaking hand. My arm hairs stood on end. Tears trickled down Al's cheeks.

Whenever the soulful sprang up to meet us, we wanted to share it with each other. Al and I, in the same place at the same moment: empathic intimacy. And that's what we experienced in the Maori Museum.

Gut-rush of a further reality

Mutinous

Woody

We tremble

Beauty-truth - a thrust Maori spear

Trust trial

Our hearts' camera clicks:

Artistry/Pride/Community

Earth roots Sea buoys

"I am"

    rooted in the belly

Goodwill

    The next day I visited the set during the filming of a scene that ended with Vampire Al climbing into a casket to sleep. A hush fell over the normally talkative crew, and it was a little chilling. When the scene wrapped, Al's makeup artist, Abbey Richardson, was at my side. "Karen, make sure Al showers. Thoroughly." She caught the puzzled look on my face. "He has to be washed with running water. He's been in a ... casket." Two stagehands nodded emphatically in my direction. "I'll tell him, Abbey, and thanks."

    When I delivered the message to Al, he wasted no time before turning the gold faucet handle in our marble shower at The Regent. "If that's what Abbey told you, I'm doing it," Al declared, as he headed into the steaming waterfall.

    Al and I nestled into the couch in our hotel suite, eating snacks from the kitchenette.

    "Careful, Al, those cheese sticks are eighty bucks a pop!"

    We had so many unbelievable impressions of New Zealand that needed sorting and processing. "I feel as if we're turned upside down, Al. While at home it's spring, here it's fall. The sky, with rainbows fragmenting William Blake clouds, and sea waves churning in transparent frothy curls. Am I enchanted, Albie?"

    Al laughed. "Both of us. They got black sandy beaches here! I thought sand was white!"

"A black beach? How about this? Today I heard that the Maori language is taught in school for everyone to learn. Unreal! That's like teaching Navajo in U.S. public schools."

"Hon, this is one of very few countries where the indigenous population wasn't killed off by its settlers. They intermarried!"

"That's a very good way to integrate!" I laughed and stole a hug.

"Know what I just read in the Auckland paper? An executive is doing prison time for dumping pulp into a river, polluting it. Not the manager. Not some poor worker, but the boss!" Al crowed. "The judge said he was responsible for the plant, and sent him to prison for five years. You think that would happen in the United States? No, there you just pay a fine and pollute again."

"You think that environmental sensibility came from Maori Culture? Their influence?"

"Of course!" Al barked. "Here Mother Earth's a living thing to be loved and respected. Hey, that spirit's reflected in the country's laws. Hear about no nukes in New Zealand waters?" Al asked. "Told the U.S. to keep out if their ships are nuclear powered. Ha!"

New Zealand's pristine beauty and the people's struggle to protect it made a deep impression on both of us. "You know, Karen, if I was twenty-five years younger, we'd move here."

In this faraway place, Al and I stepped out of time, and basked in a newly found paradise. We fell in love with each other again.

DEAR DIARY:

I've never felt so in tune with my environment and with my Al. This trip is our true honeymoon. What's happened to us in New Zealand? Did someone put an aphrodisiac in the water?! I love Al because he cares about people. About kids. About the earth. And here, we see that it is truly possible for an entire country to care about the environment and the future of the planet. Heaven.

As the week wound down, we were feted and celebrated again and again. The company had been filming for nearly twelve weeks and there was sadness in the air as cast and crew realized that this exciting period was nearly over. As a prelude to the wrap party, there was speechifying aplenty. The expected thank-yous were delivered with unexpected candor from a scaffold on the set. Now Murray gushed out his proud thanks to all, and especially his star. "On behalf of the New Zealand Film Board and all of us working to make *Moonrise* a success, thank you so much for coming all the way to Auckland to work on our film. As a memento of our appreciation, I want to present you with this traditional Maori green stone, fashioned by a native Maori Master Jeweler and commissioned for you ... Thank you, Al!" He waved Al to the impromptu podium to accept his gift, then encouraged him to say a few words. Visibly moved, Al stood for a moment, collecting his thoughts, and then let loose a tidal wave of sincere praise.

"I want to thank you, cast and crew, for this rare opportunity. It's been my good fortune to play parts that made me famous, that were shown round the world. But I've never ... never been in the company of such kind and caring, talented people. From beginning to end. Everybody on this film has worked their asses off!" Now, Al being Al, he couldn't end on that syrupy note. So ... "Now, some of you may not like me. I'm loud, opinionated, and I smoke smelly cigars, but this you can count on. Al Lewis brings the wagon home!" After a stunned silence, punctuated by New Zealand crickets chirping in the background, the crowd broke into applause which built to a riot of stomps and hoots.

The party moved to the set's living room where numerous scenes had been filmed, with the understanding that when the party ended, all they had worked so hard to construct would be struck. It was a fitting way to honor the space that had supported them during their months of filming. New Zealand wine flowed and plates and plates of delicious food were served up. Everyone was toasted and heartily celebrated – including me. I wanted to think that they were reciprocating the appreciation I felt for their hospitality and culture. When the carpenters grabbed their claw hammers and pulled down the scenery, there were lots of teary eyes. This incredible experience was over, and as Al's wife, I'd had a privileged view of it all.

DEAR DIARY:

This trip to New Zealand has changed us. Al was able to advance his career, or what he terms his "string of jobs", and also bring me along to a land where many of the issues we are fighting for in the U.S. have found just resolution. Al and I are in love and in love with the struggle to make the world a little bit better for those who come after us.

Seventy-two

SMOOTH HANDLING

On a hot August day in New York City we packed our car. Destination? Lexington, Kentucky. Al muttered with ambitious resolve, "We gotta help Paul get settled before his semester starts. He needs clothes and books. God knows what he needs for his new apartment." He was on a mission to ease his youngest son's entry into the Philosophy Department at the University of Kentucky as a Ph.D. candidate. This was a transition Al wanted to acknowledge.

We mapped out a route, scheduled a motel stop and had the car completely checked out prior to our departure. There had been some trouble with the accelerator and we didn't want any problems on this extended trip. We discovered that Al had let his driver's license lapse, making me the sole pilot by default.

After an hour on the road, while jerking through a tollgate on the New Jersey Turnpike, the engine died. I steered the powerless vehicle slowly across two lanes of toll traffic to safety.

"Albie, we need a mechanic," I quietly suggested, my heart still wildly beating.

"Let's let it cool off."

After letting Dad's once trusty Chevy Citation sit for a spell, the engine coughed to life and off we went, fingers crossed, up a steep incline to the highway entrance. Cars were merging in a dense stream, so I needed to take my turn, stop and start, until I could ease into the traffic. I was sweating, afraid that the damn motor would cut out when it was my turn to move ahead. But the opposite happened. When I hit the brake, the engine surged instead, thrusting us forward. That's when I saw the accelerator pedal lying uselessly on the floor. All that was left was a spindly shaft poking up like a three-inch spike!

"Oh, my God!" I called out to Al, "The gas pedal's gone!"

"Shit, you're right." But we kept speeding forward anyway. Something was stuck and we were wildly accelerating. We crested the incline and the car shot downhill on the open road. I managed to pull off a race car maneuver and got into the fast lane where there was no visible traffic ahead. My mind was racing. I was in a state of hyper-awareness. To the left of us, a lane of partially paved highway under construction was blocked off by orange cones and police tape, behind

203

which were cranes, trucks, and steam rollers. To the right, in the slow lane, cars were running at the speed limit. Then I spotted traffic in front of us several hundred yards ahead, but we were closing in fast! Al pretended to be calm, but he was biting his lip. I jammed my foot on the brake - no response. The speedometer continued to rocket. All I could do now was try to steer through the obstacles in front of us and we were quickly running out of open road. A collision seemed imminent. I had a decision to make. I gripped the wheel tighter. "Hold on."

"What are you gonna do?"

"Construction lane!" We bumped over the unfinished ridge between the two lanes, and kept going. At least there was no other traffic. I kept pumping the brakes, but the speedometer continued to soar. When we hit 75, I stood on the emergency brake pedal with both feet and yelled over the engine's roar. "Will we go through the windshield if I turn off the key?"

"I don't know!"

"I don't know either!"

"I'm gonna try neutral! Check your seatbelt." It was like we were in a WWII combat movie and the wings had just been shot off our bomber. Still standing on the brakes, I carefully slid the gear into neutral which disengaged the engine. Smoke poured out from all four tires, and the sickening smell of burnt rubber filled our nostrils. The car finally lost momentum and rolled to a stop. The silence was deafening. Al waited for me to switch off the key before we swung open our doors and tumbled out. We circled the car in opposite directions assessing the damage. By the time I arrived in front next to Al, I was visibly shaking. He grabbed me firmly, put his arms around me, and pulled me close to his chest.

"You were fantastic, Karen."

Right on cue, summoned from the heavens, a car pulled out of the fast lane onto our strip of road. A mom, dad and two kids stepped out.

"Grandpa!" called the mom, "I knew that was you! What happened? Let's get you to safety!" If this happened in a movie, you wouldn't believe it, but even in this remote place, Al was swarmed by fans. This was the first time I wasn't annoyed that *everyone* in the world knew Al personally. In fact, I was pretty happy about it. "Mr. Lewis, sit right up there with my husband, and Mrs. Lewis, we'll squeeze into the back with the kids." She apologized for having so little space to offer, but we didn't care. This family had stopped for us. Al explained to the father what had happened, while I sat, still shaking, beside the timid kids. We were driven past several motels and finally stopped at one that passed muster with the mom. This amazing rescue team - Al's Angels - waited to be sure we were housed before they resumed their journey, wishing us well, without even one autograph request!

Al hopped on the phone in our room and called our Road Service who promised to pick up the car for repairs. Al hung up and looked at me. I had fallen into traumatized silence and he was concerned.

"You okay?"

"I'm not getting back into that car."

"No? Why not? I spoke to the mechanic. A real nice guy. He says it'll be ready tomorrow. It'll be fixed."

"That's what they said in New York. I'm not getting back in the car."

"Come here." Al walked toward me and pulled me onto the bed in a full body hug, holding me securely, kissing my hair. "It's gonna be alright." I began to sob as the shock of what had happened finally broke loose and rippled through my body.

"We could'a been killed. We could'a died!"

"But we didn't. Because of you. I never could have done what you did."

"You're just saying that to calm me down."

"You've got nerves of steel, Karen."

"Yeh. Just look at me. Nerves of steel ..." I was trembling so much that I felt like we were on a vibrator bed.

"Not when we were in the car. Not then. This is aftershock."

"I'm hungry!" My non sequitur surprised us, and we both laughed.

"You've got to be feeling better if you can eat! Okay! Let's go!"

But after dinner I found myself back at square one. "I'm not getting into that car." I pounded my words like a flamenco dancer's feet. "Karen." Al patted his side of the bed. "Right here where I can hold you. Let's get some sleep. I'm exhausted. Kinda harrowing, wasn't it?"

"Kinda!" It was comforting to nestle next to Al's large frame. But all night I had terrible dreams. The growl of tires on unpaved cement and streaking dotted lines morphed into crashing white water, in which luge-like I plunged downward, my kayak out of control, my paddle gone. I awakened in a cold sweat; but as soon as I closed my eyes the rapids roared again. The icy river gushed up through the hole where the gas pedal had been. Whirling torrents thrashed against the fenders threatening to dash me on the rocks, shoot me off a waterfall and pitch me hundreds of feet down into a tar black whirlpool below - all the time accelerating. Then the phone rang in my kayak. I woke up and answered it.

It was the mechanic, who had stayed up all night repairing Grandpa Munster's car. I handed the phone to Al. "He fixed it, Karen. The car's ready to drive."

"I'm not getting into that car!" I hammered the words, intending to nail the issue shut once and for all.

Al looked stunned. I watched him absorb the possibility of not being able to drive out of West Virginia, but he never said a word. When the mechanic knocked on our door, Al opened it in welcome, thrusting his hand forward for a grateful handshake.

"Karen, this is the man who did the repairs." A tall fellow in overalls with floppy white-blond hair stood in the doorway. "How did it go? Is she safe?" Al prompted.

"I work on race cars and I know this is a good little car. I'd hang onto it if I were you." He was a homegrown mechanic, and I figured that if he was on a racing pit crew, maybe he knew his stuff. Mechanical genius or no, I still had my doubts.

"Oh, so then the car's okay to drive now?" Al asked, for my benefit.

"Oh, yessir. She's as sound as she can be." I felt like I was being hoodwinked. I rolled my eyes and nervously tapped my heels.

"Would you let your wife drive it?" Al persisted.

"Oh, yes, sir, and my mama, too. Like I said, that car's fit."

This mechanic's sincerity and authenticity finally won me over, despite his central casting accent and appearance.

"Got any more questions for the man, Karen?"

"What happened?"

"Cruise control burned out."

"What should I have done? We were speeding down the highway out of control!"

He nodded empathetically. "Turn the key off."

"I was afraid we'd stop so hard we'd go through the windshield."

"No, Ma'am. The car would'a rolled to a stop."

"I put it in neutral."

"Gotta turn off the key." And he gave me a gentle, radiant smile so reassuring that when he held out the keys, I couldn't help stepping forward to take them from his open palm.

"Thank you for fixing our car," I said sincerely. He smiled and shrugged as if to say, That's what I do best. Then he moved to the door and left.

Al gently acknowledged my emotions. "Fear's a terrible thing."
I took that in, feeling his empathy.

"Thank you for bringing me around, Al."

"Honey, you were spectacular," he said. I loved hearing those
words. Then moving in tandem toward the motel coffee shop he
added, grabbing me and tipping me back towards an inevitable
Honeymooners kiss, "Baby, you're the greatest."

Seventy-three

A STABLE RELATIONSHIP

SAVE, TOSS, GIVE AWAY

*A photo. I remember when I had this framed as a gift for Al. When I
gave it to him, it could have been a yacht, an ermine-lined Burberry,
or a solid gold Cadillac, he was so happy. But it's just a simple
snapshot of Al and a famous race horse ... Save!*

We rolled through the lush green rolling hills of West Virginia,
the sunshine sparkling on the ridges. Our newly repaired car purred
as we wound down through the countryside, over rushing rivers and
farmland. Unfortunately, many of the mountaintops had been
flattened by the ugly open strip mines, destroying their natural
beauty and polluting those rivers. The contrast was stark. "That's
what people do for profit," Al shouted aloud as we crossed the
otherwise green state toward the Ohio border. But we were in the car
together, the sun was shining, and I was leaving behind my fearful
feelings of the previous day. So I joyously jumped into John Denver's
"Country Roads." Every couple of miles, Al would request it again
until he finally joined me: "West Virginia, mountain mama, take me
home, country roads!" We howled it across the hollers and over the
hills. "*Mountain mama.*" Al looked at me with a secret smile. "I love
that lyric! Mama Earth calling to us just like a mother! Yeah, just like
my own ..." With that Al wailed, "West Virginia mountain *mamala* ...
take me home!"

As soon as we arrived in Lexington, Kentucky, we connected with Paul and took him on a shopping spree outfitting him with some of the items he needed for his first semester at UK. That task completed, Al scoured all the newspapers and called all the tracks for a horseracing schedule, but August was too hot for racing expensive thoroughbreds.

"Not a single race," Al grumbled. "So much for the Kentucky Derby state ..."

"Hey, Papa, how about the Kentucky Horse Farm?" Paul suggested.

"What's that?"

"It's the retirement village for American race horses."

Al brightened. "The boy's a genius! Let's go!"

We drove onto the grounds of the Farm, which were surrounded by pristine white fences marking the paddocks, and parked near an impressive statue of a mighty race horse. "Secretariat," Al reverently murmured. "What an animal. Some folks think he was the greatest race horse of all time. A power machine! I mean, what can you say about a horse that wins the Triple Crown *twenty five lengths* ahead of the next horse in the field?! He was out there all by himself. 1973." Paul and I eyed each other and threw up our hands in amazement.

"That's Al – the human sports encyclopedia!"

The three of us walked to the museum, where we paid our admission fees. Inside, Al stopped us and said, "I don't want to look at no frozen images, I want the real thing." Then he steered us toward the stalls, stopping only to read the names of the famous horses boarded there. When he read one name, he exploded, "John Henry! Whatta horse! Take me to him!"

We caught sight of him through the fenced doorway of his permanent stall, a large space, knee deep in hay, easily three to four times bigger than the typical horse pen. There was John Henry. Not too tall. About 15 hands. His groom, a strong young woman, was carefully raking around him, trying not to disturb him. Gaping with admiration, Al leaned over the gate. "John Henry! Good morning! I saw you race at Santa Anita! Remember?" The groom looked up and, impressed with Al's recollection, smiled and said, "Let me bring him outside for you, sir!"

Al introduced himself to the great horse on the walkway between the stall and paddock. I pulled out my camera.

"It's wonderful to see you again, John Henry!" The horse's ears perked and he immediately turned his head directly toward Al, listening intently. "You were magnificent," Al continued, his chin tucked in to better eye his favorite. "Do you remember your victory at

Santa Anita? Huh? No one had more wins than you. Ever! Huh?! The Arlington Million? Remember?" The dark brown horse became still and continued to listen, his gaze fixed on Al. The groom's eyes widened with amazement as she watched her normally unruly charge settle down for the man she knew only as Grandpa Munster. Al talked to John Henry as if this horse was an equal. "You didn't win it once, my friend. You won it twice! No other horse did that. Remember coming down the stretch? Your rider, Willie the Shoe, urging you on?" Al mimed galloping like the jockey. "The crowd cheering. Then you surged ahead, inching past The Bart to take the crown by a nose! Photo Finish! The crowd went wild, yelling your name! 'John Henry! John Henry!' What an uproar. The crowd loved you, John. They loved you. The richest horse in racing history!" At that, the horse's head reared back. Was it a nod, acknowledging his famous, history-making race? Had he understood what Al was saying? The groom reared her head back, too, as if to say, what did I just see? Then softly stated, "Nobody can calm ole John Henry like you just did!"

Paul and I clung to each other silently awed, trying to process what we'd just witnessed: Al with his Brooklyn accent addressing John Henry in a horse retirement home, enthusiastically taking him down memory lane! It was beyond amazing. Maybe it isn't just everyone who loves Grandpa. Add race horses to the list.

Al's tribute concluded, the champ pulled fiercely against his lead. "Okay, John Henry," the keeper scolded, "settle down." Turning to Al, she smiled broadly and thanked him. "Gotta take him back in. He's a mean ole horse. He'll stomp or eat anything in his way, including metal buckets."

Turning to his father, Paul declared, "Papa! You were incredible!"

"Oh, my god," I cry-laughed, and threw my arm over Al's shoulder.

"I always liked that horse," Al sincerely whispered, a sweet sadness spreading over him. "Did you know his name came from that song, "'John Henry Was a Steel-Drivin' Man'? Like his keeper just said, he ate steel feed buckets. He was fierce, but everything about him appealed to the common man, the racing fans with no money. Folks would gather at the horse parade before a race and talk to him! Like he was their friend. 'Hello, John Henry! Have a good race today!' Yeah. Like they knew him. He was that kinda horse. When he started winning those million dollar races, it was your rags-to-riches story. Only it was a horse. Boy, did people love him." Al snuffed back a tear.

"Oh, yeah."

"And you got to talk to him, Pop." Paul beamed.

"Yeah. Wasn't he somethin'!"

Al and John Henry. I remembered the way they looked at each other, both proud, fierce mavericks, working class personalities intertwined, like kindred spirits. My Al? A wily Horse Whisperer! And John Henry? Another famous cantankerous personality.

Al eye to eye with an equally ornery character

Seventy-four

THE MOUTH THAT ROARED

"The highest reward for a man's toil is not what he gets for it but what he becomes by it."

--John Ruskin, *Celestial Seasonings Tea box*

Both Al and I were familiar with the listener supported Pacifica Network and its five satellite stations. Living in the Bay Area, I grew up with the flagship KPFA, and later recorded poetry and plays for them. Al had been an active listener to WBAI when it first came into existence in New York City, and after his move to Los Angeles to perform in *The Munsters*, became a major donor to L.A.'s KPFK.

Spring 1996, Eighth Avenue at Thirty-Fourth Street, WBAI headquarters, the office of Program Director, Samori Marksman, an African American. And Al was there.

"What a pleasure, Mr. Lewis."

"Call me Al."

"Alright, I will. Al, you are politically astute, perplexingly hilarious, and my children adore you. You've been a guest on several of our most popular shows, fluent in various public affairs subjects. So, now shall we talk about Black History." And they did, for several hours.

As a result of that meeting, Samori wasted no time arranging an unofficial experiment, a test run for Al on "Wake Up Call", the early morning drive-time news program then co-hosted by alternative media journalism stars Amy Goodman and Bernard White. As their guest, Al pulled out all the stops. A walking encyclopedia with a solid left jab, he was an instant hit. The listener calls poured into the station. The gist: "Grandpa, we didn't know you were so political!" When the shock of his intelligence wore off, their devotion increased. They happily followed him into this new arena of self-expression.

Samori couldn't have been more pleased. "As soon as there's an opening, Al, I'm getting you your own show." And true to his word, a few months later he put Al in the spot vacated by the retiring veteran talk show host Paul Gorman. *Al Lewis Live!* debuted, and Al instantly began making waves. He asked me to co-produce with him and, delighted to be by his side, I agreed. I became the "Sorcerer's Apprentice".

Besides his successful weekly show, Al helped raise money for this grassroots station, just as he had for KPFA in L. A. He gave speeches, sat on panels and attended meetings, profoundly happy to be acknowledged for what he knew – which was considerable. He now had a ready vehicle for his fighting spirit. As Joseph Campbell would have said, Al was following his bliss.

Al rarely had guests, so he had many airtime minutes to fill. Before the show, he would take long walks organizing his thoughts. Not one to write things down or take notes, Al trained his mind to hold ideas, to "rewrite" in his head, and develop dramatic orations which he would then artfully, entertainingly deliver spontaneously. You could hear him thinking, pausing and breathing. I was getting an education in how to produce radio material and the opportunity to observe a master communicator.

Al chose King Curtis's uplifting "Foot Pattin'," as his theme song. He called out to The King under the music, a happy invitation to every listener to enter the conversation. "Come on now, yeah! Take us home, King!" The first half of his program was off-the-cuff, stream-of-consciousness commentary. The topics were as far ranging as racism, prison reform, censorship, political scams, medical fraud, and pooper-scooper laws on the Upper East Side. Al had an obsession for seeking and telling the truth.

The second half of his air time was dedicated to answering listener call-ins. He loved to interact with people, fearlessly speaking his mind. He'd call out, "I don't want you to just listen to me, I want you to hear me! And I want to hear you. But tell the truth now. I don't want no lying!" Those courageous enough to keep dialing in after Al's warning to speak the truth were rewarded with his patient attention. But if they were BS'ing him, they had to be prepared for a tongue lashing. His signature rebuke, "You, fool, you!" became a popular catch phrase. Al's war cry targeted racists, bigots, and "experts" who couldn't support their opinions with facts.

Al grew up in a poor neighborhood where he had learned to use what he had to get what he needed. He retained that modus operandi and carried to the WBAI studio, as proudly as a school boy, his plastic portfolio jammed with magazines and books, his name printed across it in black magic marker letters. He wrote quotes on 3 x 5 cards or tiny memo pads. That's all he needed. I was so proud of him.

Al's personal touch was appreciated, particularly by women, who liked to hear him talk about his mother, childhood, kids, and earlier political struggles. When they praised and thanked him he would say, "I've lived a long time and seen a lot of life. When you see the same crap coming down for the second or third time, you know what's happening!" He could sum up his views in a short phrase. Al frequently maintained, "A law is that which is paid to be written," when addressing the plight of low-income inmates in the prison system. And to articulate his opinion of the Governor, Al dubbed him "Potatohead Pataki," much to the delight of the listeners who'd lost ground during George Pataki's term in office. "Can I hear an Amen?!" Unafraid to laugh or cry, yell or whisper, his voice was expressive, heartwarming, and confidential. People loved it.

As co-producer, I wore a lot of hats: researcher, tech support, secretary, and cleanup woman. I brought to our partnership my theatrical background, organizational experience, social advocacy, and my feminist point of view. While much of my contribution was initially behind the scenes, I began at Al's urging to participate more and more during air time. I'd read an inmate's special letter, or a poem, or back Al up with facts I'd gleaned to support a specific topic. But my reticence to weigh in when I hadn't been asked to speak irritated him. He had more confidence in me than I had in myself. "Why don't you speak up when you have something to say!" he'd scold. I disagreed. "The show is called 'Al Lewis Live,' not 'The Karen Lewis Show', I shot back.

One Saturday a caller ranted about lazy mothers on welfare. I had been Al's silent partner – up to this point. Pissed off and without hesitation, I firmly challenged her to come to my office at Eviction Intervention Services for a reality check. We served hundreds of mothers on welfare who were about to be evicted. "Lazy?! They're trying hard to keep their families stable when the system is obviously failing them. Do you know what a family of four gets in Food Stamps each month?" I challenged. I continued like a defense attorney to clue in this "fool" about what real life was like. When I looked up from my microphone, Al was staring at me in awed shock, his mouth a fallen O. His wife had just righteously corrected a listener! That moment was clearly a milestone for me and probably for Al too.

My stunned husband was delighted with my on-air response, and after the show praised me over lunch. "I couldn't believe you did that! It was wonderful! I always knew you had it in you. So are you ready for more on-air responsibility?" I was. And whenever New York City housing issues threatened tenants' rights, for example, Al urged me to host programs on the subject.

Our weekly talk show and our interaction with the public made us both feel great. Al was like a pig in shit. He was performing. But not somebody else's script. He had his own soapbox, a platform from which to teach, preach and reach. He loved the listeners for their ardent efforts to make sense of the crazy world around us. He also loved the purchase his position provided, allowing him to freely mingle and contact the stars of his heart, the movers and shakers on the progressive front. The more courageous and outrageous they were, the better! And of course, the mavericks were also attracted to him. Father Lawrence E. Lucas, Catholic Chaplain on Riker's Island, became a frequent commentator on *Al Lewis Live!,* and a dear friend.

Outspoken, anti-racist, and brutally honest, this Catholic priest provided the political extension we needed to lengthen the program's reach. Together we acted as a united front against the outrages perpetrated against the black community.

Through Al's visibility as a political force, we met forward thinking brave fighters in The Struggle. We met people from prison and legal advocacy groups around the country, and most importantly, we worked with those very people whom these organizations were trying to help. We built powerful relationships with programmer comrades at WBAI who, like us, were committed to fighting oppression. I felt like I was a fast-tracked Ph.D. candidate in a progressive studies and journalism school!

Seventy-five

DUMBER AND DUMBER

During that time of serious political analysis and commentary, there was still time for playful nonsense. Al had been a guest numerous times on "The Richard Bey Show," a low-brow audience participation entertainment extravaganza. They loved him when he played a crazy, hilarious judge for their silly contests. Al would pound his gavel and whirl out his punch lines like Judge Judy on laughing gas.

But this time, Richard Bey himself was on the line and he was asking for *me*. We knew each other from Berkeley when he had been one of my first husband's prize acting students. "We'd like you and Al for a show about couples with age differences. Not exactly Shakespeare," he chuckled. "Definitely low brow, but I'm sure you can handle it!"

"Sure, why not? Sounds like fun!"

At the TV studio in Secaucus, New Jersey, we were paired off against an older woman in love with a younger man. Then we women were separated from our partners and coached. "Here's the premise. Whose lover is better? When the bell rings, come out fighting." Our coach grinned like a victorious mud wrestler, goading us on. "Just let loose!" Soon the cameras were rolling.

The 40-something, dominating her boy toy, bellowed, "I've got no use for saggy, baggy, or craggy." Then I countered, "But an older man is like good wine - aged to perfection. You want a baby? Fine. I want a man with experience!" This was nothing more than a

214

silly party game, but I loved my glamour make-up and red cowboy boots, and I kicked up a sexy fuss. When the guys went head-to-head, Al maneuvered away from his usual attack style and softened his punches, behaving like a debonair clown, which got him tons of applause. Richard Bey was thrilled.

And so were we. All the way home in our chauffeured limousine, Al and I compared notes. "Do you think the audience knew it was a put-up job?" I tittered.

"No way," Al retorted. "They were cheering like crazy! Wasn't it a hoot?!"

I grabbed his hand like we were on a date. "Not exactly Shakespeare, but definitely a hoot!"

"Hell, it's entertainment! There's always got to be earthy low-brow comedy." Heading into the Lincoln Tunnel, we snuggled into the limo's luxurious interior, wallowing in our inanity.

"Albie, we make a <u>much</u> better couple than those two!" I cooed.

"Amen!"

"I like you just the way you are. Saggy, baggy and craggy!"

Seventy-six

IMAGINING

SAVE, TOSS, GIVE AWAY

A photo of Al and me. Sitting next to that surprising and appropriate statue. Save. Oh, yes, save ...

Al had been to Cuba in the 1950s to gamble, taking one of those pleasure-ferry rides from Miami to Havana, and he had followed with interest the subsequent Cuban Revolution, an on-going social experiment. I, on the other hand, knew little about the island situated 90 miles off the coast of Florida. In 1993, we had the opportunity to travel there thanks to Global Exchange, as participants in the Latin American Film Festival.

We visited Cuba during The Special Period, a time marked by hardship and harsh conditions following the fall of the Soviet Union, their strongest trading partner. Adding to their misery was the continued U.S. Embargo or Blockade. As a goodwill gesture, we packed medicines and clothing as gifts for the Cuban people, and set about studying their history and customs. Armed with reading materials provided by Global Exchange, and led by our guide, Jennifer Carino, we flew into Havana.

We were housed at the Escuela Internacional de Cine y Television, or International School of Film and Television, in San Antonio de los Banos, which was established by the brilliant Mexican novelist, Gabriel Garcia Marquez, as a way to develop the Latin American film industry. The school was a training ground for students who could not afford, or whose countries did not have, film schools. Marquez said, "We in Latin America are tired of shit American Films. Why can't we make our own shit films?" This school aimed to provide the education needed to promote a viable film industry.

It was a fascinating, exciting place, where creativity trumped poverty. Frequently we ran into established directors, editors, cinematographers, and actors who were teaching courses, supporting programs, or bringing their expertise to the hand-picked, promising students. People like Francis Ford Coppola, Danny Glover, Terry Gilliam, Jim Sheridan, Harry Belafonte, Paul Mazursky, Estella Bravo, and Mexico's Arturo Ripstein. As guests, we were given the best the school had to offer. We watched Cuban films and took classes taught by Cuban actors, editors, and directors.

When the Festival started in Havana, we had our choice of dozens of films playing in every venue that had an operating film projector. I saw lots of movies, but Al, the guest of honor, saw very few films, preferring to smoke Cuban cigars on the patio of the famed Hotel Nacional. He did talk to hundreds of film buffs from around the world, attend press conferences, and he frequently gave interviews. Apparently, countries like Argentina and Brazil were still airing *The Munsters*.

Several fellow travelers expressed an interest in visiting a Cuban Day Care Center, so Global Exchange organized it. This simple, spotless gem of a pre-school was voluntarily constructed by the parents who lived in that quarter. The young children played at cooperative games. Not once during an hour and a half visit did I witness any selfish behavior, a common occurrence in the U.S. The Day Care's nursery had adult-sized cribs, because, as was explained to us, "A child's crib is too uncomfortable for the adult assistants who need to cuddle the kids." What a shame that this practice could never be permitted back home where for a teacher to even touch a child would be illegal.

I got a real lesson in Cuban Sociology when we were invited to the school principal's office for a strong cup of Cuban coffee and a chat. All of our comments were immediately translated by our group leader for the teachers and principal. When my turn came, I reported that I was the director of an organization in New York City that prevented indigent tenants from becoming homeless. Following the translation, I watched confusion pass over the faces of the teachers.

"What's wrong?" I asked Jennifer.

"They don't understand the word *eviction*."

"Didn't you translate it?"

"Oh, yes, I used the right word. They just don't understand the concept."

"*Eviction*," I said. "That's when a landlord throws a tenant out of her home." Jennifer quickly translated my words. Immediately, a shockwave passed through the group of Cubans. Tears flowed from the eyes of one teacher. Another cried, "*No es possible!*" Jennifer said, "The idea of eviction is literally unthinkable to them."

"I don't know why it's not unthinkable in America ..." In this country everyone cared deeply about each other. And I wasn't used to that.

Al and Danny Glover
Latin American Film Festival

Al and me, Hotel Nacional, Latin American Film Festival

The temperature dropped and I caught a cold that settled in my sinuses and moved into my ear, making me feel miserable. I went to the school infirmary, an incredible place. There was a room for "green medicine," where alternative therapies were used. The Medical Director, warm and friendly Dr. Maximo, explained. "Students come from countries that mistrust Western Medicine, and we try to

218

accommodate them. Besides, we often learn about new herbs and traditions. Let me examine you, Karen." He looked into my mouth and checked my throat with a disposable tongue depressor that came out of a sterilizing unit. "We must recycle," he told me with a smile, and placed it back into the sterilizer. To look in my ear, he repositioned me by the window and then, placing a reflector on his forehead, bounced the sunlight into my ear.

"I'm curious. Why don't you use a flashlight?"

"Ah ... batteries. We have no batteries."

I was embarrassed. "Of course. This is The Special Period." After the examination, his assistant heated up a pot of water until it steamed, dropped in eucalyptus oil for me to breathe, and gave me instructions for doing it myself. She also massaged my shoulders and pressed acupressure points on my fingers. Doctor Maximo handed me two or three antihistamine tablets, no doubt the same ones that Al and I had given the clinic on our arrival as part of our medical gift package. I felt much better after inhaling the steam, and I didn't even have to come up with a co-pay!

I told Al about my visit to Dr. Maximo. He became very emotional as the small details of the Cuban Emergency registered on him. "Batteries? We throw them away by the millions in huge toxic dump sites. But Cuba, who supplies the world with medical technology of the highest order doesn't have fuckin' batteries!" That was the beginning of a serious campaign on Al's part to bring attention to the medical emergency in Cuba. Nothing like personal experience to put a face on a crisis.

Jennifer enthusiastically informed our small band of travelers that she'd successfully scheduled a tour for us of the Partagas Cigar Factory. She was especially excited to offer this treat to Al, the biggest cigar smoker in the group.

Surprisingly, Al didn't want to go at first, but I pressed him. "Don't you want to buy your Cubans at the source?"

"Yeh, I do, but what will I have to endure to get 'em?" He laughed a dour little laugh. Al simply could not abide boredom, and as this was a tour, he expected just that. But in the end the lure of the freshest Cuban cigars he'd ever smoke got the best of him and he relented.

We found our group of Americans in the Partagas lobby talking to the guide. While extremely bright, she spoke in a monotone like a scared history professor. Oh, great. Just what Al needed, a guide with no confidence. He got to work immediately. He grabbed her arm and pulled her and the group toward a corner of the factory where the tobacco leaves were sorted in bundles.

"Smell this!" he said to her and the group at large. "Cuba's got the right soil for tobacco. Now touch this!" he pointed to some other leaves in better condition, with fewer holes and tears. "See how good that is? This is for the outer wrapper of your cigar. Cuz it looks so nice." Al was so energized and entertaining that we instantly followed his lead. We began to sniff and delicately run our fingers over the darkened two-foot-long leaves. The Cuban women in charge of grading and piling the tobacco bundles began to chuckle, hiding behind their hands. They pointed to the *Viejo* with knowing nods. It was amazing to watch this rehearsed tour figuratively go up in smoke as the participants began to *experience* the factory. The guide began to have fun as well and felt more confident in speaking about her subject. My Al is at it again! A man on a mission. At each juncture of the tour, Al and our guide playfully tussled, trying to top each other with accurate and ample information.

"Top of the line Cuban cigars don't have filler. It's like sawdust. Cigars loaded with that crap taste like cardboard."

"Yes! And we have no cardboard in this factory," our guide added.

Next we entered the rolling room, a large sunny chamber fitted with long pew-like benches occupied by seasoned cigar rollers. "*Buenos dias!*" Al greeted them, shaking their hands as the rest of us eased into the room. "See? That there's the reader," Al explained, pointing to a man on a podium. "For generations, they've been reading books, newspapers, all kinds of stuff to the workers. They use actors, poets, professors ...You don't see that at your average American workplace!" Al proclaimed. He moved at a fast clip toward the front, still causing a stir.

Al surged up to the reader, grabbed his hand and shook it, interrupting his oration. By now our group had caught up with Al, and work had come to a complete halt. Our guide took a deep breath and in Spanish formally introduced us. "These are friends from Global Exchange!" We were warmly welcomed with a cheer. Then she moved closer to Al. "This is Senor Al Lewis, a famous American actor you will soon see on Cuban Television, where we honor him in Raul Fidel Capote's documentary on comedy."

Suddenly, taking their cue from the reader who raised his hand to direct them, the rollers tapped their cutting knives, building percussively to a crescendo of noisy praise in celebration of Al. The cigar rollers' salute! Bang, bang, bang, boom ... reverberated in the air like Fourth of July fireworks. This unexpected tribute to my beloved's humorous spirit arose spontaneously. My husband, a radiant Buddha, basked for a moment in the musical afterglow. Al wrapped his arm over our guide's shoulder and hugged her. Then he added, "Isn't she wonderful?" which set off a spontaneous round of appreciative applause in our little troupe. Al swiftly turned to the reader and slapped him on the shoulder several times to thank him, too, and our party slowly trickled into the tobacco shop next door. I watched Al as he backed out of the rolling room, hands folded in prayer position, bowing to the workers.

Al stood on the sidewalk outside Partagas, grasping his two new boxes of Lusitanias. "You were wonderful," I gushed.

"Life is what you make it," he stated quietly, acknowledging my praise for his creativity and guts. "My former wife, Marge, used to say about herself, 'I had a wonderful life. Too bad I wasn't in it.' You can't be a passive observer of your own life, Karen." I took that as my cue to take action. I grabbed his hand very tightly ... and yanked him into a nearby ice cream shop.

Al was waiting as promised outside an improvised bookstore, its porch piled high with books, a few patrons clinging to the shelves like bees to honeysuckle. After the 1959 Revolution, like the cars on the streets, most of what lined the shelves was old, dusty and frozen in time. Great! We eagerly went in and looked around.

I spotted a theater section off to the side, displayed on raw wooden packing crates. A title grabbed my attention. *Theatre World Season 1955-56.* Al had lovingly mentioned a special date many times: May 8, 1956, the opening of Eugene O'Neill's *The Iceman Cometh* at Circle in the Square. My fingers flew to the index. Page 147. And I suddenly found what I was looking for, my husband's image squaring off with that of Jason Robards on the shabby barroom set. My heart pounded.

"Al! Al! Can you believe this!"

"Whadda you got there? Wow, can you beat that! We had to travel all the way to Havana in order to find this!" The memories flooded back to Al as he read aloud the cast list from his most memorable acting job.

"You must have been a fantastic Hickey, Al, a real fantasy-buster. I wish I could have seen you in that part. I really do."

I met the creative genius, Santiago Alvarez, known as the father of Cuban documentary films, when he lectured at the film school. I already admired his powerful short documentaries. But I was also drawn to the artist for personal reasons. He suffered from Parkinson's disease as had my father. I suspected that his illness was severe and that his Parkinson's would incrementally progress, decreasing his creative ability as time went on. This gnawed at me just as it had with my dad.

I made a point of introducing Al to Senor Alvarez at the next opportunity. They were from the same generation, had a lot in common, and sure enough, they enjoyed each other's company. Frequently, Al invited his new friend for a meal where they shared quips and talked about politics and films.

Due to the Embargo, many medications were difficult for Cubans to get. One such medicine was a rare and expensive treatment that held great possibility for bettering Santiago's condition. He asked if we could get it in the U.S. He handed us a prescription. We promised to try to fill it when we returned home to New York.

Documentary film maker, Santiago Alvarez, and Al

One day we had arrived in Havana too late to see the tribute ceremony to John Lennon on the anniversary of his assassination. I was determined to visit the park in Vedado to see the commemorative bronze sculpture, an homage by Cuban artist Jose Villa that depicted a welcoming Lennon sitting on a park bench. "Come with me, Al. This'll be great!"

"I came to Cuba to be with Cubans, not a dead English rock star!" Al declared.

I insisted, and pulled him into the limo. Driving toward The Vedado district, Al asked Giovanni our faithful limo driver, "What was the ceremony all about?"

"Oh, Senor Al, very *importante*. Rock and Roll was banned for many years. But The Beatles were different. They sang about revolution. Even Fidel made a speech to say he was sorry for the mistake. *Si*, The Beatles and especially John Lennon write very good words. *Si. Si.*"

"Why didn't you say so before? Step on it, Giovanni!"

We arrived at the park, one of those flat urban public spaces with a few trees and lots of dead grass. When I spotted the sculpture I did a little bouncing dance on the back seat. I flew out of the cab and raced to stand in front of John. He looked peaceful and engaging at the same time. Al and I sat on John's bench and felt connected to our favorite Beatle and his message of peace. When I caught sight of a plaque engraved with the lyrics to *Imagine* in both English and Spanish, Al recited them along with me because he knew those lyrics by heart.

Giovanni quietly quoted Fidel. "'John was my favorite Beatle, because I am a dreamer, too.'"

On our very first trip to Cuba all the members of our Global Exchange Reality Tour received numbered and embossed invitations to a reception following the official closing celebration of The Latin American Film Festival. They were issued by none other than Fidel Castro himself. "This is hush-hush," Al said, noting that there was no designated address for the party. Our group leader, Jennifer Carino, was informed that the event could be called off without notice. "I wonder why?" I innocently mused aloud during a group meeting. Al spoke up, "Do you know how many attempts have been made against Fidel Castro's life?! Most of them by American operatives!" My jaw dropped.

The day of the party arrived and we were still wondering if the celebration would be cancelled. But two hours before the scheduled time we were told where it was. After a 15-minute bus ride we were deposited at the curb in front of The Palace of the Revolution, Cuba's version of The White House, which was heavily guarded by armed police. In the lobby all of our hand items were searched and our cameras were secured in a guarded cloakroom. This high level of security put us on alert. We were then escorted into a huge majestic hall.

For the first time during this trip, and after 12 days of low-calorie meals, there appeared before us a mirage. Long tables heaped with delicious appetizers! I felt like Oliver Twist, a newly released prisoner, and a party crasher rolled into one. The food arrangements looked opulent after what our Cuban diet had been. But when I honestly compared this spread to parties back home, this offering looked frugal. There were trays of meat and cheese which we devoured appreciatively but with misgivings, knowing that those living outside these walls were struggling to get any food at all on their tables.

I was enjoying a serving of crudités near Al in the rear of the room, when suddenly one of the wall panels slid open and out stepped El Commandante himself! Stunned to see Fidel standing two feet in front of him, Al stepped back. The Commander in Chief offered his hand which an uncharacteristically speechless Al shakily reached out to embrace.

"Good evening. And thank you for coming," Fidel uttered sincerely in Spanish, which was instantly translated by the woman at his side.

"Good evening!"

"I like very much this bolo," he continued, touching gently the jewelry at Al's throat.

"It's carved. From shed antler," Al stammered. "You know...you have deer here in Cuba."

"Very nice. I remember you from Harlem. We met there in 1960, Mr. Al Lewis." Al's eyes bugged out.

"At the hotel ..."

"Yes, at the Hotel Theresa."

"At 125th Street! I also heard your wonderful speech at the U.N."

"Yes! Thank you for your solidarity in 1960 and today." With that, Fidel moved gracefully toward the center of the room. Al shook his head in disbelief.

"Fidel was talking about the incident in 1960 in New York," Al whispered as we watched to see what would happen next. "He was supposed to stay at another hotel. But they wanted to charge him thousands of dollars for added security. Ha! The Hotel Theresa, you know, they were very progressive. They welcomed him with open arms. I was there! Greeting Fidel!"

Al and I looked at each other, trembling. Either El Jefe had a fantastic memory or a great research staff! When we looked up, Fidel was standing right next to Jennifer Carino, our diminutive trip leader, towering over her. Then the Cuban President extended his heartfelt thanks to her and Global Exchange for being courageous enough to travel to and assist his country during the crisis of The Special Period. His words rolled from him in such a simple, direct way that it made one feel embraced. Fidel then thanked all the guests who had made sacrifices to attend the Festival, thereby helping his people.

Al had followed the Cuban Revolution for decades, and admired much of what had been accomplished, such as a free health care system and education, an end to the gambling and corruption that had marked Batista's Cuba, and until The Special Period, the

dissolution of prostitution. It had been a dream of his to shake hands
with Fidel, and it had happened. It was rare for me to see Al
overwhelmed, and I secretly enjoyed watching my wisecracking
husband made speechless.

Our vacation time over, we reluctantly flew back to a freezing
New York City. As I unpacked our summer clothes to put them away,
I came across the prescription for Santiago Alvarez and remembered
our promise to help him. "What are we going to do about this, Al?"
"Well, let's make a list of all the doctors that we know and call
on them." And that's what we did. We called and called, but no
American doctors were willing to fill a prescription for a patient they
hadn't seen, let alone deal with the U.S. Embargo against Cuba.
"Why'd you say we'd get this?" I whined in defeat, knowing
how much Santiago needed the medicine.
"I never said we would," Al gently counseled. "I said we'd try,
Karen. We have to try. Do our best." Back on course, we
brainstormed and decided to ask friends in countries that had
relations with Cuba to help us. Finally, through a doctor friend in
Europe, we were able to buy the medicine and she agreed to have it
delivered directly to Santiago in Havana.
We received a letter from Cuba, hand-delivered by an
American traveler, as the U.S. Embargo against Cuba did not allow
any official mail service. The letter was from Sr. Alvarez and he was
overwhelmed with gratitude. How do you describe your feelings when
he calls that simple act a miracle? It is humbling no matter how you
look at it. My life with Al continued to surprise and change me. His
insistence on simply trying gave me courage. "Just try. Don't look
back. Just try."

Returning home also meant returning to our show on WBAI.
Of course Al wanted to report about our trip and, as we anticipated,
there were objections to our vacation choice.
"Cuba! Hanging out with Fidel, huh! You, you, Commie! Why
don't you go back where you came from!" Click. Clunk. Hit and run.
"Guess the caller didn't know I'm from New York. Brooklyn. I
know you're still listening, you fool, you." Al responded, his volume
intensifying. "I'm not here to defend Fidel. I'm here to tell you about
Cuba. Every culture has successes and failures. Isn't it exciting to see
how other countries handle life's challenges? When my wife got sick
and had to go to the doctor, we never paid a cent. Do you have that
here, in the wealthiest nation in the world? There they have one
doctor for every 125 citizens! Everyone has a doctor in the
neighborhood where they live. Do you have that here? I don't think

so. Why do you think they have so many doctors, huh? Cuz medical school is free! My nephew went to medical school in Boston and now he's up to his neck in school loans. Ya gotta think about these things. That's all."

I reported on how our group took medicine to this country in crisis. "How can you give medicine to a dictatorship?!" Another caller bleated in anger.

"The people are not the government!" Al boomed. "They're innocent human beings. They should go without aspirin? *You* go without aspirin. See how you like it!"

No sooner had that attack ended when a caller complained about a different topic. "While we're at it," he yelled, "how could you do that horrible Richard Bey Show? You have no morals!"

Al took a big breath. "Listen, you! I didn't hurt anybody. My wife didn't hurt anybody. Everybody had a good laugh. Have you no sense of humor? The only person who could ever tell me what to do was my mother. So get lost!"

Seventy-seven

AND THEY'RE OFF

One evening I came home from Eviction Intervention Services after a tiring day of writing grant proposals. Al didn't say hello or kiss me. He was ranting. "I can't believe it! I just can't believe it."

"What, Al? What happened?"

"Jimmy-the-waiter?" Al said it all in one, as if Jimmy's last name was TheWaiter.

"What happened to Jimmy?"

"You know he has AIDS." Yes, I nodded.

"Well, they wouldn't let his partner Adolfo in to see him. Can you believe that? At the hospital! Tomorrow I'm going over there to kick some ass."

"Take Adolfo with you!" I was now almost as upset as Al.

"Of course. Of course I'll take Adolfo with me. He cares more about Jimmy than anybody, including his parents. They washed their hands of him years ago. If anything happens to Jimmy, Adolfo won't get his Social Security, and I doubt Jimmy has a will. I mean, how cruel can you get? He has no say in his partner's treatment."

The next day Al stormed the hospital ready to read them the riot act, but because he was Grandpa Munster, they gave him a warm welcome. In fact, Al reported, "I didn't even have to raise my voice." The unfair treatment of unmarried couples angered both of us and Al might have been disappointed that he was deprived of a righteous rant.

Then it dawned on me. "You know, in the eyes of the law we are also an unmarried couple!"

Later that week Al approached me with a strange look in his eye, working his eyebrows like Groucho Marx. What was he up to? "Wanna get married?" he cooed.

"To you?" I teased back. "Forget it!" He chased me across the living room like a clown with a huge heart painted on his chest until he caught me in his arms and hugged me. Then he said, "Let's go to Vegas!"

"You don't want to get married!" I laughed, "You just want to play the horses!" He had to kiss me, to prove me wrong and to shut me up just in case I was a little bit right about those horses. But it was a very nice kiss.

We started to play around with wedding plans, and after we let our imaginations run wild, improvising hilarious scenarios, embellished with outlandish details, we soon agreed that we wanted to keep it simple. There was the fact that we'd both been married before, with all the wedding hoopla, and felt no need to repeat that. In the end, we invited our families to the Hotel Monte Carlo, in Vegas, where the grandkids could enjoy the pools and water slides. "It's an all out family vacation" was the cover story and we told no one of our secret agenda.

Al and I arrived there two days before the others and immediately hopped a cab to City Hall. A lady judge presided over our marriage, which tickled Al no end. He teased her throughout the ceremony as she asked how we'd met, how long we'd known each other and why we wanted to get married. "Well, Your Honor, does it matter that we're not virgins?" Caught in public with his heart on his sleeve, Al had to produce hilarious answers or be drowned in his own shy, sweet feelings. "The truth is, Judge, we have to get married. I knocked her up." She quickly replied, deadpan, "Then you're doing the responsible thing, young man! I now pronounce you man and wife." We drove back to the hotel for a special celebratory supper, courtesy of room service.

Our family members soon arrived in groups from various states unaware of our new marital status. And I greeted them in the hotel lobby while Al (I knew it!) bet on horse races around the world. We enjoyed several days of entertainment, meals, swimming, sightseeing, and, oh yes, horse racing. Then, as part of our family get-together, we invited everyone to a special meal in one of the hotel banquet rooms.

When all had gathered, Al tapped his glass, welcomed both families, and then leaned back in his chair, a serious expression on his face. It was clear that he had something on his mind and it looked like bad news. The faces of our guests tightened. My mother looked worried.

Al slowly began to speak. "Two days ago ..." Dramatic pause. "On the 6th day of August, in Clark County ..." Another inordinately long pause, during which Al bit his lip and sucked in his breath. "In the State of Nevada ..." He let that sink in. "In front of Judge Victoria Sanchez ..." Al shook his head grimly as if looking for a way to soften the mortifying news he was about to impart. "On that day, before Judge Sanchez ..." David Lewis's face grew ashen. My mother grimaced. "Karen and I joined our hearts in wedlock!" He grinned like a goon, pulled me over to him, and repeatedly kissed my forehead through his own gurgling-brook laughter. The crowd was greatly relieved. Then happy for the couple. Then mock angry at Al for pulling that stunt.

The room exploded in celebration as our families rushed to us with congratulations. Al was forgiven for his audacious practical joke delivered with perfect comic timing. So, in the privacy of our own banquet hall, our families laughed, ate, and talked, getting to know each other better. It felt good. I was legally wedded to my dear unpredictable Al.

Seventy-eight

DANCIN' FOOL

SAVE, TOSS, GIVE AWAY

This award brings back memories. It's heavy and needs to be carefully packed. Save.

"This one's a biggie, Famous Monsters of Filmland. A fan convention put on by Ray Ferry, that guy who edited the magazine all those years. It's gonna be at the Universal Sheraton right near Universal Studios where I filmed *The Munsters*. And listen to this, Karen. They want me to judge the costume contest."

"Whoa! Sounds great!"

"It's a three-day weekend package. For the fans. They got awards, a radio play featuring old time guest stars of radio and TV. And it looks like they're giving me an award for the Best Comedy TV Series. What a line up! We gotta go!"

"They send you tickets?"

"Right here. JFK to LAX."

Twentieth Century Fox television producer, Kevin Burns, a good friend whom Al met when he was still teaching film at Boston University, met us in the lobby of the Sheraton. He guided us through the sea of costumed guests and led us into the middle of the crowd.

The hall was huge and inviting, a sea of people. "Wow, Al, what a party!" Every time Al and I turned around, another star from the past grabbed Al and kissed him. It was better than a high school reunion. The atmosphere and excitement were overwhelming. Fans in costume cruised the celebrities in the room. A few persisted, waiting for Al's attention. "God, Al," I whispered as the volume in the room zoomed up. "Is this country totally obsessed with nostalgia, fantasy, celebrity, and bad B-Movies, or what?"

"Yeah, Karen. It makes us look normal!" We both laughed.

A fan dressed as The Tin Man rocked up to us. "Mr. Lewis, did you know that you did an episode of *Naked City* where you played "Gus"? Remember when the police chief asked you how many fingers were on your hand? Ha! Fun-ny! You were awesome."

"Oh, yeh. Heh. Thank you. That episode was pretty good, wasn't it?" As The Tin Man creaked off, Al turned to me and said,

"Geez, I don't know what he was talkin' about. But these fans, they know more about my life than I do!"

Boris Karloff's daughter, Sarah, was there and I asked her if she'd mind taking a photo with Al and me. Fans, movie buffs, and industry movers and shakers acknowledged that this was a night to remember.

The Awards Ceremony was announced and the crowd fell relatively silent. When his name was called, Al marched to the podium to uproarious cheers and applause. He was wearing his glamour tux, black with silver accents, and sporting a pink bowtie and matching cummerbund. He gratefully accepted his award, the coveted Hall of Fame Readers Choice plaque for the All-Time Best Comedy TV Series for his work in *The Munsters*. "For once, I'm gonna be brief. Thank you so much for honoring me with this award, which I humbly deserve!" The cheers and applause started up again. Kevin Burns squeezed my hand. With tears in his eyes he said, "We'll never see this again, this line-up of celebrities from the golden age of television and film." Then he sputtered, "They're aging."

Another highlight of the evening was the costume contest. Fans had designed their outfits months in advance, hoping to be singled out for their inspired interpretations of roles from vintage films or their own fantasy characters. One contestant was entirely covered in black: shoes, trousers, jacket, Darth Vader helmet and cape. The only exception was white gloves. No one knew who this was, as he had signed in under an obvious alias, "John Doe." But there was a growing buzz in the hall that Mr. Doe might be a well-known performer who was filming a music video at Universal, that the mystery contestant was in fact Michael Jackson!

Following the program, as people were slowly dispersing, a folded hand-written note was delivered to Al's palm. "A secret invitation, non-transferrable, not even to be mentioned, to visit Mr. Michael Jackson on the set at Universal. RSVP ASAP." So it *was* him! We looked at each other in shock. The note continued, "A guide will meet you tomorrow morning in the lobby, wearing a Michael Jackson baseball cap."

"Is this for real, Al?" I asked. "Or is it a spoof, a set up, or something worse?"

"I don't know," Al sputtered. "What do you think?"

"We could be taken for a ride!"

"Nah, most of my fans are nice people. Remember Bryant Park? Even the hoodlums are respectful. The worst thing that could happen is nuttin'."

"What do you mean?"

"If it's a joke, the guy who signed this message won't show! There we'll be at 9 a.m. with no place to go. Big deal." In spite of his blasé exterior, I knew Al was excited by the prospect of meeting Michael Jackson! So we agreed to go along with this invitation wherever it might take us.

9 a.m. The lobby at Universal Sheraton. Sure enough, the Baseball Cap showed up. We were escorted to his van, and whisked away to Universal Studios.

"I spent lotsa years on this lot," Al said to the driver, trying to get a clue from him about the day's agenda. The driver was friendly, but a gofer-guide and tight lipped. Al's eyes scanned the gate to the entrance of the lot and beyond. "Yeh. Yeh. The Tower. Just a big amusement park now. I wasn't too amused when I was here. Heh, heh." The gofer-guide was poker-faced. That was a rare bird, a non-Grandpa fan.

The van weaved around buildings and we pulled up to a new set construction, scaffolds still visible. We were then dropped into the hands of Guide Number Two, and the mystery continued. Speaking in hushed tones, Guide Two warned us that noise and talking were off limits in this studio. I whispered to Al, "Where were we going?" Al gestured to me, palms up and shrugging, clueless. The guide led us into a dimly lit hangar, through a series of labyrinthine walkways until we came to a suspended set which looked like a huge tubular balloon positioned several feet off the floor. A fantastic dream scene. Guide Two apologized for asking us to remove our shoes, but stated that it was mandatory since the set was all white. Shoes off, we climbed a ladder-like stairway, moving upward until we entered the elongated set. As our eyes adjusted to the whiteness and light, there stood Michael Jackson. He moved forward to welcome us. Al immediately offered his hand in greeting.

"I'd shake hands, Mr. Lewis, but my costumer will scold me," he said languorously, smiling his sweetest Michael Jackson smile, and displaying snow white gloves. "Excuse me a moment, I'm just finishing this sequence." Michael moved back to a set on an open stage. The music began -- his latest hit -- and he danced in his signature style, including his famous moonwalk. Michael was a demanding perfectionist, so it was start - stop, start - stop. Then he was done. He gestured to us to follow him to another area of the set. We ducked under a padded connector tunnel into what looked like a white cockpit where his sister, Janet, was waiting for him. Seeing Al, Janet jumped up and down squealing, "Grandpa! It's you! It's you!" How tiny she is, I thought, and so beautiful. She and her brother were decked out in sexy spacesuits, like rock star astronauts.

"They are at the Universal Sheraton for the Famous Monsters of Filmland weekend," Michael informed Janet. Hmm, was Michael at last night's costume contest, or not? Janet enthusiastically embraced Al. Tickled to see him, like a little girl, she threw her arms around him and giggled in irrepressible rounds. Michael glared at Janet and quickly put an end to this bubbly scene of fan devotion, which made me now wonder if Janet was the mysterious person in black at Al's gala. Michael tersely asked us to stand to the side for the next part of the rehearsal. "We need to practice our dance sequence for the lead song. It's called *Scream*." It was obvious that Michael didn't like his sister fussing over Al. He wanted her devoted and undivided attention. The music was cued and Michael moved, turned and danced. Then Janet moved in for a *pas de deux*. It was mechanically and seamlessly executed, and performed at a breakneck pace. Michael yelled, "Cut," and an earphoned assistant asked us to please refrain from moving, applauding, or making any sounds. Michael and Janet then repeated this choreography several times, while we stood watching in enforced silence. When they finished, Guide Two escorted us back to the original stage and asked us to wait for Michael. "He wants to say goodbye," she whispered reverently, as if we were in the Vatican and the "he" she referred to was The Pope.

Michael respectfully returned to Al, and I truly believe he expected to hear words of praise and awe pour out of us. But that just wasn't Al's way. In his mind, all the Masters of the Entertainment Arts were equals and educated by the past.

"That's some routine! Did you ever see John Q. Bubbles? Best tap dancer that ever lived!" Al threw out this bait to Michael as a test to see if he knew his forebears, the dance masters on whose shoulders he stood. But he looked subdued, as if stifling his shock. I could almost see Michael thinking, Hey, *I'm* The King. But he quietly replied, "No."

"Yeh. John Q. Bubbles taught me all my tap dance moves," continued Al. As Michael watched, stunned, Al instantly threw himself into a passionate dance sequence across the space in stocking feet, exploding with a fleet footed "Shuffle-off-to-Buffalo" in one direction, returning with a "Grapevine" and a "Ta Dah" finish, an adventurous split (as wide as his arthritis would allow), completed by pulling his feet together into an erect posture, ready to deliver a straight-backed bow.

Michael was speechless, but I don't think it was because of Al's performance. After a few seconds of silence he muttered a listless, "Wow, Mr. Lewis, that's really something. And at your age."

"I knew you when you were this high," Al bubbled with pleasure, gasping a bit. "When you were singing in the Valley with your dad!"

"Is that right?" Michael said tensely, clearly wanting a different conversation.

"Yeah. I knew your dad and your brothers. You were this big. What a cute kid."

"Thank you, Mr. Lewis. Thank you." Guide Three had apparently received a secret signal and we were peremptorily dismissed. Eager to move us out, Guide Three tugged at our sleeves like a security guard. But Al turned around to face Michael, leaned into his Asian bow, palms pressed together, and nodded as he backed out.

We sat in a trailer on the back lot waiting for the van to pick us up. Al whispered sarcastically, "Well, that went over big, huh?" Then he chuckled.

"Obviously your exuberance poked a hole in Michael's perfectly controlled universe."

"You mean I screwed up?"

"It's not clear. But he might have been a trifle upset."

"Perhaps we've made a dreadful mistake."

"If that's the case, do you think we'll ever work in this town again?" We looked at each other, and burst out into uproarious laughter.

"Well, Professor Lewis, here's a perfect example, proving your theory, of what happens when a star starts believing his own PR."

Back in New York, I kept thinking about the Michael Jackson incident and wondered how Al was feeling about it. "Who knows what's going on in his head. He's big, Karen. He can do it any way he wants." Al paused, considering something. "He's fooled a lot of people."

"Yeah, but we got to meet *Michael Jackson.*"

"Never forget that. He didn't have to invite us. But he did. We met Michael Jackson. Yes we did!"

"And you out-danced him!"

Al was high on the experience. For weeks, everywhere we went, Al was bursting with the news that Michael Jackson invited us to meet him. "You shudda seen it! All white, the set. Everything. Oh, yeah, and I danced for him! I showed him a thing or two."

Seventy-nine

AL-TRUISM

Back in New York we were passionately researching material for our weekly radio program. We were digging up stories about racism, corruption and oppression, which weren't that hard to find. And whenever our investigations involved drugs, they always seemed to involve the unfair Rockefeller Drug Laws. Born from hysteria, these draconian laws were hated by dealers and judges alike. Due to mandated sentencing, people who were convicted of minor drug infractions were doing prison time that even convicted murderers didn't face.

Once a week, while I was at work, Al spent the lunch hour in front of Rockefeller Center in a silent vigil. He was protesting in solidarity with the families and friends of individuals unfairly incarcerated under these unreasonable drug laws. Each demonstrator held the photo of an inmate unjustly imprisoned for a minor drug-related offense.

Through Al's participation at the vigils, we got to hear the real stories from the families of those sentenced, the attorneys who represented imprisoned clients, and drug policy advocates. We learned that too many were doing hard time for petty crimes such as acting as a courier, selling tiny amounts of weed, or taking the hit for someone else, often a drug kingpin. The whole thing stank and the overwhelming odor began to burden Al's sense of justice.

I went to find him at the vigil. And there he was, in his cowboy hat and boots. I kissed him and he put his finger to his lips in a silent "shhh." I had to admit I was thoroughly enjoying this rare and wonderful experience - Al's silence, that is! But the atmosphere there was deadly serious. I saw the literature-laden table set up right near the curb, the demonstrators, mothers and grandmothers who were looking sad and worn, a few little kids, children of the wrongly incarcerated, essentially parentless, walking quietly with the adults. They were holding laminated photos of a loved one, who was someone's mother, daughter, father, son. The words underneath the faces floored me. They stated the conviction and the time served. The sentences were unbelievably harsh. Arrested for $5 worth of marijuana, serving 15 years to life!

Al held a sign with the image of 50-year-old Rufus Boyd, who served 22 years of his 25-year sentence for a first time drug offense. When Al went to see him at Green Haven Correctional Facility, Rufus told Al that he was his first visitor. Al asked him, "First visitor today?"

"No," Rufus said. "First in 22 years."

When Al came home and told me about this, he was visibly shaken. "I just can't imagine it," he murmured. His eyes were filled with stinging anguish.

After that, Al and I began to visit prisoners. We experienced the chill of the cold metal doors slamming behind us locking us into a security cell until our visitor permits were checked. It rattled my nerves. I felt the militant hostility directed toward us as probable "soft-on-crimers" and it angered my righteous core. The worst thing was being denied access to the people we'd come to visit based on whatever reason the warden or commissioner decided to give us that day. It was a horrifying glimpse into what those locked inside experienced daily.

Al at silent vigil protesting the Rockefeller Drug Laws

At the beginning of December 1998, Al asked me what I wanted to do for New Year's, and without hesitation I looked into his eyes and said, "Let's visit someone in prison." Al smiled a very sweet smile and took my face between his palms.

"Yeah, let's bring in the New Year right."

On New Year's Day, our old friend, Randy Credico, director of the William Moses Kunstler Fund for Racial Justice, and professional stand-up comic, drove us to Bedford Women's Correctional Facility. The Kunstler Fund was awaiting the Governor's year-end clemencies.

All the way there, Randy hilariously imitated Al. "Heh, heh, heh. We gotta get rid of those drug laws. Crap! That's what they are. Crap!" Al rolled his eyes, pretending to be annoyed while I laughed at Randy's spot-on impersonation. At the prison, the three of us sat in the visitors' room as the warden marched in, wearing a military style overcoat. She informed Donna Charles that her clemency was denied. Donna had already served nearly 12 years on a 17-to-Life sentence for a first-time offense, and her family collapsed where they sat, their hopes shattered.

Possibly the most far-reaching and miraculous result of our efforts was the case in Tulia, Texas, in which an overwhelming percentage of the town's people of color found themselves behind bars. Randy Credico flew out to Tulia and filed this on-air report by phone during our program. "This corrupt Texas town has been cashing in by abusing The Rockefeller Drug Law's unfair tough-on-crime stance. They've been framing black citizens so they could boost incarceration quotas which – surprise surprise – brought in more money and perks to the police force!" This travesty of justice was exposed over far-reaching WBAI airwaves on the *Al Lewis Live!* show. It was the starting point for a movement that built nationwide, exposing the truth about how the Drug Laws were manipulated for profit.

We kept the faith even though inside we both believed that we might not be around to see any real change. But then a few months later, a miracle happened. The tide turned! Stunned, we watched the news of the Tulia story unfold as the Texas court released dozens of innocent and falsely incarcerated citizens! It was so rewarding to realize that our initial reporting had helped shed light on this terrible story.

We were so happy for the release of those who had been unjustly thrown in jail and for all their families. We celebrated quietly, to register our gratitude without angering the gods of justice! "It took everyone to do this, Albie."

"Yeh, it did. But you know, my Karen, we didn't do anything but follow our hearts."

Eighty

BUSTED

One hot evening in Flushing, Queens, after the devastating funeral of a dear friend, wilting from the heat, emotionally drained and hungry, Al and I checked the menu posted outside a local Chinese restaurant, hoping to find a nice meal. Suddenly a car sped down Main Street, slammed on its brakes as it cut across the opposite traffic lane, careened over the curb, and screeched up onto the sidewalk inches away from where we stood. We nearly suffered a double cardiac arrest. The car doors flew open and out jumped four rough looking men in worn out jeans, bandanas and beards.

"Ohmygod, Al!" I gasped. He grabbed my hand and held tight, his eyes darting over the scene, reading the men's body language. "Leo!" they shouted, "Leo Schnauzer!" As they whipped out their badges we realized that they were undercover cops -- and fans of Al's. We burst out laughing in relief. Al shook hands and slapped shoulders. "Al! It's so good to see you. We spotted you right off. You look terrific. We were over here in Flushing. Yeah, just pulled off a big sting!" Each man moved in, vying for a friendly hug.

"Geez, I thought we were getting mugged!" Al teased. "You scared the crap out of us." Al had to sign autographs for each officer or "face arrest"! He loved every minute of it, especially when the cops warmed up and sang the *Car 54* theme song in four-part harmony!

Eighty-one

IT'S NOT EASY BEING GREEN

SAVE, TOSS, GIVE AWAY

A box of political campaign materials, posters, leaflets and buttons. I can't face going through all this now. Save.

It was a Saturday afternoon in the spring of 1998 when Al and I finished broadcasting *Al Lewis Live!* and we hurried home eager for a nice nap. Our eyelids were drooping as we dragged down the hall to the bedroom. My husband sat down to kick off his shoes, and then noticed the message light blinking on the answering machine. He rolled over onto the bed and pressed it.

"Hello, Mr. Lewis. I represent the Brooklyn Greens. We'd like to talk to you about running as a candidate for Governor on the Green Party ticket." Al deleted the message.

"Another nutty DJ!"

"And on Saturday even!"

"But, you gotta admit that was clever!"

"Turn off the phone. Let's go to sleep."

Several days later at home reading, Al answered the phone. "Just checking, since we never heard back from you. My name is Craig Seeman, and I'm with the Brooklyn Greens. Did you get my message?"

"So you're for real after all. What can I do for you?"

"We'd like to talk to you about running for Governor."

"Governor, huh? Why'd you think of me?"

"You'd make a great candidate. Can you come down and meet with the Committee?"

"Yeh. Just give me the time and place."

A week later, Al reported to me following the meeting. "They listen to me on the air." He made a Kermit the Frog face. "Geez, you never know who's tuned in, do you? They want to get the Green Party on the ballot. They've never had a big enough candidate to win the 50,000 votes needed to get on the ballot."

"And they want you, Al? That's great!"

"Heh. But no one gets in except Democrats and Republicans. Ever been to the Election Board and seen what an exclusive club it is? New York's election laws are impossible." Al rolled his eyes.

"So, what'd you tell them?"

"I gotta talk it over with my wife and family."

"I'm excited that you're considering running for office, but I'm afraid it could be too exhausting. In a few short months of electioneering, politicians seem to age horribly and grow all gray. And their wives ... ! I could probably handle it, but you're no spring chicken, Albie Lewis!"

"No, but I'm a tough old bird! I'm gonna call the kids and their mother and see if they think I should do it." Al laid out the basic situation for them and everyone agreed to respond before he had to render his decision to the Greens. Each family member had one vote.

Marge, Al's former wife, was worried that Al's lefty past would be thrown in his face and hurt his acting career. She voted NO. Dave, the oldest son, was concerned about how strenuous this campaign would be and wanted more information. Pepper, his wife, voted a loud YES, declaring Al would be the kind of person to get energy from all that stress because he thrived on challenges. Convinced by Pepper's rationale, Dave voted YES, too. Ted, the middle son, and his wife, Andrea voted YES. Paul, the youngest, and spouse Jennifer didn't like the game of politics and voted NO. Echoing Pepper's confidence in Al's ability to transform stress into positive energy, I added my YES. Three NOs and five YESes. Al thanked us for our opinions, and with much mock bravura he loudly proclaimed, "I vote YES for myself!"

Well and good, but we both had to be vetted. Al and I were placed in front of a panel ranging from 35-year-old urban farmers with dirty fingernails to 20-year old bicycle messengers to well-dressed 45-year-old political pamphleteers. We were videotaped while being questioned about our lifestyle, green orientation, and desire to win the election. We were quizzed about our political party affiliations, where we'd gone to school, even what we ate. I wanted to break the tension by yelling "greens" but I bit my tongue. We were interrogated about sustainable agriculture and energy sources, organic farming, gender politics, ecology, and the balance of power in our marriage. We bought organic groceries from a local food collective, and I had a vegetable garden. That translated to The Greens as "Thinking globally, acting locally!" My job as a tenant advocate and our roles as radio co-hosts on *Al Lewis Live!*, a progressive oriented broadcast, highlighted our ties to the community. All in all, we were seen as an excellent candidate package. Besides, I think we moved The Greens with our crazy love for each other.

But Al was not the only candidate. Of course, he had to make it through a Primary. There was a wearying meeting in Montauk, Long Island, with numerous candidates representing themselves with platforms and speeches. But, in the end, Al received the nomination from the Committee.

Next, they had to pick a slate. Al asserted, "I will not run on an all white male slate! I know Johann Moore's gay, which is wonderful! But that's not good enough!" While to some extent Al had been chosen for his tenacity, this was the first time that the Committee realized that he was also truly his own person. Their hopes were instantly deflated. Oops.

Because Al insisted upon it, the party had to come up with a running mate who was a minority woman. They found Alice Green. Besides having a totally appropriate name, she was a brilliant African-American woman. As an Albany-based prison rights activist, she would be a powerful partner for Al. When Alice agreed to run as Lt. Governor, he was sincerely satisfied.

The period from August, when Al's race was officially announced, through Election Day in November was a time of tremendous growth for me. Not only did I meet brilliant people from all walks of life, I also met the worst. I knew politics was dirty but I hadn't yet had my face pressed into the mud. Al's entrance into the race disturbed the bottom feeders as well as the big fish at the top. Other candidates selfishly worried about how many votes a popular figure like Al Lewis was going to "steal" from their campaigns. Now Al was "taking meetings" with politicians of every stripe, even from the extreme right. And he enjoyed the hell out of this opportunity. As he loved to explain, "Al Lewis, where Left and Right meet!"

Luckily, I still had my work saving people from eviction, because those political encounters upon which Al thrived put my digestion into knots. "You don't have the stomach for it, Karen!" Al chortled, happy to protect me from the mud slinging. "Gotta expect that." He did get energy from a good fight!

Al and I were required to attend many Green meetings which were very politically correct. They were so purely democratic that it took forever for the tiniest motion to be carefully explained, discussed and voted on. Al would walk out of the meetings, ostensibly on cigar breaks, and rely on a handful of political soul mates to run out and advise him if anything really important required his attention. And, yes! Those cigars were also a point of contention as we had predicted. "If I was Churchill, they wouldn't ask me to quit! What's greener than Cuban tobacco?"

WBAI Pier Party.
Al and I petition to get Al's name on the ballot

Political activist, Randy Credico, wanted the Campaign Manager job. Al explained to him that that wasn't in the Greens' game plan, but he wouldn't take no for an answer. Even without the title, he insisted on playing the manager's role. Randy, a brilliant standup comic, a wonderful writer and political animal, put into place fundraising events that had broad appeal. He produced popular political variety shows at Gus's Place, a Greenwich Village eatery with a large banquet room set up like a cabaret. Randy called in his friends: Professor Irwin Corey, Soupy Sales, Art D Lugoff, Terry Waldo, and Lewis Black, who volunteered entertainment for Al's campaign. After years of generously supporting others' political efforts, Al was seriously humbled by being on the receiving end of the

243

Green Party Campaign Meeting in Hudson, NY

gifts and goodwill of these brilliant professionals.

Al traversed most of the State of New York by bus, train and "goodwill ferry," picked up and dropped off by friends, passed off like a baton in a relay race. To say the campaign was strenuous would be a complete understatement. In scope, it was like organizing for a different huge wedding every three days. Al described it as "climbing up Mount Everest barefoot."

His bold humor and pointed political message made him an instantly popular hero. People who had never voted, or had given up on the political process because they were disgusted with what they encountered daily, got on the band wagon. "You're being screwed without Vaseline!" Al would exclaim. "You know what's happening! You're not stupid, you're being robbed. No wonder you don't vote! I see what's going on here! You're being downsized, abused, cheated, and disenfranchised." They loved Al for not making promises he couldn't keep.

In the late '90s, politics appeared to be far less about caring for humanity than about profit. Al spoke of lobbying as bribery, and dramatically spelled out B-R-I-B-E to illuminate his view on the corporatization of government. He refused to worry about how his professional life might be damaged by his opinions. "I'm so old! What can they do to me!?" he chortled, and continued to use his fame to shine a light on the problems of the middle class and the poor.

I felt such stirrings in my heart for him as I began to see more clearly where he'd come from, what he'd overcome to be a star, and why people adored him. My Comic Wizard passed his magic wand over the issue of poverty, making it leap humorously into public awareness. I was awed by his depth when he accurately read the signs of hypocrisy and spoke directly about the sources of racism, job loss, factory closings, welfare payment reductions, and victim blaming. When I heard him speak his truth, using his signature audacious humor, I watched myself fall more deeply in love with him.

October was always a huge month for Al because Halloween was Grandpa Munster's big holiday. He had some Halloween appearances lined up prior to his nomination by the Green Party, and turned down others so that he could hit the campaign trail. One morning following one such Halloween appearance for hundreds of fans in Albany, he was awakened by upstate DJs on the phone. An aggressive young female and male team.

"Oh, Grandpa, how many groupies swarmed you last night, eh?"

"So many I lost count! Heh, heh, heh!" retorted Al. The banter went back and forth with this drive-time foolishness which Al enjoyed engaging in. He refused to cool his comedic heels because the political spotlight was on him. Then Al was challenged with the following question: "So, Grandpa, what's your type? If you could have any girl? Huh?" asked the young man. He was topped by his female sidekick who added, "Come on, Grandpa, what do you want for Christmas?!" Al responded without dropping a beat. "A sixteen-year-old Japanese girl with heavy thighs and a round black hat!" Straight out of vaudeville! I shrieked with laughter. I was making breakfast in our kitchen and had to put down the spatula to cover my mouth, afraid that my laughter would be heard on the air.

Immediately after the interview ended, the telephone rang again. It was an outraged Green Party officer demanding to know how their candidate could say such a thing! The Up-Staters who'd heard the show wanted to know if he was a pervert. Meetings were already being scheduled for damage control. We were suddenly caught in a humorless hell. But Al absolutely refused to take any meetings around this incident, declaring it too ridiculous to pay any attention to.

"They're nuts!" he growled. "That interview'll get me more votes than any politically-correct meeting they can come up with. Don't you remember Howard Stern and the FCC?"

I was afraid that the Party would turn on him, so I met with Greens from Brooklyn to Queens, and basically briefed them on humor, low-brow comedy, and the history of sexism in vaudeville and burlesque. From Shakespeare to Commedia Del Arte to afternoon TV. I took them to school on comedy. I pointed out that these Greens hadn't understood or appreciated the wild creativity behind their candidate's absurdly brilliant line. Only Al could conjure up "and a round black hat!" I got it off my chest, even though I was met with angry stares. But The Incident divided the party for and against Al. Realizing they had already invested too much in their candidate, after about a week all the party factions came back together to vote for Al Lewis.

Al scheduled a visit to an upstate prison during the time he was running for governor, only to be told he was not allowed entry. When he asked then Commissioner Glen Gourd his reason, he was told, "No electioneering is permitted in the facility." Al protested, saying, "Prisoners don't vote!" Commissioner Gourd responded with, "You're right, Mr. Lewis, then it's because I say so."

Right before the election, Al was invited to be part of a TV special themed around successful elders, featuring the great astronaut John Glenn. But two days before the event, Al was disinvited. In a flash, he was on the phone attempting to get to the bottom of this rude turn of events. No one would come clean, except for one contact who actually cried on the phone, in essence admitting that the producers refused to take a chance on a "wild man like Al Lewis" so close to Election Day, even though he'd promised to say nothing about his gubernatorial race. "I've hit the glass ceiling," groaned Al, "I don't know whether to laugh or cry. Sonofabitch. It's all connected. They aren't going to let me on the show. I'm not a politician. God forbid! I'm a political animal." Even though Al vented and exploded, he actually had more reasonable expectations than I about dealing with wheeler-dealers and the power elite.

While the schedule was brutal, demanding and exhausting, Al kept pace in the race and never even alluded to the high physical and emotional cost of earnestly running for public office. I was running along with him, puffing by his side, and every few hundred yards I handed off my full support as if it were Gatorade.

In the few quiet moments we had, we talked about the campaign. Al confided, "My true mission's to meet people and talk to them about what's really going on in their lives. You know, why they're feeling so desperate. Hell, Karen, I know it's impossible for a Green to be elected Governor. But I think I can still get the 50,000 votes needed to put the Green Party on the ballot for the first time in the Great State of New Y-a-w-k!" He committed himself to the task as if he had had a chance, giving the campaign his all.

Al was not elected Governor, but he did get the Green Party on the ballot. When I think about our Green Party endeavor -- the political, social, and emotional aspects of Al's run for Governor-- I have to smile. It was the roller coaster ride of a lifetime. Those months were packed with excitement and eye-opening experiences for us, as Al, the modern day Sisyphus, repeatedly pushed that huge rock of ecological hope uphill. Was it scary? Yes. Was it worth it? Yes, indeed.

Eighty-two

ANOTHER LOSS

Marge, Al's former wife, was in a serious health crisis. Almost thirty years earlier she had been in that terrible automobile accident in Florida and had lost so much blood that she needed numerous transfusions to save her life.

"Blood in the 1970s was donated anonymously and wasn't screened the way it is now, Karen. The transfusions saved her life, but she also got hepatitis which attacked her liver. Now her liver's failing." This crisis brought the family together in a way that surprised and touched me.

Like a mini-medical team, each of Al's sons tried to find ways to save their mother, even by offering to be liver donors themselves. "Pop, if Mom needs a transplant, I'm ready," Dave stated unequivocally.

Marge's doctors were resistant to the idea of a liver transplant. She had lesions which they believed would be transferred to the new liver and therefore they refused to operate.

So Al and his sons continued questioning and researching, hoping to find that needle in the haystack that could save this woman who meant so much to them. Marge grew weaker and weaker, and Al turned sullen and despondent. His former wife, 12 years his junior, was supposed to outlive him, but she was now losing ground. He called her daily. Then when telephone calls became more difficult for her, she responded only when she was strong enough to talk.

One day she asked specifically for me. Marge told me in a voice that sounded like my own dying grandmother's, "I see you standing by Al's side. You're the keeper of the flame now."

I told her I loved her, and said what was most difficult for me to say ... "Goodbye, Marge." Over and over, Marge's words echoed through my mind as if in a fairy tale: "Keeper of the flame ..." I wasn't at all sure I wanted that mantle, but the stories were already inside me ...

"When are you going to Florida, Al? Would you like me to go with you?"

"Let the kids go, Karen."

"Al, what are you telling me?"

"I'm not going. Marge is in my heart. I've said everything to her that I can say."

The three sons made their pilgrimages to Florida and reported to us by phone. They stayed with their beautiful, diminished mother until she was no more. A few days later, we gathered together in Brooklyn for her funeral.

Marge's death hit Al hard. He grieved for weeks. I was worried about his health which was already compromised by the long, arduous Green Party campaign. I needed to find some immune system support for Al and me. And it came to us from a surprising source.

Eighty-three

PAT ANSWERS

Whenever Pat Priest, "Marilyn" from *The Munsters* TV series, called to say hello to Al, they would talk for quite a while. Inevitably, the phone would be passed to me with a smile. Al was delighted that Pat and I got along so well. She was down to earth and affable. She and I immediately connected, probably because we both adored Al. "Oh, Al was such a blessing on the set. He was like a father to me. He kept us all in balance."

One time when Pat called, Al handed me the phone and it was my turn to get my "Pat fix." We talked a bit about what it was like to act with my husband, but quickly discovered that we had another interest in common: alternative health care. "You and Al have got to come and stay with my husband Fred and me in Idaho. The air's so fresh."

The conversation turned to Marge's funeral and how it had emotionally exhausted the family, leaving us tired and moody. "Diet can play a huge role in restoring health," Pat said enthusiastically.

She was a non-Hodgkin's lymphoma survivor and faced her health challenges with curiosity and passion. "You know, Karen, I'm now a spokesperson for the Lymphoma Research Foundation. I help educate and support other cancer patients. I'm not acting so much any more, but I have to admit, the theater prepared me for what I'm doing now - talking at conventions about cancer treatments and prevention. It's so important ... And I love it! Diet is really key. For example, sugar is no good. It will deplete you. You need fresh fruits and vegetables. I have a garden ..."

"Thank you, Pat, for another inspiring conversation." This was just the kick I needed to get us back on track with our health.

To boost our physical well-being, we shifted our on-going nutrition program into high gear. Al made an appointment with a highly recommended herbalist and we brought home armloads of supplements from him and from the health food store. I bought starter plants and seeds to grow herbs and vegetables in our community garden. Al declared, "Hey, if Pat's taking charge of her health, we can too!"

Al and Pat Priest at an Autograph Convention

Eighty-four

REMEMBER THE AL-AMO

In 1999 when Al and I returned home for the holidays, mellow and tan from warm weeks at the Latin American Film Festival, we were met with icy weather, then icy messages on our answering machine from our WBAI comrades. "We've been locked out, Al! They changed the lock at the radio station! They're trying to take over the place." Apparently an opportunistic faction of the Pacifica National Board, in direct contradiction to their mission as public radio board members, wanted to sell WBAI. It was advantageously positioned in the middle of the FM dial, and so worth millions. We immediately returned the first call and heard the following from Executive Producer Sharan Harper.

"I've not only been locked out of the studio but banned from reporting to work!"

"That's like an illegal slumlord eviction! You can't lock people out of their businesses! That's illegal," I blurted in anger.

"It's like a fascist takeover!" Al bellowed. "It's a power grab."

After the seventh message, Al turned to me and said, "We've been *di-rec-ted* to take a meeting before our show starts tomorrow! Ha!"

After being away on vacation we were determined to report back to the faithful listeners of *Al Lewis Live!* And now we were determined to get to the bottom of this apparent coup. At the crack of dawn, we pulled our boots on and struggled through a fierce blizzard to get to 120 Wall Street, WBAI's new address. At the main entrance, we stopped at the door station to sign in as usual, but were questioned about our identification by an unfamiliar security guard. After his confirmation phone call, he gave us permission to proceed. "What's with all this security?" I asked, frustrated. The guard was tight lipped.

"Come on. Let's sort this out," Al replied.

On the tenth floor, where our studio was, we were buzzed in by a flabby temp security guard in an ill-fitting uniform. "More guards?" I questioned. "What the hell?"

"This is a community radio station!" Al boomed, scaring him off. We were immediately intercepted by a Pacifica National Board Member, Bessie Wash, and her partner in crime, Utrice Leid, a popular talk show host who was an apparent turncoat and had actually supervised the previous night's lockout. For some reason she had asked Al for this meeting. We had arrived well before our show was scheduled, allowing ample time for a conference which never evolved into anything more than an uncomfortable meet-and-greet. So why had they demanded a meeting? They never stated their agenda, yet they acted like they were already running the place. Oppression hovered like smoke from a book burning.

Despite these road blocks, our program launched at noon as usual with our theme song, the uplifting "Foot Pattin'" by King Curtis. But we were under a gag order and were unable to discuss any station business on the air -- including this takeover. Though clearly glad to be back on the radio, Al was silently fuming about being censored. But he put up a good front with welcoming remarks, news of our trip, and current events.

Twenty minutes into the show, National Board Member Ms. Wash burst into the studio in clear violation of the same station rules which Al and I, with great difficulty, were laboring under. After only one sentence, Al slammed down his fist. "This is my show! You have no right to be in here. Get out!" Cowed by Al's vehemence, she left!

Al had drawn a line in the sand. He would never tolerate such cowardly behavior or do anything to facilitate the "enemy." It all went out over the airwaves and every listener heard it. The chutzpah, the guts, the moral righteousness of my wonderful husband! So what was going on here? Bessie Wash wanted the audience to witness "the meeting" which she hadn't allowed privately before the show. It was an on-air ambush of Al's very popular program to announce the changes she meant to implement.

Al's first courageous stand immediately inspired other at-risk staff members, programmers and supporters to proudly unite in solidarity.

It's important to remember that WBAI from its inception was a non-profit, commercial free, listener supported organization owned by the public, not private corporations. Its mission statement and guidelines are for unorthodox programming that is the opposite of the usual top-down management driven programming content. The takeover faction was out to change the entire content of this completely progressive media outlet into more profitable mainstream commercial programming. The atmosphere at WBAI became stifling, as each week a few more of the outspoken voices were banished. Some colleagues became sellouts, thereby defecting to the other side. References to the McCarthy Era were often heard.

Al railed against those who wished to destroy and remake the radio station, despite the gag order, by speaking in metaphors and parables, the meaning of which every loyal listener understood. His show continued to survive as one of the few remaining voices of truth. Judging from the enormous amount of mail coming in for him, it was apparent that Al couldn't be silenced without a severe backlash from his avid supporters. The takeover group seemed intimidated by the fact that many of his supporters were "scary" ex-prisoners and former felons, not to mention cops! So his program prevailed. For the moment.

This illegal occupation of the airwaves was countered by rallies, demonstrations, teach-ins, and fundraising held all over the City for the "banned and fired." Al was called on frequently to speak at public forums away from the radio station because on-air discussion of the takeover was still not permitted. To raise money for the cause, we worked evenings and weekends using our industrial audiocassette copier to create hundreds of copies of the popular, now infamous, show in which Al had laid down the law to Bessie Wash.

Errol Maitland frequently called on Al for stirring updates and provocative reports for his underground Internet podcast WBIX. Errol valued Al's agitating skills.

Brilliantly, Juan Gonzalez, a reporter from The New York Post who frequently joined Amy Goodman on *Democracy Now!,* and Leslie Cagan, a nationally revered progressive organizer, began rallying support. They summoned the aid of professionals on the left and held meetings with relevant non-profits and attorneys to launch a legal case against the occupiers.

Al fought to remain on the air as a rebel intermediary for the listeners. "We gotta stay on for the voiceless. Like the people behind bars." Although stalwart, he was physically feeling the strain of not only this battle but the Governor's race and the loss of his former wife. Difficulties with his health escalated.

In April 2000, a meeting was scheduled by Pacifica Board representative and traitor Utrice Leid to "talk about Al's show." The meeting quickly deteriorated into a bad-cop movie interrogation, at the end of which Al was blamed for an alleged break-in of her home! "One of the participants of that rally outside my apartment building was the perpetrator," she proclaimed. "That rally was your doing. You're responsible for a crime." She figured Al would refute the charge, but instead he jumped to his feet and roared, "Are you out of your friggin' mind?" I watched in horror as Al's left eyelid instantly dropped, nearly covering the entire eye.

"You can't prove any of this," I retorted. "This wouldn't hold up for one second in a court of law." After more than an hour of Ms.

Leid's provocative and hysterical harangue, we still held our ground and maintained our innocence. She continued to wave her flimsy accusation at us until she realized that we would never give up. She abandoned her attempt to establish a justification for firing us, but did so anyway.

Banned from the station, we were escorted out of the building by another rent-a-cop. We were outraged beyond belief. Out on the street we tried to regroup.

"Al, that traitor, that sorry excuse for a station manager, used to be our friend! We bought her dinner, talked to her on the phone dozens of times. We supported her recovery after her accident. Now she'll be collecting kudos for taking down 'BAI's star performer, Grandpa Al."

"Yeh, I know, hon. I ain't goin' there."

"Huh? She just stabbed you in the back."

"You can make yourself sick going over all of that. That's what happened during the McCarthy era. Friends became enemies in a flash. She's not my friend. I've closed that door."

"I don't know what the lesson is from all of this," I said.

"Power corrupts and absolute power corrupts absolutely," quoted Al, his thumb stroking my cheek.

"I'm proud of you for standing up to them." I kissed him.

DEAR DIARY:

The hypocrisy! The same individuals who have up until recently promoted democratic principles, equality, and civil rights now behave like back-stabbing fascists. I still can't believe the scene we endured, interrogated by Utrice Leid in the 'BAI conference room. It contained all the elements that define oppression. I could have been an incarcerated person sitting in front of a corrupt parole board, a battered wife, a farm worker asking for restitution for chemically induced cancer, or an Argentine student about to be disappeared. Of course I wasn't, but sitting under that single light bulb in the station's conference room, flanked by yes-men, I saw how it worked. I feel, paradoxically, both numb and enraged.

Thousands of supporters mobilized for months, desperately trying to save their beloved station. The court ordered, in a David v. Goliath style triumph, in favor of David. The Court came down on the side of all those that held democracy foremost in their hearts and minds. And the true meaning of the WBAI Mission Statement was ultimately upheld. The faction was legally required to end its rule, and *Al Lewis Live!* along with the other banned programs, returned to the airwaves. Jubilation! We had mourned the loss of our radio time, that meaningful interaction between us and the audience, but now we had it back and it was better than ever.

Eighty-five

A BITE FOR SORE EYES

"I can't see, Karen. Well ... I'm seeing triple." Al was scared stiff. He sat in his big reading chair with his hand over one eye. "I can see out of the other eye," he said, as the uncovered orb moved in a slow circle, taking in items in the room.

"Triple?" I queried softly, to hide my concern.

"Yeah, three. I can't tell which is the real one. Like on stairs. Which one I should step on!"

My heart sank. "We gotta get you to a doctor."

Al's doctor, who wanted to rule out possible causes for the problem, confessed, "I'm not sure what it is."

"I've got to find a solution," Al stammered. "I don't want to live if I can't read."

My terrified husband was sent to a top New York neurologist who quickly delivered a diagnosis. "It's myasthenia gravis of the eye, Mr. Lewis, a rare autoimmune disorder affecting your facial muscles." And the reason why Al's eyelid had drooped so dramatically during the infamous WBAI interrogation. The doctor prescribed a long list of medications, all of which had <u>bad</u> side effects, ranging from bad to worse. Diarrhea pretty much summed it up. Al was offered numerous complex treatment options that had no guaranteed results, and there were many neurological tests to be carried out by various specialists. Ultimately, he was fitted with a contact lens that successfully covered the affected eye, but usually got lost under his eyelid because he couldn't see to put it in correctly.

After several months of never knowing when the terrible symptoms would strike again, or how long the episodes of near blindness would last, we asked "Dr. I." in Buffalo Grove, Illinois, for help. He was an alternative medical practitioner and frequent guest on WBAI. There was a lengthy three-way conversation over our speaker phone during which Dr. I. questioned Al about recent medical exams and tests, and heard the lists of all of his prescriptions and complaints. He then offered the following.

"After all you've told me, Mr. Lewis, my guess is that your immune system is distressed from your exhausting political campaign, the loss of your ex-wife, and the political strife at WBAI. I know from my own association with WBAI that that experience had to be stressful. People don't want to believe that stress can do serious damage. But it can. Grief, especially. If you want, I can help you build up your immune system. Go on my detox diet for one month and see if you get any results. You'll know after three weeks. After four, you'll feel better - no matter what. If the diet doesn't cure your eye problem, you'll still feel better."

"I gotta try it," Al confirmed. "I'm desperate."

"Mr. Lewis ... Don't try this unless you're going to commit to it one hundred percent. It's just too hard." Al clamped down on his cigar like a steel trap.

"I can do it."

"Okay. Ready?"

"Yeah. Karen, write down everything the doctor says." Which I eagerly did.

"The diet is simple, but most people won't do it. No sugar ..."

"I don't eat any now. I'm a diabetic."

"Good. But none of those artificial sweeteners either, please. No caffeine. No alcohol."

"Fine with me."

"No processed foods."

"We hardly eat any now," I chimed in, "unless it's in the restaurant food we get."

"Great. Chemicals have to be eliminated. Simple ingredients are what you want. And organic, if at all possible."

"Oh, yeah. We order from a local supplier," Al offered. "Fruits and vegetables." He smiled, looking proud of himself.

"As much as you can. I know it's hard. No white flour."

"Yeah, we've pretty much cut out white flour already."

"Fine. Ahh Mr. Lewis, I can hear you sucking on that cigar ... No tobacco." Al pulled his lips down and backward in a rubbery grimace, revealing gritted teeth, as if to say, 'Oh shit.' Glancing up from my pad, I shook my head, a tacit It'll-never-happen.

"Alright. No tobacco!" Al affirmed. Wagging my finger, I mouthed the words, You're lying to the doctor! "I mean it, Doc. No tobacco," Al promised. Then he gave me, in the seclusion of our living room, "The Wrist." Which this time meant, 'You don't think I can do it? Get outta here!' Ralph Kramden just sent me to the moon.

"That's it," Dr. I. continued. "Simple. Yet impossible for most people. However, my wife and I stay on this diet all the time and we eat very well."

"Then I can, too."

The doctor laughed warmly at Al's resolve, then added, "I'm a pretty good cook. I'll send you some recipes."

"Thanks, Doc!"

I knew that Al had made up his mind and would keep his word. Relieved at having a direction that restored hope, we started the new routine that same evening by happily munching on a huge organic salad, grateful that we'd already been buying and eating foods for our new regimen. While we ate we made up a shopping list of all the necessary supplements to take including Oil of Oregano. "Were you telling the doctor the truth about quitting smoking?"

"I gotta do it."

"Then hand over those cigars."

"Look, I got three in my pocket. After that, it's cold turkey."

"Cold turkey? Good thing that's on our menu!"

"Har de har har."

Dr. I.'s theory was that Al's cholesterol medication might be leaching fat off the myelin sheath of the eye nerves. So if he could lower his cholesterol naturally by eating properly, he might be able to slowly, safely, wean himself off the medication and restore the nerves. His cholesterol would be routinely checked by a local doctor. In the meantime, he would simultaneously be building up his immune system. Needless to say, we took this all very seriously.

It was important for Al to have plenty of filtered water and animal protein, including game (cold turkey) and organic liver of the purest quality. Finding pure foods in New York City was not an easy job. I was charged with the daunting task of preparing these new meals, and coordinating supplements and medication. But I was also benefitting tremendously from learning more about nutrition. Did I forget to mention glorying in my husband's smiles?

"Albie, honey, why don't people know about this diet?"

"Corporations don't want 'em to. Think about all that junk food in the front aisles of the supermarket that nobody'd buy!"

While we were already benefitting from taking proactive measures provided by this so-called "kook," Al's mainstream doctors, who hadn't yet come up with a workable treatment plan, cautioned us against being taken in by alternative medicine, which they seemed to think was witchcraft or voodoo. But not one of them had provided a positive alternative of their own for revitalizing Al's health. It was crucial for us to continue with this strict but beneficial diet, so fresh and delicious that we thought we were back in our childhood kitchens.

After two weeks of our healthy diet, Al's spirits were up. He was detoxing! By taking action against this debilitating problem, hope was alive and kicking. Within three weeks, Al was reading with more regularity. After only four weeks, he was essentially "cured."

Meanwhile, back at the neurologist's office, the doctor was amazed that Al was doing so well so quickly. His point of view was that there was no proof that the detox diet had or had not provided Al a cure. He was convinced that Al had simply gone into remission. True, this can happen with those dreadful neurological disorders, but it could be that Al's condition was really a false myasthenia gravis instigated by cholesterol medication. We might never know. But it didn't matter. Because, along the way, we'd been blessed with greatly improved health, a better diet to guide us, a lower food bill and, as a bonus, a lower doctor bill.

After two months and good test results, Al was able to reduce both his cholesterol and diabetes medications as his eye continued to improve.

By the way, Al did it. He went 75 days without a cigar! It's a good thing I didn't bet against him. On the 76th day he celebrated by smoking a well-deserved Cuban Partagas.

When Al's crisis was finally over, he continued to go in for regular check-ups. At one of these appointments, Al and I sat side by side in "Dr. R.'s" office. The doctor entered and asked, "Well, what can I do for you, Al?"

"I'm in love with my wife. How about giving me twenty years?" The doctor pulled out his prescription pad and obligingly scratched out an Rx: "20 years," then signed it with a flourish. With a smile that acknowledged the power of love, he warmly handed it over to Al. "I'm in love with my wife, too."

Eighty-six

GROWING TOGETHER

Our time together was rich and satisfying. We felt lucky and grateful for the life we had woven on the loom of our relationship. Every day felt like a blessing and it was the simple things that made us happy.

Music poured from our old-fashioned multi-format boom box. The justification for our buying so much music was that we were testing songs for our radio show. But we were really feeding our ears and souls on nurturing sounds.

Al filled our home with plants. He busied himself potting, watering and divining their ideal locations. It was half Feng Shui and half Botanical Social Work. Among his babies there was an abundance of cacti, several impressive spiky boarders with which we shared our space.

We had our own plot in the Roosevelt Island Garden Club where we grew vegetables and lots of spring flowers. We shared the work. I did the digging, planting, watering, weeding and harvesting. Al's half of the labor was to puff on a cigar and supervise me. I loved to watch my spouse lick his lips when he eyed the muddy harvest that the little garden patch yielded.

Probably stemming from our theatrical background, we both shared a love of clothing. Clothing as self-expression, as costume, as dramatic derring-do. Al shopped and I organized our closets for easy access to colorful shoes, hats, coats, and accessories. Al loved it when I picked out his outfits. "You're lookin' good, Al! We know who dressed you!" neighbors would tease. When he dressed himself, he also got a loud reaction -- folks doubled up with laughter. But he simply couldn't resist klown kouture. Or, does an orange vest go with purple plaid pants?

In short, we were in love. Everywhere we went, our hands, like eager tentacles, reached for each other. The Shaker song says:

> *When you find yourself in the place just right,*
> *You will be in the valley of love and delight.*

Our marriage loom shuttled from left to right, back and forth, with comforting regularity, weaving a bright and tightly woven tapestry of love, surprising us with its emerging, vividly colorful images.

Lewis Family Thanksgiving 2002 in L.A.
Rear (l to r) Dave, Andrea, Ted. Seated: Jennifer holding Raphael,
Paul, Bryce holding Keenan, Al holding Julia

Eighty-seven

RIVER OF SORROW

The alarm had gone off and I was quietly pulling on my clothes, getting ready for work. I didn't want to waken my snoozing husband who had stayed up late the night before, reading. The phone rang. Before 9 a.m.? What idiot would call me at this hour? It was irritating. I didn't want to be delayed. I needed to get to work. Grumble. Grumble.

"Hello," I snapped, in a whispered tone.

"Karen? This is your mother." Oh great, now what? She needs crossword help? "Have you got your television on?" she asked with some insistence.

"Mom. I'm getting ready for work. Is *The Munsters* in re-runs again?"

"Just turn it on!"

"Geez, Mom, I gotta get to work."

"A plane ... it ... well ..." My mother's thoughts seemed to converge into a confused log jam.

"What? What is it, Mom?"

"A plane crashed into the World Trade Center!"

"I'm turning it on, Mother. Hold on." I watched news anchors, like deer in the headlights, feebly trying to patch together a narrative.

"Dear God, Mom. Thank you for calling me. I have to contact my office. I'll call you back."

I woke up Al. He said, "Holy shit," and stumbled to the TV set. I made my calls to all the workers on our early shift at Eviction Intervention Services and told them to go home at once. I figured the roadways would soon be blocked to and from the City. I was responsible for my staff and I had to be there. I headed for the subway station and my mind raced as I tried to anticipate what to do next. Roosevelt Island is just across the river from the United Nations, which was already under high security alert. I got to the subway stop and it was closed and guarded by the police. I tried to take our famous tram across, but it was closed too. It seemed like nobody could get in or out of the City at any point. My brain clicked into hyper alert. The picture suddenly became clear. This was extremely serious! I ran back home not knowing what else to do. Al and I sat on the couch, tugging at each other's fingers. Eyes glued to the TV, we wondered if we were looking at a bad Hollywood sci-fi flick or a malicious prank like Orson Welles' *War of the Worlds* broadcast.

We turned on WBAI, hoping for their usual fast-breaking news coverage. What?? They were playing elevator music! Oh, right. WBAI, founded on maverick fearless investigative journalism and on-the-spot coverage of important stories, was now under control of the takeover hijackers who'd not only banned us, but apparently the news as well, in favor of playing 1001 Strings.

In surreal stark contrast the day shone, the sky a perfect September blue. The water in the East River sparkled, sunlight crisply refracted off the crests of tiny waves. But not a boat in sight, other than the Coast Guard patrolling up and down past our windows.

We watched the unthinkable story unfold for several hours, until we realized that no one was reporting anything new, just a loop of a loop of earlier speculation. We'd seen the second plane hit, heard the breaking stories of the attack on the Pentagon, and reports of the plane crash in Pennsylvania. And still no one could explain it. "What do you think the real story is, Al?" He sat pensively for a moment and then spoke, "It looks goddam fishy to me."

We went outside and walked around talking to people, hoping to learn more, but no one knew any more than we did. They were all completely panicked. So back to the TV set, hoping for any information. The day stretched out like gooey, tacky tar on a hot street that grabbed up speculation, rumors and fierce anxiety and pulled them all into its sticky core. How to understand? What was real? Where to find the truth? Already there were rivers of tears on Roosevelt Island as word on the street had it that numerous local firefighters and WTC workers had disappeared in the Trade Center vapor, leaving spouses and children, friends and neighbors bereft.

Concerned about work the following day, I hugged Al for a long time and went to bed, leaving him in his armchair, a cigar between his fingers, leaning into his thoughts.

Two days later, an acrid stench announced the arrival of a massive wall of white toxic smoke from the burning Trade Center rubble. As it roiled up the East River, we locked our windows, but the putrid chemical smell leaked in through the air conditioner louvers until I covered them in plastic and taped them shut.

In

      the moment

Chumbe!

Mental defense systems on high alert

      Karate inhale

      Eyes scan

      Exhale

      Chi flows

      Target in sights

      Strike-ready!

We hold hands

Four days after the attack, producer Errol Maitland, our ally at former WBAI, called Al and asked for a live phone interview to give his take on the events of September 11th. For 30 minutes Al stood by the window overlooking the East River, phone in hand, pulling up facts, speaking directly and knowledgeably without a single note. That program was aired over the on-line radio station WBIX, the alternative to WBAI.

Al began with a heartfelt acknowledgement of the horrific events and compassionately noted the efforts of the First Responders who continued dauntlessly to uncover survivors in the rubble. He then went on to question the identities of the nineteen alleged perpetrators who were "officially" blamed for the attacks. Al decried the mainstream news media for encouraging revenge. "At the moment what we have is banging the war drums ... Will that solve the problem? Let us say that this alleged person, Osama bin Laden, is the Svengali, the Mastermind, and they capture him or they nuke him or they obliterate him. Will that solve the problem? No. The problem still remains. There will be another Osama bin Laden. Whatever name."

Al was also concerned about the racism implied in identifying the perpetrators as Muslim. "Have you or any of them ever read the Koran? I have. The number one sin in the Koran is to commit suicide. Read the Koran. Read it! Don't just repeat like lemmings. Read it ..." He also urged people to dig into history to discover patterns and historical facts. "You cannot disregard historical events. History doesn't move by the fact that you like it or dislike it." Then he punched us with this pithy quote: "Just this past year, George Bush the Elder said at a meeting – this is a direct quote, 'You can fool some of the people some of the time. That's what we have to concentrate on.' Don't be one of those people. Don't accept. Don't accept what I said. Question."

We were scared alright, but not in the same way that those around us were who were asking 'Why do the terrorists hate us?' Al, as usual, encouraged everyone to keep questioning and not to accept the official story, or the official conspiracy theory either. Our ideas were different from mainstream thinking. It was all that reading and probing we'd already done. What guided us and gave us balance was our passionate quest to learn the truth about what was really happening behind the media veil.

"What are we going to do now, Al?"

"Let's do what the President said, 'Go shopping!'" he sarcastically jabbed.

Eighty-eight

KING OF HEARTS

Six months after 9/11, there were still no official answers about why it happened, but we knew the world would never be the same.

Yet some things never changed, like Al's legion of adoring fans.

The phone rang. It was Mancow Muller calling from Chicago. "I'm getting married, Grandpa!"

"Congratulations! To you, Mancow, not to the poor girl!" Al wisecracked. Mancow was the Midwest's version of Howard Stern and Al had been a frequent guest on his drive-time radio show, *Mancow's Morning Madhouse*. Now he was inviting us to his Valentine's Day wedding.

"Look, we'll fly you in to do the show the week before, and then you and Karen'll be here for the wedding!"

"I ain't givin' nobody away!" Al teased.

"Her father'll do that," Mancow retorted.

"You mean he agreed?!"

Al signs Mancow's Munster memorabilia

"Yeah, Grandpa, this is a big church wedding, and I want you and Karen to be there," the radio host proudly stated.

He seemed to be over-emphasizing the legitimacy of his upcoming marriage which must have been tough, given his reputation for illegitimacy. We had flown out to Chicago about a dozen times before to be on the show, enjoyed ourselves and the city each time. Besides, Mancow put us up in really nice hotels.

A week before the wedding we flew into frigid Chicago. At the radio station Mancow greeted us. "Great to see you again, Grandpa and Karen!" Mancow hugged us and jumped up and down with excitement. "Grandpa, come into the studio! Do I have a surprise for you!" It was a coup! Mancow had secretly lined up Jonathan Harris from *Lost in Space*, via telephone, for a surprise on-air interview with Al. Those two seasoned performers drove sweetly through the back alleys of their shared past, including the times when Al played "Wizard" on several episodes of *Lost*. When the segment concluded, the phone lines were burning up like the Chicago fire.

"Wasn't that great, Grandpa? Huh? Huh?" begged Mancow, needing an attaboy for that morning's brilliant airtime and his casting ingenuity.

Al couldn't resist. "Geez, Matthew," he ribbed, using Mancow's real name. "You're just like a little kid! Yes! It was wonderful to talk with Jonathan again. Okay? You actually do know your stuff!" Mancow settled down for a minute to suck up the acknowledgement. "Thanks, Mancow. It was wonderful talking to my old friend again."

"Yeh, well, you two were great," Mancow excitedly blurted.

During the *Madhouse in the Morning* week, snows fell and it was still bitterly cold, as only Chicago can be in February. Al didn't feel well, and after each early morning show we would head back to the hotel to hole up and rest.

On the day of the wedding, we took a cab out to the church and sat with hundreds of guests witnessing Mancow's gorgeous, but unexpantly traditional wedding. Afterward we headed to a huge hotel banquet room for the reception where the newlywed bride and groom greeted us with warm delight, clearly thrilled that we had been part of their celebration. After about an hour, Al whispered to me that he was too tired to stay the course and had to lie down. Without a word to our hosts, I gathered our coats and we slipped off into the blustery, freezing Chicago night.

Eighty-nine

MILES AND MILES OF HEART

When we returned home to Roosevelt Island, Al still didn't feel well. He looked gray and was sweating. He rubbed his chin to ease an unfamiliar pain. I called "Dr. F.," Al's primary care doctor of many years, and got his answering service. Too early. I wiped Al's feverish face and saw him wobble when he stood. I didn't like this at all. I tried Dr. R., our local doctor, and when he listened to my description of what was happening, he whispered, "I hope Al isn't having a heart attack. Call his primary again and let me know what happens."

Within an hour, Al was on Dr. F.'s examination table, covered with electrodes. He was hoping to prove to Al that he was *not* having a heart attack. Al, who was going on 80, wasn't an easy patient. The usually confident and overbearing Al became like a frightened child offering his own naïve guesses as to what ailed him. His doctor worked to direct Al away from those dark scenarios, but then had to give him some bad news. "Al, this is unbelievable. You've had a heart attack. But a rare, right-sided one. They don't present in the normal way. I'm calling the hospital. Meet you there." Emergency! Off to Dr. F.'s Dream Team in Cardiac Care.

Al was into Cardiac Non-Invasive by noon. I anxiously waited in the visitors' room, eager to see my husband. At 3 p.m. he was rolled out after two angioplasties. "Well, get my clothes, Karen. We're going home!"

"I think the doctors want you to stay here for a while, Albie." I was handed a card that stated Al had stents in his arteries, and should carry this card everywhere. "Why?" I asked Dr. F. "Because he could set off metal detectors at the airport." Oh, great. Modern medicine. It's like a bad sci-fi movie.

After six days, with his doctor's blessing, Al was given permission to return to work at WBAI. Things had gone well, but the doctor said a third artery would need attention in a couple of months.

Two weeks later, Al returned to his radio program completely up to speed. He plowed into the hour with added vigor. He started out with his tease during the opening theme song by King Curtis: "Come on, King! Come on! I'm back. Yeah, come on, King. Ohhh. I'm back. Hot diggety dog!" The music faded and Al continued.

"First off, I want to say hello to all the men and women behind the walls of the gulag. My wife and I haven't forgotten ya. We're doing the best we can. I'll be speaking at the demonstration in front of the Governor's Office to demand that they get rid of the Rockefeller Drug Laws, the mandatory minimums. I especially want to thank all of the hundreds and hundreds of people who sent me get-well wishes both at the hospital and to me at home. I'm fine. I kicked the rear end out of the grim reaper. I sent him to an early shower. He wasn't too happy about that! I want to thank my doctor for saving my life."

I always carried a little notebook with me everywhere. In it I'd kept a record of all the hospital staff who'd assisted in his recovery. I handed it to Al and he read out their names: all the doctors, nurses, orderlies and volunteers. That was his special way. To remember the workers and the people who helped him.

Al's three sons and and guardian angels, Paul, Dave and Ted

Ninety

ONE DOWN

SAVE, TOSS, GIVE AWAY

A dog-eared crossword puzzle magazine, almost completely filled in, purchased at the hospital gift shop. Toss.

"Karen, I'm going to be alright?"
"Yes, my sweet."

266

"Good. Because I believe you. Now I can go to sleep." Well, I couldn't, because my heart was pounding. No jokes? He's worried. He's not taking this in stride.

The next night. "Are you sure I'm going to be okay?"

"Yes, my love. You had two arteries cleared. And imagine how much better it will feel to have the third one done."

June 30th 2003. As we crossed the threshold at an early hour, I saw it scribbled on our appointment calendar. "Op for 3rd Art."

We hovered in a tiny hospital room waiting to check in. Lockers, four beds, a small table. A tiny window with an old-fashioned air conditioner stuck into it. The hospital hadn't rehabbed this wing yet. This didn't do much for my confidence. Al sat at the end of a narrow bed looking out the window beyond the city. But my awareness was yanked sharply, as if someone had grabbed me by the collar and given it a tug. Was Al daydreaming? He was the realist. I was always the dreamer. I'd never seen Al daydream before. I thought: He's with his mother. And it scared me. "You okay, Al?" Before he could answer, an intern walked in. Young, lovely, white coat. She greeted us, clipboard and papers in hand. Warm professional smile. She'll be a good doctor, my heart said. Al was still withdrawn. How strange ... no funny lines or teasing for this beautiful young doctor.

"Name?" Al dutifully whispered the answer. "Date of birth?" And so on down the list she went, winding up with a disturbing disclaimer. "Are you aware, Mr. Lewis, that there is a .001% risk involved with this procedure?" Al shot me a this-sounds-fishy look.

"Is this a waiver, a release of responsibility?" I asked. She nodded.

"Nothing to be concerned about. Only one in 1000 patients has a problem. Sign here." Al reluctantly picked up the pen and signed off, shaking his head. With that, the young doctor vanished with his autograph. I didn't know what to say to comfort him. Unfortunately, all I could think of were the many negative stories about hospitals that we covered on our radio show. So I bit my lip.

Al changed into his hospital gown. An orderly arrived with a huge plastic bag. "For your clothes, sir." We dumped everything into it except Al's wallet, which landed in my purse. One more piece of his identity taken away. Just another man in a cotton cover-up, strings flapping up the back. He seemed so vulnerable. But Al was not just another old man, and there was no way they were going to strip him of his dignity.

We were escorted to the waiting area outside the operating theater and silently held hands. The noon sun lit up our gurney and chair. A smiling orderly broke into our peace, "Mr. Lewis. Grandpa!" His stride lengthened. He really was beside himself with delight. "Ready to go?"

"Just a moment," I said, addressing both men as I edged between them to sit next to my husband. We grabbed each other's hands. I scanned Al's face and eased toward him as he lifted his head to meet my lips. A tender kiss. Eyes locked. "I love you," we uttered at the same time. I walked with him, but got stopped. "You gotta wait here, Ma'am." The two men were sucked into the doorless corridor behind the nurses' station.

"I'll be right here, waiting for you, Albie!" I watched the orderly leaning into the gurney, pushing. Then his shoulders bounced up and down like pistons. He was laughing. Hurray, Al was at it again!

Three hours, they told me. I could handle that. I managed last time under far worse conditions. Today it was an ordinary angioplasty. We can do this. Noon. I had time for a quick bite and still get back here for Albie's homecoming!

Ate, stretched, checked messages at home. Al's sons called to wish him well. He'll be happy when I tell him that. Called my office. Got back to the nurses' station. The seats were a little hard. Two back-to-back waiting rooms. Cardiac Invasive/Cardiac Non-Invasive. I was a "Non" so I sat there. Reminded me of a cheap motel lobby. Same upholstery. Same old magazines. I finished my article about volcanoes in an antique National Geographic.

"Any word?" I asked the desk nurse.

"Not yet." By then it had been three hours plus. Guess they're running late. Decided to take a walk. Somewhere in that labyrinth behind one of these walls doctors were clearing out Al's clogged artery. That made me smile. I couldn't wait to see my hubby feeling better.

I popped a Lifesaver. I chatted with other anxious waitees. We formed The Waiting Room Club. We cheered when one of us got to rush toward a gurney coming out of the OR. "Who does he belong to? You! Oh! Congratulations!" It was a game that helped the time pass.

I checked my watch and sprinted over to the nurses' desk again. He was not ready. "Why?" I questioned. "Be patient." I'd been patient. Okay, I'll be calm and keep trying to stay patient. Wouldn't want them to rush the job.

A walking meditation. Relaxation techniques. Mindful breathing. Still, I couldn't keep my eyes off my watch. It seemed to be insistent about that three-hour promise. I looked across the room at the nurse. She saw me but she shook her head, saving me a trip.

Suddenly, the lovely intern was standing in front of me. She clutched my hand then quickly let it go. An uncomfortable attempt at empathy. "Not professional" flashed across her face. "Mrs. Lewis, your husband ... delay ... difficulty ... plaque ..." Her brow furrowed underneath beads of sweat. I tried to decode her message and realized that she was simply young and inexperienced, but I needed clarity.

"Yes ..." I urged, wanting more. "Yes, go on."

"Need more time. Doctors are working ..." She turned on her heel and walked off. But I was pretty sure she was <u>fleeing</u>. Yes, my gut agreed: The lovely young intern just <u>fled</u>.

It was code. She hadn't told me anything directly. But I didn't have the code book. It would be like my crossword puzzle book – but with no solutions. What were they really saying? Nobody was telling me anything. Of all people, I had the right to know. Didn't I? But I'm stuck here, clueless, sitting on my badly upholstered waiting-room chair. A little alternate nostril breathing. If I relaxed, I might get the insight I craved. I took out my pen and idly doodled the words *Artery Plaque Delay* in the margin of my crossword book. Trying to make sense of that cryptogram.

Two gay guys were still in a holding pattern, waiting for the tall one's mother. They have been so kind to each other and me. "Nothing yet?" they asked. I shook my head. They put their arms around me making me the icing in their sandwich cookie. Two men I did not know, and their love was like manna from heaven, an elixir. The kindness of strangers.

I looked at my watch. 5 p.m. There he was! Dr. F! I rushed toward him. But he was not looking for me. He was going somewhere else. His face distorted by heart-sinking panic. "Dr. F! What's happened? Where's Al?" His eyes widened, "He's in there bleeding to death. They're doing everything they can ..."

"What? What did you just say? BLEEDING TO DEATH whatwhatwhat are you talking about? Why? This is a hospital! You're a doctor. Just make it stop!" My legs turned into rubbery licorice sticks and the floor was coming up to say Hi. "Elevator going down." My palms flew out. Dr. F. clutched my arms and held tight. My legs were back but they'd become two columns of shifting sand.

"They're in there trying to save him!" he blurted. I stumbled toward the nurses' station.

269

"Save him?? Save him?? You've got the wrong patient. Let me in there! Albie!" I rushed towards the OR, but the nurse's arm clanged down like a signal gate at a railroad crossing, blocking my way. I ricocheted off her arm and back into Dr. F's grasp. He silently and quickly escorted me back to the hallway in front of the waiting room.

My gut was buckled and knotted up. When did I get punched? I leaned against the wall. "More time ..." "Be patient ..." "Trying to save him ..." "Bleeding to death ..." I called out, "Dr. F!" He was gone. I slid down the wall. Licorice legs again. Why couldn't I breathe?

"Hello, darlin'. Let's get you off the floor." Cheery voice. Positive face. Older nurse. She likes me. "Why are you so cheery? Can you get me in to see my husband? They say he's bleeding." I used her arm to haul myself up from the linoleum.

"You look like you could use reinforcements! Better get some food while you've got the chance. Cafeteria closes soon."

"I'm not leaving here until I hear about my husband."

"Gotta eat."

"I'm not going until I hear about my husband."

She stared at me, a no-nonsense TSA Officer.

I fake relented. "Okay, I'll go. I'll go."

The nurse smiled and gave me the victory sign and left. But I didn't go. Once everything stopped spinning I could get off this rickety, gyrating, nauseating ride and go find Al.

Soon the nurse angel flew back with some crackers and a juice box. "I figured you'd still be here, Hon."

I woke up in my chair. My head was still spinning. Cracker crumbs on my blouse. I must have passed out. It was 7:35. But what day was this? Or night? And Al was still not out yet. They would've told me. Oh, God, what's happened?

The gay guys came to me again and hugged me just as the mother emerged. I felt happy for them and envious. I leaned over their loved one's gurney. "Did you see my husband in there?"

"She's still asleep. Here, take this," one said tenderly, pressing a religious medal into my palm.

"Thank you. Thank you for your kindness." I watched them disappear around a corner, leaving me alone in this purgatory.

I tried everything I knew to stay conscious and alert. I paced, walking a circle up the hallway and back mentally uttering my favorite walking meditation. Left foot Right foot Allah Allah. Left foot Right foot Allah Allah. I pressed through one foot and then the other. Left foot Right foot.

I got to the corner and there she was again, the Tough Love Angel Nurse, who had wanted me to eat. Was she glowing? Smiling? She raised a huge, dingy white wing that flew around my shoulder. "Honey? You got anyone you can call? A girlfriend? Someone who'll come over here and wait with you? Can I help you make a call?"

"I'm fine. I'm perfectly capable of making a call." I took off in the wrong direction. She caught me and spun me around heading me toward the pay phone. She was serious. "I'll do it if you can get me in to see my husband."

"Do it!"

I knew the number by heart. I heard Heather's voice on the answering machine, and then loud coughs. "Karen, I've got the flu, but don't worry, I'm a doctor and I'm used to phone calls night or day. Anytime." I finally felt grounded. "I can't come, but I'm here for you." We talked for a while.

"Mrs. Lewis. Mrs. Lewis." My heart jumped into my throat. My Al! Finally! I raced to the nurses' desk.

"Pick up your husband's clothes."

"Why?" I thought the worst. "What's happened to him?" I felt I was about to go under again. Water would flood my nose and choke me. I was going down. I had to convince myself that I couldn't drown if there was no water. "What's happened to him? What are you telling me?"

"To pick up your husband's clothes. That's all. That bag there. He's been moved to Cardiac Invasive. They don't belong here any more. Come on, Ma'am, my shift's over."

I felt the medal I'd stuck in my jacket pocket earlier and looked at it. St. Anthony, saint of miracles. I rubbed it between my thumb and forefinger, saying a silent prayer. I grabbed the huge plastic bag marked LEWIS, AL and stumbled into the hall with it, holding the top close to my mouth. Maybe I could muffle the panic sobs, the blurting breaths, the sounds of air sucked into a pillow because no person was there to calm the soldier's widow. *There's been a bloody battle and the B Movie chaplain says, "A keepsake, Mrs. Lewis. Your husband's personal effects."*

I dragged the pitiful bundle to the Cardiac Invasive waiting room which was now empty. He was alive, I kept telling myself. I sat down on the loveseat next to the bag. Don't cry. These clothes belong to a living human being. But I'd been blind-sided. Didn't see it coming. Didn't get it. Too late. I stuffed my face into the creases of the bag and sobbed out the shock. "Let it all out, girl," Al's voice whispered in my head. Thanks, Albie. I'm here waiting for you.

Voices in the hall. Nurses joking. Shift change. They're all going home, but not us.

I remembered something from Al's last hospital stay. I got up and pressed the ICU Intercom buzzer. "Mrs. Lewis here. Is Mr. Lewis ...?" Not yet. Not yet. No need to call Heather again. Oh, shit, I hadn't called Al's kids back.

I dialed up one after the next. They agreed that I should call Ted with updates and he would relay messages to his brothers. Their voices calmed me. *Ted and Paul's graduation ceremony, in my pink linen suit, waiting outside the UNM stadium, after. I see them emerge in their gowns. A huge smile on my face. Paul grabs me, flips me sideways, and tosses me to Ted, then back again! Al shakes his head, but he sees how happy his sons are. I'm in good hands. They won't drop me. We laugh our heads off.* They're so smart, so strong and loyal. They will hold me to my course.

I lean against the bag of clothes and tune in and out of these dreams. Happy times with Al flash before my eyes. *We glide through West Virginia in our car, windows down, singing to the mountains, "Take me home".* Take me home.

I opened my eyes. My memories vaporized. It was 11:45 p.m. In the doorway stood Dr. F. Expensive jacket. Impeccable shirt and tie. Brooks Brother's loafers so cool now with those summer slacks. "Karen. They said I'd find you here."

"Where else? Al's still here." Maybe sarcasm isn't good here, Karen. I need to hear the truth and I need to hear it clearly. I'll politely ask him exactly what's going on. I straightened my jacket. Realigned my blouse. He sat down on the far end of my sofa. I sat erect and moved to the edge, showing keen interest. I said as calmly as I could, "Good evening, Dr. F."

The carpet was green with repeating diamond patterns on the diagonal. The doctor crossed his legs at the knee and exposed his very expensive socks. They looked fabulous with his shoes and slacks, but I didn't like his look. It was cold and alienating. I would have preferred talking with a scruffier working doctor in rumpled scrubs who would tell me plainly and honestly the whole truth about Al's condition. He hadn't said anything yet, and suddenly, "How are you, Karen?" Was this a joke? How am I? My mind didn't know what to do with this. Al trusted this doctor. I wanted to listen but he hadn't said anything. Why was he here? Sitting with me? A waft of fine red wine. Oh, I get it. His wife had made him come. Was she the compassionate one in the family? I needed to break the tension. How could I loosen this man up to get the truth out of him? Ah, I remembered, his family went on vacation. "How was your vacation?" Did I just say that?

"It was great!" he said, clearly relieved, and happily continued telling me all about it ... Damn, I'd just given him permission to chicken out. I'd clearly lost my compass. Why hadn't I asked him about Al right away and made him explain everything to me? Why was I being so damn polite? Al might be dying. I followed the angles of the diamonds on the carpet. "Blah blah, sandy beach, nice tans, blah blah, a few days, blah blah, what we needed. Blah blah, my wife told me! Blah blah blah. The sound faded and I knew Dr. F. had finished his travelogue.

Silence again.

"And Al?" I finally ventured.

"It turned into bypass surgery. We'll have to wait and see." Glancing at his Rolex, he quickly rose. "Wait! I want to see him! I've been waiting for hours!" But he was gone.

Wait and see? Wait and see! I started walking again with purpose. Wait and see. Wait and see. I knew exactly where I was headed.

Chapel. I charged through the stained glass doors. I wanted help. I needed to talk. I smelled candles burning.

I paced up. Paced back the chapel aisle. Turned a corner. There it was. My niche. No religious icons. Just flowers and low light. My chair.

If I could talk to anyone right now, then who? The names tumbled out of my mouth like jewels with magical healing powers. I bobbed at the waist, half in ache, half in prayer. I stood up. Called roll, my arms outstretched to bring in their energy. "Roikja, Al's mom. You're here. Al's brother, Philip. Here too. My dad. Here. My Grandma Mayme. Here. I want a pow wow. I'm calling you all. Begging. I'm in trouble." I heard the drums and the wailing, chanting voices. Now our families' souls were dancing into the circle. Dancing into my supplication. "My Albie is on the edge of the cliff. Will he jump? Must he? Am I wrong to hold him back? Tell me?" Hold him Hold him Hold him, my heart beat. "Roikja, Roikja! Your son loves you. Is he coming to you? Dad? My dad danced away. "Don't quit, Kid. Get the facts!" Grandma smiled. "It's all about Love, the greatest force in the world." "Stay calm, stay calm, stay calm," they all sang. "Breathe, breathe, breathe," they all chanted. "He stays with you!" Al's mother barked. "He stays with you!"

Was I making this up? Hearing what I wanted to hear because I needed to hear it? Was it a dream? Sleep deprivation? Wishful thinking? I didn't know, but I did know I felt the confidence I needed to go on.

I drove my heels into the hospital's floors – wood, marble, rubber mat, linoleum, institutional carpeting until I landed in the waiting room with the diamond patterned rug. How quiet, this holding area abutting the ICU. It was cold. Had they turned up the air conditioning?

I pressed the intercom buzzer for the second time tonight. But this time the door opened and the head nurse placed her arm around me. That gave me a chill. Before I could panic, I heard, "They're still working ..." She waved to another nurse, ordered me a blanket, and ushered me out like a whimpering pup. Outside! Sit. Here's your blanket. Good girl.

Still locked out, but I'm not going anywhere. Why don't I rearrange the furniture? I fashioned a bed out of a chair and a loveseat, turned out the light, and crawled under the blanket. My consciousness – an eternal conduit to Al, a river, a jet stream of encouragement. Energy. Life force. Your mother says you belong here ... with me, Albie. Listen to your mother.

Quiet. Quiet. Quiet. Then footfalls. Someone moving fast. Suddenly in the backlit hallway, a large figure in a white coat emerged in the doorway, radiating... What? Good news?

"Mrs. Lewis?"

I scrambled to rise, but the blanket had swallowed my legs. "Me. That's me. Yes?"

"Don't get up," he said. His tone was oddly settling. After 21 hours of hanging by a thread, I was suddenly comforted by his presence. He sat down near me. "I'm Dr. A. They called me in when your husband went into Cardiac Invasive. We had to do an emergency bypass."

"But he's been in there for... so long." This doctor looked at my eager yet worried expression, taking me in.

"A very strong man, your husband! He was bleeding and we had trouble finding the source so we could stop it. That's what took so long." He was smiling because he'd managed all this. He had done a good job. He had saved Al.

"The good news is your husband's alive. The bad news is he's not quite out of the woods."

"Should I call his kids? Right now?"

"No, not yet. No need to alarm them. This isn't a vigil."

He stood, gestured toward the ICU, and asked, "Would you like to see your husband?" In exhausted sarcasm, I quipped, "No, Dr. A. I just did a 20-hour vigil in this waiting room because I'm really into crossword puzzles!" In an instant, I was on my feet, racing to the door.

Dr. A. swung open the ICU door and stepped back as Al's gurney passed in front of us. My husband looked beautiful. The doctor said he was strong. As Al glided into his ICU space, the doctor continued his rundown. "More surgery later... Couldn't close the chest until we're certain all the bleeding's stopped ... A meeting in the morning with the whole medical team." But I was taking in the miracle of my husband's survival, the message from his mother in the chapel, the radiance of this doctor. "Why don't you go home, Mrs. Lewis. We'll meet tomorrow to go over all of this." But I had one more thing to do before I left. I leaned into Al's good ear and whispered, "I'm here, Sweetheart. Thank you for staying with me. You made me and your mother very happy." I kissed his cheek. "Goodnight. I love you."

5:30 a.m. I hailed a cab. I was on my way home. As I fell into bed, images lingered on my retina. I saw the high tech bed, the bandage on Al's chest, the beauty of his face, and tried to relate all that to those loving spirits who came into the circle tonight to help Al. Send them our gratitude. Thank you Roikja, thank you Dad, facts, yeh, thank you Phil, thank you Grandma ...

But I'm back at the hospital at 11:30. July 1st.

It took a while for all of the medical team to arrive, but eventually I was ushered into Al's ICU room. Five of them stood at attention, hands behind their backs, eyes lowered, as the lead doctor introduced each one and his specialty. A bank of high-ranking medical experts around Al. And me alone on the other side of the room. It was lopsided. The weight of the moment made the room appear to tilt away from me. Would I now find out what really happened to my husband last night? Only my desperate need to hear about Al's condition kept me from bolting. But Al was breathing. I could see his chest rise and fall. So why were they acting like he wasn't?

"Good morning," I stated, "I'm Mrs. Lewis and I'm eager to hear about my husband's condition." Each expert made a comment, and his words fell and ricocheted off the spotless linoleum: "We don't know what will happen." "We have to wait and see." "Too soon to tell." Each delivered his euphemism, as if he were a Fox News talking head.

One monotone M.D. said the angioplasty had "gone wrong," and that "some of the plaque that should have been cleared got pushed through the arterial wall, creating several holes through which blood had poured into your husband's chest cavity." He continued this gruesome account without expression. Was he trying to appear to be *scientifically objective*? "The rest of the plaque showered through his veins to create a dam at his knees, blocking the flow of blood to his lower extremities. Mr. Lewis is – let's put it this way – in a kind of coma."

Shocked, I blurted, "What do you mean a *kind* of coma? Please speak English!" My question was ignored and the next doctor in line continued the briefing. "You see, Mr. Lewis is on blood thinners which we hope will break up the blockages in his legs." They pulled the sheet away just enough to reveal sickening red blots down Al's normally flawless white skin. Oh my God.

They asked me if I had any questions. Oh, yeah, I had questions alright. "What's this about blood thinners? What does *pooling blood* mean? What kind of danger is he really in? Are those blockages at his knees life threatening? What are you planning to do about all that? And, when will my husband come out of this so I can talk with him?" And the answer was ... "Let's wait and see." I was handed lots of business cards, which I suppose was meant to be a comforting gesture, but they weren't even answering my questions now face to face. So it meant nothing. The doctors suddenly scattered like roaches do when you snap on the lights. I wrote what little they told me in my notebook, a daily log I kept, documenting all their words to have on record, even though none of their words seemed to make sense to me. Not one of the doctors was really saying anything.

I leaned in close to Al, the person I always discussed things with. "I'm here, darling. I'm by your side. Did you hear all that 'Maybe, Maybe not,' crap, Al? I know who'd get an earful if you were awake right now. Your mother says you're staying with me. Isn't that good news? I'm with you one hundred percent, Love. They may kick me out, but I'll never leave you." My weight shifted from left foot to right and back again. I believed he had the right to die, but I didn't want to lose him. "Albie, what do we do now?" After a long quiet moment, hoping in vain for an answer, I carefully wove my way through the tubes and kissed him. "Bye for now, Sweetheart. I'll be back."

When I returned later, "Dr. C." was waiting for me. "May I have your permission to perform a colonoscopy?"

"A what?" I screamed. "Why?"

"Your husband is bleeding from somewhere," Dr. C. casually stated, "and perhaps I can order a blood slide which might reveal the site."

"Bleeding?!" I gasped. "What's the potential risk?"

"There's more risk if we don't do it."

"If it's absolutely necessary, then yes."

"It is."

"I agree."

I pulled out my diary. "Al has had eight units of blood because so much is pouring out of him. I prayed for the doctor to be imbued with brilliance." I really wanted to *explain* to Al what had just transpired, but a nurse came in and I was asked to leave the ICU. "Sorry, but we have work to do. Come back later." The doors slammed behind me like prison gates, claiming my husband.

I sat there in the waiting room in a helpless daze. I watched the ICU visitors routinely ignoring the large NO CELL PHONE sign which had small print declaring that the phone signals might interfere with sensitive cardiac equipment. All that seemed to mean nothing to these phone users. I found myself in the unseemly role of Wicked Witch of the Waiting Room and quietly asked everyone to read the sign. One irate man yelled at me, "What, I shouldn't call my daughter!?" He gave me a deadly, savage look. I screamed in frustration, "Your loved one's equipment could go down because of that call! It could be life and death." But that meant nothing to him or any of the other self-absorbed phone users in that room. Infuriated, I marched to the first floor Administration Office to complain.

"Well, cell phones have changed since we put up that sign," said the administrator. "They're mostly not so dangerous now."

"Then take down the sign!"

"Oh, we can't do that," she said patronizingly, her chin lowered touching her corporate suit collar.

"Oh, I'm sorry, of course not. You're only job here is to keep people alive. And what's your plan if cell phones harm a patient? Deny it," I spat. In angry defeat I noisily let myself out of her office.

Back in the ICU waiting room, a few minutes later Al's cardiac surgeon appeared, and in a loud voice, asked everyone there to refrain from using their cell phones, and to use the payphones right around the corner. This was clearly an attempt to appease me. Maybe I had at least done something to raise awareness in the waiting room. For the moment, anyway.

When I returned home and opened our front door, I stood there surveying the wreckage: dirty dishes, takeout food boxes and an unmade bed. It hit me that I was really strung out, stretched way too thin. It won't help Al any if I end up in the hospital too. I drew on my knowledge of ways to protect myself through grounding, breathing, and relaxation techniques to keep me strong for what might come next. I stretched out across the bed and ....

The next day, when I arrived at the ICU, a little more rested and grounded, I was met by an impeccably dressed doctor in a Madison Avenue suit. He was looking for Mrs. Lewis. When I identified myself, he introduced himself as the staff gastroenterologist and surgeon, "Dr. Y." He said, "I don't mean to alarm you, but if your husband's intestines have to be removed, I'm the doctor who will be operating. I thought it best to alert you."

"What? Why? Remove his intestines? What the hell are you talking about? Nobody said anything about that. What's going on in there?"

He continued matter-of-factly. "You see, your husband is bleeding rectally. If we can't pinpoint the site, then I'll have to operate." He added his business card to my collection, wished me well and left. I sank into the same couch I'd slept on two nights earlier, and covered my face with my hands. Breathing deeply, I wrote in my little book: "... the doctor said he wanted me to be prepared, not shocked. But he's the one that's shocking me. Stephen King couldn't have thought this plot up in a million years. Go in for a stent, go into a coma, and come out with a colostomy bag?"

Just after that I found Father Lucas, the Catholic Chaplain for Rikers' Island, standing in the hallway. He had heard the news about Al and rushed over to the hospital. I escorted him to Al's bedside. Our dear friend and priest looked shy in the face of Al's plight. But he took my husband's hand and close to his ear, told him to be strong. Feeling Father Lucas's power, I considered what he did best and asked him to pray. So he started out with The Lord's Prayer and then continued into an improvised spontaneous prayer expressing Al's purpose on earth. "Dear Father, we humbly ask Your blessing for our brother Al. Such a good man, caring, caring, caring for Your children. Helping those in need. Surely there are more good works for him to do here on earth ...? Thy will be done. Amen." Tears came to my eyes as this Catholic priest blessed his ailing Jewish friend. How lucky I felt, to be in the presence of Father Lucas, a real person in an unreal scene. But he had other people in distress to visit and said goodbye. Just before his arrival I'd thought, I don't know if I can keep riding this wild bull of a nightmare. And now, the positive energy this man gave to us made me forget for a few moments my stark reality.

Alarming news. The blood flow to Al's feet was weak and the doctors feared the "feet would die" and they would be lost. Whoa. Hold on. From angioplasty to amputations? I was psychically scrambled: *this does not compute.*

278

From what I gathered, Al's feet had begun to poison him, and he was put on dialysis. It didn't seem possible, but I felt even more helpless and inadequate. "Desperation makes people do desperate things," Al used to say. I noted that I was now one of the desperate, but I determined that I must not do anything desperate. Must not.

But, what could I do anyway? I missed hugging my husband. I missed lying next to him in bed. Now he was physically off limits to me, held captive by machines, tape, tubes, sheets, and wagging fingers. I stood near him, staring at his face and hoped I could try to get through to him without touching him. I moved closer to his ear. The right one. The one that heard the best. It became my hijacked radio station and I was the DJ.

"Al, it's Karen, my love. Today is July 2nd at ... (and checking my watch), two-thirty p.m. And now for the weather update. Looking out the window, I see that it's sunny and warm here in New York. It's a beautiful day outside. From California and Texas come bushel baskets of love from your kids, Dave, Ted, and Paul. And also sending his love is Richie the overworked mailman whose sack contains hundreds of cards and letters from all your friends, neighbors and folks at WBAI." I reminded Al of his address and phone number, which were words he used to like to roll around on his tongue, and I assured him that he was always welcome at that address, and that his phone calls would be answered. His home was still there waiting for his return. I made all those promises, in a sea of not-knowin'-nuttin,' simply hoping on some level that he was "aware."

I was sure Al could hear me so I sang. I sang of love, going through my fractured repertoire, phrases missing, whole songs gone except for the choruses which I tra la la'd to until I wound around to the essential, soulful message: love exists. I love you. "*Love me tender, love me sweet, all my dreams fulfill ... I found my thrill on Blueberry Hill ... Caro mio bene ... Somewheeeeere over the rainbow, birds must fly. Birds fly over the rainbow, why then oh why can't I?*" I sang in singing-lesson Italian, a few bumpy Danish tunes, French ballads, pop and show tunes in English. When I ran out, I started all over. I was aware, even over the hum of the machines, that I might be disturbing someone else's loved one. But no one had complained, and frankly I couldn't help myself. I kept pulling tunes out of my chest to deposit into Al's ear. My medley continued with, "On the Street Where You Live," followed by the French National Anthem. I wished like crazy that I could manage the "Internationale," because I knew that Al would consider that a love song. I launched into "Stand by Your Man." Then I heard footsteps and felt certain the nurse was going to throw me out. Instead, Nurse S. joined in. We didn't know many of the lyrics, which made us laugh, but still cruised into the chorus, "*Staaaaand by your maaaaaaaan.*"

"He knows you're here," she hummed with conviction. That song had never meant so much.

On July 7th, Dr. A. scheduled the operation to close up Al's chest, and this time my doctor friend Heather, who'd held a lifeline for me by telephone since the night of the botched angioplasty, was by my side. I wrote:

> *About 4 p.m. they rolled Al out the door toward the OR. I tried to wave and call to him. They said it'd be about two hours. Along about 6 p.m. my heart agitated a bit. Here we go again. Heather told me to be patient. She cited delays, preps in the OR, and the doctor's desire to do it right. At 7 p.m. I took a walk to get myself aligned. Al already had those two disasters, so my thoughts turned anxious again.*

> *Waiting ...*

> *The scariest flight I've ever taken*
>   *with air pockets that send me up*
>   *and down*
>   *until I am hanging onto the seat in front of me*
>   *begging to land or die*
>   *whichever comes first*

> *Waiting: A boot camp for Zen Monks*

At 7:20 p.m. Dr. A. appeared with a smile on his face. "Mrs. Lewis, everything went well."

"See!" Heather nudged me with her shoulder, but she too had tears in her eyes.

Luckily for me, plans were in place for the arrival of support troops. Al's sons were on their way.

*Notebook entry: July 8ᵗʰ. It was a dream come true
to see Ted standing next to his dad, saying, "Pop,
I'm here." I cried in relief and awe.*

Later that day, just as we were being shuttled out of the ICU,
Paul arrived and we asked if he could say hello so Al might hear his
voice. Afterward, Paul looked shaken, and he and Ted went for a long
walk. Shortly after, their older brother called to say he'd safely
landed.

At home, in an effort to address Al's predicament and
consciously fight our fears, we brainstormed. We pooled every idea
and every creative measure we could think of to further Al's healing
process and wrote IT ALL down.

During our next ICU visit, we started to implement those
ideas. Dave taped a flashlight to the TV stand to radiate green,
curative light onto Al's chest, neck and face. I brought Bach remedies,
flower essences. Aroma therapy and essential oils were soon wafting
through the ICU. The doctors were okay with what we were doing,
while they also avidly followed and documented the restricted blood
flow to Al's extremities, establishing a timeframe for irreversible
damage to his feet. We asked permission from Dr. A. to have our
acupuncturist treat Al and he gave his approval. So Steve, our family
acupuncturist, joined our team in an effort to get Al's blood moving
south. We felt we were doing everything we could to save his feet. As
Steve applied his needles, our family formed a circle of love around Al
and experienced a gentle easing of the pressure we were under. We
felt if this didn't directly help his feet that the acupuncture would at
least build up his strength. I was certain Al could sense that we were
there, his love a magnet pulling us to him. We were taking action and
our ICU space hummed with hope.

Enter Dr. F., who marched in with a bedside manner from
hell, roughly prodded open Al's eyes, and grabbed Al's right foot for a
cursory observation. He glared at us as if he had walked in on a
witch's coven or a hippie love-in. Then without a word, he abruptly
left.

*Notebook entry. July 9th: Even though his dad is
comatose, Ted began verbally coaching him to*

mentally send blood to his feet. "Pop, the mind is a very powerful thing ..." The nurse said she'd seen feet in a lot worse shape, but also pointed out potential blisters on Al's heels that definitely had to be watched.

July 10th. According to the night nurse, Al had bitten down hard on the tube when she'd cleaned his mouth. As we approached the bed, Al began to cry and move his shoulders! My arms flew out like an octopus to grab the others. We just witnessed the motion we had longed for. It was an affirmation of our hope that he would return to us.

July 11th. Doctor E. sought me out to get permission for a tracheotomy. Oh, no, another dip on the roller coaster! Why on earth would Al need a trache? Are these doctors trying to drain Al's medical coverage with extraneous procedures? Ordering every possible treatment provided under his medical plan? Was that what this was all about? But Nurse S., the most open of Al's nurses, encouraged the procedure, saying it would "ease the patient and possibly protect his vocal cords." Of course, I thought, Al Lewis was a performer and needed his voice. I signed his request.

July 12th. Al's three sons and I arrived en masse at the ICU where we learned that the overriding concern was for Al's feet, and things did not look good. Much damage had been done to them from the heart balloon in the right groin and the plaque shower during the angioplasty. Dr. A. reported that amputations were looming large because Al's feet were not getting enough oxygen.

At home, Paul cried, then Ted, then I followed. Dave teared up and bellowed, "We don't accept that, and we don't quit!" Yes! We agreed to do everything possible to prevent amputation of Al's feet. Ted pulled us into a huddle and we ritually vowed that our team would utilize each of our skills to the max. That sparked Paul, who said he'd heard about medical maggots and leeches used against necrosis. He raced to the computer. We were gathering ideas. Ted said, "Let's ask all the doctors we know if they can help Pop." Good. I had heard about gangrenous feet being brought back to normal with hyperbaric boots. Paul volunteered to approach Dr. D., Al's vascular surgeon, about this. We collectively refused to give up. Like Bruce Lee when pushed too far, we moved into another, more aggressive level, and fighting energy filled us as if from nowhere.

Dr. D. surprisingly agreed to look into hyperbaric treatments and how they might work to supply oxygen to the feet. When Dr. F.

came to examine his patient, we asked him as well, hoping he would order them. "No," he said simply. "Your concern is misplaced. It's his brain you should be worried about. There's been no sign of frontal brain movement." Oh Dear God. Feet? Brain? Our enthusiasm turned to lead.

July 14th. When we walked into Al's room we found him with his eyes open looking at us! I couldn't believe it. I stifled a scream and rushed to his side. Dave cried and held his dad and kissed his forehead. We were so happy that we didn't know what to do and just cried out of pure joy and relief.

The doctors informed us that while this was a good sign, Al was still in trouble and although his consciousness might well return, his feet could not be saved. Once the gangrenous parts were removed, they said, his brain fog might lift. My mind was reeling. The sons were not taking it well, either. The doctors are flipping a coin. Heads they win. Tails Al loses. If it goes one way, Al's feet will be gone but his mental ability will return. Or if it goes the other way, Al's mental ability will be gone and he'll never dance again. We were powerless to do anything. In my numb desperation, I heard this question come out of my mouth: "Dr. D., can you do a leg transplant? I have very good balance."

"Sorry, no," he said very softly. I hauled out the Serenity Prayer.

Notebook entry: July 15th. The inevitability of Al's amputations looms over us. But Dave is totally clear; this is a lifesaving measure and his father will have to rise to the occasion. This commitment to a positive, simple approach gives me strength.

Notebook entry: July 17th. When I arrived, Al's brother, Hank, was just emerging from Al's room looking spent and red eyed. I watched him turn to Al for one last look and he yelled, "I saw Al smile!" I saw it, too! I ran to my spouse and once again his face yawned into a full-blown smile!

"Al! You smiled, for us!"

Dr. A. appeared. "Yes, it's a good sign. But remember, it's just a sign. Technically, he's been in a coma for, what? Nineteen days?" Still, the three of us stood by Al's bedside, hugging each other. Hank thanked me profusely for caring for his older brother and told me he couldn't do what I was doing. After he spent a few more minutes talking with Dr. A., he left feeling hopeful about Al's recovery.

July 18th. When I arrived at the ICU, good old Dr. F. was making his rounds. He said, "Based on the depression that Al experienced when he suffered from myasthenia gravis, I am certain that he will not be able to handle the missing foot."

I asserted, "Our family has discussed this at length and I respectfully disagree with you."

"Besides," he continued, "after the amputations I don't think Al will regain mental capacity anyway. And what are you going to do about that?" *What could I do about that*? To demonstrate his point, he roughly rolled Al's head from side to side and lifted the lids, looking into Al's eyes. Dr. F.'s point seemed to be that Al was brain-dead! My emotions bounced off the floor and rolled into a hard little ball. Oh, no, don't snap at him, I begged myself. Do not alienate Al's doctor! I looked into Al's face for myself, garnering strength from what I saw. I called out just as Dr. F. disappeared through the ICU curtain, "He's going to make it! You'll see!"

Notebook entry: I just learned Al's brain stem is healthy!

Yes, I mused, this *is* a boot camp for Zen Monks. I desperately wanted my husband back, but I had to keep warning myself not to get ahead of this story – to stay in the moment. Then I might be able to let go of expectations.

Finally, Al's amputations were on the surgical calendar. Since the operation was scheduled for the following day, Paul and I were permitted to stay with Al during his dialysis treatment. I sang "Imagine" to him knowing that when I stopped I'd have to say goodbye to his feet. There was no fairytale wish I could utter, nor special magic spell that would keep the doctor's knife away. When the time came, they wheeled away the dialysis machine, and I reached out to my husband, my partner, my mate.

"G'bye-beautiful-feet," I stuttered, lifting his knee a few inches so that I could kiss it. It was also goodbye to the special pleasures I'd enjoyed: clipping his toenails for him, soaking his feet in bubbles, giving him foot massages, and watching him tap dance for a shocked Michael Jackson. I shook. The tears rained down. Paul threw his

284

arms around my neck and held me. The nurse stood by supplying me with endless tissues, and in an unusual gesture of empathy, she softly rubbed my back. God, I felt empty.

So, after Al lay in a coma for twenty-two days, the day of the amputations arrived. Paul had to leave, but Ted flew in from California. I was grateful for his presence. We nervously waited for Al to emerge from the operating room and finally exhaled when the doctor gave us the thumbs-up sign. We grabbed each other and shook with relief, crying into each other's shoulders. As soon as we were permitted, we were at Al's bedside sending him healing energy.

The next day, Dr. A. found me in the waiting room and handed me off to a colleague who needed to finish up some paper work. Could I please sign off on the disposal of Al's severed parts? I stood there speechless. I was coldly handed an inventory list: five toes; one foot. Finally I managed, "Is this nightmare ever going to end?" This white coat needed my signature and his pen was extended toward me. Just another functionary. I took his pen, but before signing off, there was something I had to say. "You know, you need an acupuncturist in this facility. You may not think it works, but a billion healthy Chinese people do. And it may have prevented this loss." He may not have been listening but I needed somebody to hear that. He averted his eyes, gently wrested the pen from my clenched fingers, and quickly removed himself. I laughed. Or did I cry? At this point they were the same.

> *That night I dreamed of debris*
> *washed up on a beach*
> *caught in a net of seaweed*
> *discarded plastic bottles*
> *syringes*
> *pop-tops*
> *chewed-up styrofoam cups*
> *and feet*
> *the sound of my own voice behind my ears*
> *a low moan of recognition*
> *woke me*

It was Paul's turn to visit. Following the amputations, the doctors believed Al might regain consciousness, and we had asked for some medical advice regarding what to expect. A highly recommended psychiatrist, Dr. P., warm and avuncular, arrived in a tweedy, English-style suit. I was mesmerized immediately by his soothing manner of speaking, but then very quickly realized that he was saying absolutely nothing. My heart sank. He clearly manifested what I called "the undertaker effect": the placid visage, noncommittal tone and statements that seemed to be full of hope and meaning but were in fact empty. In essence, he told us everything we already knew and then said it was foolish to speculate on what might happen, and that it was wiser to wait and see. In other words, he was no damn help at all.

I turned to Paul. "You know what your Pop would say if the tables were turned and you were stuck in this hospital, and he heard what we just heard? 'Dr. P., I'm going to your medical school to get your parents' money back!'"

Paul smiled for a second and then in a cold fury asked, "Why do we need Dr. P.?"

"Unfortunately, we asked for his assistance," I said. "If the report on your dad's mental status is bad, they'll send him to a facility that won't help him recover. They'll, you know, warehouse him!"

Concerned about Al's future referrals and care, Ted (who had returned yet again) and I asked for a second neurological opinion. That's when "Dr. B." stepped into our lives.

Notebook entry: July 27th. Dr. B. said, "Al is clearly awake, often at different levels of awareness, and he is very tired at times and therefore not always consistent." He noted that Al was deaf and because Dr. B. was too, he made sure to raise his voice and include him in the exam. "Tell the other doctors that in case they're mumbling."

Dr. B. urged us to work with Al a lot. "Tell him clearly that he is getting better, that he is able to move, and there is no medical reason why he couldn't. Reassure him again and again." Finally, we had a doctor who could take us to the next level, who realized what terrifying conclusions Al may have come to about his own condition, and who treated him not as a case, but as a fellow human being. Dr. B. was a gem.

There were several calls on the answering machine from *The National Enquirer* asking for confirmation of their latest tip on Mr.

Lewis. I let them lie there like birdshit on my picnic plate. The idea of those vultures calling our home when we were in complete crisis had my blood boiling. Later, I picked up the ringing phone by accident, thinking it was the hospital, permitting a scandal-seeking paparazzo to catch me off guard, his slimy voice sending a jolt of revulsion through me. I said, "You have some nerve disturbing my family when you know we're in crisis," and hung up on him. But he remained hot on the trail, and after a few more days of phone slamming, Ted took the call and graciously gave *The Enquirer* an interview. The phone calls stopped. Why didn't I think of that?

We began to take notice of, and document, Al's progress. His fingers twitched. His eye lids fluttered. Then there was a rippling in his forearm. A smile. And we witnessed Al's eyelids flicker and open. He seemed to be checking out the scenery. "He's looking around!" I cried. "Papa!" Paul screamed. Al smiled and went back to sleep.

We ran to report these exciting, hopeful signs to the doctors but we were met with deadpan looks and patronizing sympathy. "We can't ascribe too much meaning to these events." "These anomalies can happen." "The autonomic nervous system ..." We soon realized that this is what the doctor's cynically called "loved-one dementia," in which family members imagine things that aren't there, because they want to believe more than anything that their loved-one will get well.

But hope is a powerful thing. Those tiny signals from Al reinforced our resolve and strengthened our love. When I would leave the hospital after one of those signs from him, I would skip to my bus stop. But then I would superstitiously repeat the Serenity Prayer, asking myself to remember that Al had his own plan, his own trajectory. Yet I believed I had to demonstrate "the courage to change the things I could," as advocate for an unconscious man in the hospital. I simply had to.

Notebook entry: In the waiting room, a suspicious figure emerged weighed down with photographic equipment. Paparazzi alert!

His shoes, bags and camera were covered with grass stains and dried dirt, as though he'd been slithering through some starlet's backyard trying to sneak a shot of her cellulite. He picked up the phone to the nurse's station inside the ICU. "I'd like a visit with Al Lewis." Ted and I watched quietly. They put him on hold. I told the photographer, "Sir, ONLY family." When the nurse got back on the phone, she apparently said he could go in! Ted jumped to his feet to diffuse the situation. I sped into the ICU to fend off this media raid. I was amazed that this crude mercenary parasite felt he had the right to enter the unit, at the risk of further compromising Al's survival with his grossly unsterile presence, just to snap a sensational photo for his scandal rag. I was even more amazed that the nurse allowed it. After that close call, we had Al moved to a room away from the ICU entrance.

By hanging out near the nurses' station, Ted learned that the neurologist's diagnosis of Al was "Zero," that he would not mentally recover. But armed with Dr. B.'s encouragement, he assiduously began training his father to tighten his eye muscles on cue, his love a strong energetic force. He stood by Al's good ear and began his session. "Pop. If you hear me, 'scrinch' your eyes tight." That was a word they both shared.

Notebook entry: July 25th. Al responded to Ted's commands and closed his eyes very tightly, scrinched them in fact! He did it three times with Nurse J. as witness. I raised my arms spontaneously in triumph and began to sob out of sheer joy. Al looked into our eyes and tracked the movement in the room. Nurse J. gently asked us to leave when Al's blood pressure started to rise, no doubt from over-stimulation.

July 26th. We began a progress review with Dr. A. who had heard the buzz about Al through the nurse's report and wanted to hear directly from us about what we had witnessed. Confidently, Ted told the doctor that he'd show him right then and there. "Pop, this is Teddy. I'm right here. If you can hear me, scrinch up your eyes real tight." Al scrinched, a big full wrinkled-up blink.

Dr. A. was bowled over. "It's one thing to hear you say it happened," he nodded, "but another, to see it for myself." Ted and I were thrilled and we stood next to the doctor making sure our shared observations were written into the official record.

Notebook entry: July 30th. The nurse told me how happy she was for me, to see Al doing so much better. And he was! His fingers were moving now. He turned his head. He was moving his tongue and his lips.

Notebook entry: July 31ˢᵗ. I sat next to Al. He looked a bit tired today, but I got a big smile. I talked to him about moving his arms and rubbed them with rosemary oil. He engaged me with his eyes, but eventually closed them. I got the Walkman and loaded up a Louis Jordan tape, upbeat and fun.

Louis' playful voice sang, *"Crazy 'bout that woman cause Caldonia is her name/ Caldonia! Caldonia!/What makes your big head so hard?"* Al's eyes sparkled and he smiled. "Caldonia" had always been a favorite, one that had him slapping his thighs. I pulled up his earphones and asked him if he liked it. He nodded yes. My heart was singing right along with Louis. It was a great day visiting with Al. He was winking at me and the nurses. He formed, "I love you," with his lips. I can't believe this.

Notebook entry: August 1ˢᵗ. Dr. A. left for his vacation. Later Dr. F. came by and said Al is terrific. I asked him to speak loudly to Al. When he repeated to him, "You're terrific," Al gave him a comic grimace, which I clearly read as: "Why am I in bed then? You're nuts! Take a flying leap!" Thank God, Al hadn't lost his sense of humor!

The psychiatrist, Dr. P., re-emerged with solid admonitions about breaking the news of his amputations to Al too soon. He cautioned that since Al was going in and out of waking up, "like a waning and waxing moon," we must be very patient. When I mentioned my fears about Al discovering his amputations he reassured me that my husband was in a "protective level of consciousness" and could not absorb the facts right now. "Even patients who know they are undergoing amputations have trouble realizing that their limbs are gone due to phantom limb syndrome. That's the sensation that their limbs are still there. Keep things very simple and when the time comes we will have to tell him the truth." I wondered how soon that would be. By the next day, Al had had his first physical therapy session, and I became concerned that no one had discussed his amputations with him.

Dear Diary: August 5ᵗʰ. Paul spent the afternoon with Al, watching a Fred Astaire movie and listening to a cassette, a family favorite, "Tuva of Siberia." He had Al squeezing his hand.

Dr. C., the gastroenterologist, came by with unsettling news; there was once again blood in Al's stools. As he moved closer to include Al in the discussion, I saw confusion and alarm in Al's face. When he told Al that he had had this kind of procedure before, Al mouthed very distinctly, "With Doctor W.!" That completely stunned us. Al had just recalled the name of the doctor who had administered an emergency colonoscopy several years earlier! Take that, Dr. F.!

As the gastro team filed in and began to gown up, Al moved into panic. I asked Dr. C. if I could have a moment with my husband before they began the procedure. I settled Al by rubbing his neck and asking him to go deep inside himself, to relax and call up hidden reserves. Al obliged and receded into peaceful relaxation. I turned to leave the room and gave a stunned Dr. C. a gesture which said, "You see, it's as simple as that." I hope that the immediate effectiveness of this loving hands-on, drug-free technique was not lost on this medical expert.

I forced myself into a walking meditation up and down the now familiar halls, recognizing all the cracks, stains, and subtle inconsistencies of tile colors. Right foot. Left foot. Ten minutes, twenty, thirty, forty, sixty. Then Dr. C. appeared with a smile and photos of Al's colon! The rectal tube had created a lesion which he had cauterized. I grabbed his arm and thanked him. He flashed a warm smile and said, "We can't go on meeting this way," which made me laugh. "Yeah, I sure hope not!" I answered. Then I thought, doctors can be so cheerful when the news they have to deliver is good. A cynical reminder of the tightrope I was still on. Good news or bad, I had to keep putting one foot in front of the other.

August 6ᵗʰ. Al was doing so well that he was moved from the ICU to the Step-down Unit. Dr. A. came by. He mumbled with pleasure, "I'm tired of waiting for this," and proceeded to unwrap a metal trachea device. Al became nervous and agitated. I helped him to gently relax, and told him that the doctor promised this would not take long. In short order, Dr. A. removed Al's plastic device and replaced it with stainless steel one. Al blurted his first audible words in six weeks, "That's it?!"

"Al!" I squealed, "You're talking." And couldn't resist adding, "And it used to be so quiet in here!"

With a huge comic frown he retorted, "Get over here, Prudence!" My Al was back! What a pleasure to have him back with sense of humor intact and to hear his gritty, musical voice again!

"Oh, you're in for it now, Doctor A!"

Ninety-one

CARE IS JUST A FOUR-LETTER WORD

Notebook entry: August 14th. Al is agitated, trying to understand what happened to him. "They did the angioplasty, right? So why am I still here?"

My heart is pounding in my chest. What do I do? Al always needed to get "the scoop" and his brilliance at doing just that was amply rewarded as a radio journalist. Now he can't even get the scoop on himself, and I've been advised not to tell him too much. Shit.

It was the psychiatrist, Dr. P., who warned us not to bring up the matter of the amputations unless Al initiated the conversation. We tip-toed around in clouded apprehension about this mortifying lie-by-omission, afraid we would slip up and say something inappropriate or not be up to the task when Al began to sense his missing parts. The thought of messing things up made me jumpy and unsure. How would Al react to such a blow? It felt like I was hiding a miserable, dastardly secret that I needed to confess. I was agitated about not telling the truth to the person I respected and loved more than any other, quietly, as I would a true friend and trustworthy confident. Al's sons and I drove each other crazy with speculation.

Foot Dreams

I now slept on Al's side of the bed facing the phone. I dreamed that all the world's missing feet were flying through a sky tossed by a hot Santa Ana wind, like socks flipped and tumbling in a huge dryer. Whose feet were they? I wanted Al's foot. Where was it? I needed to know. I searched with nightmare vigilance looking for it; the shape I knew so well, the alabaster skin, long toes, and narrow ankle. Was I being tested? Could I identify the missing limb? No. No. Not that one. How would I prove it was his?

I burst through, awake, sweating; the dream wind had been so hot. Al's foot was lost. I needed to get it back.

Several nights passed, dream free.

Then it returned. This time, feet - like hundreds of charms from broken bracelets - flew through the air looking for their owners. My wet face awakened me. Tears not sweat. I couldn't bear the thought of Al's foot not finding me.

Al was pushed, "boot camp style," as they proudly termed it in that hospital, to work as hard as he possibly could on his physical therapy or they wouldn't continue to rehabilitate him; he'd have to go elsewhere. I didn't know why they pressed him, and given some of my husband's serious medical issues, I was alarmed on several occasions to see how they ignored his concerns.

I got an anxious phone call from Al. "I'm in trouble, Karen! I'm in physical therapy on the lounge chair. You know, where they teach you to sit up. And the blanket falls off, Karen. And it wasn't there! Jesus Christ, my leg is gone, Karen! I asked her, the therapist, what she did with it. I guess I yelled at her." Knowing Al, he must have let fly a burst of colorful four-letter words. "She wouldn't answer me! She said she didn't like my behavior and left. What did I do?"

I rushed to the hospital immediately and I found him in a terrible state. "For God's sake, my leg is gone. Karen, why isn't it here? Karen, answer me!" I felt guilty, angry, and full of sadness that I hadn't figured out how to protect Al from this unnecessary shock, but for his sake I tried to stay calm and keep it simple.

"When you were asleep, they had to amputate, Al, to save your life."

"Save my life? What the hell happened? Who did this? Why? Why didn't they tell me?" How was I going to explain all that? I wasn't even sure I knew what had actually happened.

"It's complicated, Sweetheart, but I promise to tell you everything I know ..." I told Al the whole saga of his twenty-two days in a coma in as much detail as I could muster. But looking into his eyes, I realized that he couldn't make sense of it. I knew it would be quite a while before things would settle for him. It had even taken me weeks and I had been conscious. I was interrupted by the social worker who wanted to hear if Al had been accepted at Coler Hospital's Cardiac Rehab. "Yes. Yes," I told her impatiently.

"Good," she hissed, "Because he no longer qualifies for our facility." What?! Then I took a deep breath.

The next day, Dr. P., the same psychiatrist who had strongly advised us not to tell Al about the amputations, called me into a conference. "So sorry to inform you that your husband has verbally abused the therapist and will not be allowed to continue therapy in our clinic."

"Dr. P., your therapist abused Al. She stepped over the line with him. My husband had been in a coma for 22 days when those amputations were carried out, and with no conscious awareness that any of this had happened to him. You instructed us not to tell him, leaving him to find out for himself. Why wasn't she professional enough to expect his reaction under those circumstances? What would have been your reaction, Doctor, had that happened to you and you were never properly informed? You never took responsibility for breaking the news to Al. But it's moot now, Dr. P., he's just been discharged to another rehab facility. Thank you very much for all your *brilliant advice* and *compassionate caring*." Showing no expression, he turned and left.

Finding an appropriate rehabilitation facility covered by Al's insurance had been an exhausting, frustrating task so wrapped in red tape that I would wish it on no one. Around and around I'd gone with the hospital social worker, trying to find a bed in a suitable setting. When Coler Hospital on Roosevelt Island came up as a possibility, I called our local gerontologist, Dr. R., for his opinion. He thought it was an excellent choice and that Al would love it there. Al's new temporary residence was only a few blocks from our home.

Ninety-two

HIT MAN

I'd noticed it when I first walked through the long halls of Coler Hospital. A warm, friendly feel. "Dr. K.," the head physician of Al's wing, was a gregarious neighbor we'd known for years who loved to greet us on the street. He took a personal interest in Al's admission to his medical facility and met with me to fill out the necessary forms.

"Not another HIT patient!"

"What? HIT? I don't know what you mean."

Dr. K. explained, "HIT means Heparin Induced Thrombosis."

"Never heard of it before."

"Those blood thinners sometimes do the opposite of what they're intended to do. They clot instead of thin! And there is no test available to check the patient's reaction beforehand."

"Oh, my God. You just gave me the first explanation of what might have happened to Al. I mean, the glaring implication is that the doctors lied to me or covered up a mistake." Dr. K. saw the stunned look on my face.

"I promise to help you and Al understand what happened at the hospital and how HIT may have contributed to his complications. But you have to realize that Al has made an unimaginable recovery

294

which is tantamount to surviving a high-speed car crash." After hearing about HIT, it was even more unbelievable that Al had recovered at all. At age 8o, this was a miracle and testimony to his powerful life force.

"Thank God it wasn't his hands, Karen." Thank God, indeed, I thought, but his feet were also a means of artistic expression. Still, Al had suffered a terrible loss at the hands of those doctors.

At Coler, Al began the arduous task of standing, moving, and working out at the facility gym, under the direction of his cardiac doctor and beloved physical therapist, George. He practiced almost every day and was learning to walk on his new prosthetic by holding on to parallel bars. The first time I watched his workout, I stuffed my knuckles into my mouth so I wouldn't cry. He was trying so hard, flinching as his weight pressed into the new leg, hands inching along the bars. But his spirit was running high. "That George doesn't bullshit, Karen. He's the real thing."

Ninety-three

S-O-R-R-O-W

My mother, in Tucson, Arizona, was following Al's progress and was happy that he was doing so well, but she was also having her own serious medical problems, as she underwent out-patient chemo for lung cancer. Mom called me on her bedroom phone in severe panic, unable to breathe properly. I could hear her struggling to speak as her breath failed her. After her doctor admitted her to the hospital, I knew I had to go to Tucson.

By the time I arrived, my mother had been referred to a nursing facility. I drove there immediately and found her sitting on her bed, looking out the window. I grabbed her up in my arms and held her close. She kissed me with all her might. How tiny she looks, I thought, and hugged her again.

"Listen to this message from Al," Mother enthused. "I just can't erase it. I play it again and again." She pressed the replay button on her cell phone.

"Hi, Mom, it's me. Al. I just wanted you to know that I walked seven steps today. Yeah. With the parallel bars."

"Isn't that wonderful?" Mom cried, as she patted my arm over and over and looked at me, her hazel eyes memorizing my face as if she was going to paint it.

For six days, my brother and I explored alternative living spaces for my mother and spoke to numerous health care facility administrators in preparation for her next step. Mother would soon need another type of care, but no one was sure which she would qualify for: long term care, alternative care, or perhaps even hospice. Finding options for all of these possible outcomes was a daunting and dehumanizing process. As soon as I returned home to New York, my mother did qualify. Not for alternative living, but for hospice. That meant she had maybe six months to live. But just three weeks after I kissed her goodbye in Arizona, she was gone.

Her body was flown to her family home in Pennsylvania for a final farewell. I joined my brother and drove there for the service. Al was bedbound and deeply regretted not being able to take the trip with us. He and Mom had bonded early on and had enjoyed a mutually supportive relationship.

It was a sunny day in October as we formed a circle around the family plot in Bath, sharing loving stories about Mom. Looking at my grandmother's gravestone next to hers, I wept and sang "Grandma's Eyes" for Mom, just as I had for her mother, Mayme. My cousin held me. He could see that my legs were shaking.

I stayed behind after the others had moved on, hoping to have some alone time with my mother, to find some way to express the deep affection I felt for her in a language that we shared. "Hey, Mom, here's a crossword puzzler for you. One down. Starts with 'L', ends with 'E', has four letters. The clue is: What I feel for you."

Family Portrait for Mom's 80th birthday.
Rear (l to r): nephew David, sister-in-law Mary Anne,
nephew Jason, Al.   Front: Brother Jon, Mom, me.

Ninety-four

ONE STEP FORWARD...

Meanwhile, back at rehab, Al had made friends with doctors, nurses and staff. He would tease them and engage them in discussions about their families, interests and jobs. This lovely setting had become Al's new home. He had everything he needed at his fingertips, including me when I was there. Each day I would walk to the facility to visit my husband before I went to work. Then after I closed the office, I would head back again to spend the evening with him. I often brought movies from home that we could watch together. "Hey, Karen? Do we still have *Cabin in the Sky?* I love that show. No one can top that talented black cast. Their musical numbers!"

"We do! I'll bring it over, your Special Request." After dinner, I'd climb into his hospital bed with him to enjoy this favorite of his. We would sing, laugh and comment through the whole film and glory in the performances. Then we'd rewind the dance sequences to view them again, especially the John Q. Bubbles tap extravaganza. We never discussed the painful irony that Al's dancing days were over.

During the holidays of 2003, there was talk during our weekly Rehab staff meeting of Al returning home! On the surface, it was the gift we both were hoping to find under our tree, yet beneath the obvious joy, was the impending profound change. On one hand, at home, Al and I could have privacy, whatever we wanted for dinner, control over who walked through our front door, and most of all, we could have each other night and day. But on the other hand, at home, Al could not press a buzzer on his bed and expect a doctor or nurse to respond immediately to his needs. He would not have the flow of staff that he'd come to know and enjoy cruising in and out of his room, bringing smiles and quips. He would not have the captive audience to share his schmoozing and joking. We discussed these changes at length and I asked him if he was ready to leave. "I'm not sure I'm ready. What do I do if I need a doctor right away? Anything can happen."

But all these points were moot anyway because the rehab doctors decided that Al would do just fine at home, and since they no longer had any medical reasons to keep him, they set up a discharge date. I was excited but Al was still leery. Home specialists were sent to our apartment for a safety inspection, to organize our living space with a hospital bed and other equipment as part of the discharge plan. It was then that I decided that Al's hospital bed would be in our living room, not far from the front door, so that he could follow all the comings and goings in our household and outside. I had to remove carpets and any objects that might impede his movements, and I rearranged the furniture hoping to make our apartment as inviting as possible.

The night before his discharge date, I arranged plants and flowers, put the video player by the bed, got the snacks he enjoyed, and planned his favorite dinner. I even picked out an outfit to wear that I knew Al liked.

The next morning the phone rang and it was Al. "Albie, when can I have you back?"

"Something's wrong, Karen. Doesn't my voice sound funny?"

"A little, I guess. It does sound a bit higher in pitch."

"My hand's funny, too. It doesn't go where I want it to."

"Uh-oh. I'm on my way over."

Alarmed, I headed over to Coler. When I walked into his room, a neurologist was finishing up her exam and stated that Al had suffered a mild stroke and advised him to go to the hospital. "Do we really have to go?" I asked the doctor.

298

"You can't take a chance with this sort of thing," she said. All of my hopes and dreams of going home with Al were crushed.

"Any way around this?" Al asked. "Can't I stay here?"

The doctor looked terribly sorry. "We're not a hospital ..." After having gone through all those months in recovery, we couldn't give in to this bitterly disappointing irony now and allow ourselves to be devastated. We had to stay focused on Al's health. Instead of driving down the street to our Roosevelt Island apartment, the ambulance took us back to the hospital.

Al had to endure more testing. Hoping someone would take pity on us and discharge him, we kept up constant pressure to get his release. We just wanted to go home. We told everyone on the staff how much we needed to be home, how important it was for us to go home, and by the way, could we go home now? After three days of neurological probing, Dr. R. finally admitted that the tests showed only minimal involvement. He signed the discharge order to release Al. I gave the doctor a big kiss on the cheek and we got the hell out of there as fast as we could. We were going to return to our home for the first time in over six months. Yes, we were Finally Going Home!

When the ambulance attendant wheeled Al over the threshold of our apartment, Al's eyes grew full. He looked like a prisoner of war who'd returned home and was about to kiss the ground. His eyes darted in every direction, checking to see if he really was back where he belonged. Were the rooms where they should be? His prize possessions where he'd left them? The East River still there?

"Karen! You made it beautiful! I'm home!"

"For you, Albie. For you." We hugged and kissed as the ambulance attendants shuffled their feet and looked uncomfortable, clearly touched by Grandpa's homecoming.

Our personal life was – to a certain extent – private again. We reveled in the intimacy of living together. We had a new team of health professionals, therapists and nurses from the Visiting Nurse Service, coming in and out of the apartment. We also had the kindest and most responsive home health aides you could ask for in Troy, Charlie, Eleanor and Nelson. This crew could handle just about anything their tough, demanding, hilarious patient dished out. In return, Al delighted in sharing his stories, advice and humor with them. He was back in his element.

Dr. R., the local gerontologist, made house calls, which kept Al's life from being turned into a series of roundtrips to the hospital. This good doctor even visited Al when on vacation by sending his assistant to our home where he examined his patient via SKYPE. How lovely life is when Hope is on the horizon. Al kept improving!

Thoughtfully, Ted gave his dad a computer, complete with large-letter keyboard, to encourage him to use it. Hopefully, Al would spend time researching issues he loved and be able to keep in touch with family via the Internet. Ted's gift also served me well and significantly shortened my to-do list. I could access medical supplies from home and communicate swiftly with my office. Al was skeptical about this monster on his lap and never cottoned to it. When the aides used the computer, he would holler at them to "Get off that damn machine!"

When Al and I talked this over, I took their side, insisting that they had to have time to check their messages. Al stood firm. "You're not here, Karen. You don't see it. That computer sucks them in. I thought I'd have to grab Troy by the ankles and pull him out."

Ninety-five

GOODBYE AMERICA

Al received a call from Sergio Oxman, a Spanish film director, who wanted to schedule another shoot to complete his documentary, *Goodbye, America!* about Al's political life.

"They didn't finish it? How much did they shoot?" I asked my husband.

"Karen. Well, so far, they have me in a barber chair backstage getting into my Munster make-up for a Halloween gig. As I talked to my make-up man -- and he asked me questions -- they cut to historical footage of what I'm telling him about. Or they cut to me performing in another setting. It's so creative!"

"If you want to do it, Al, we have to tell him things are different now."

When Oxman called to go over logistics for the next shoot, I told him, "Things have changed, Sergio. Al is now ostensibly homebound ..."

"I'm so sorry, Karen. May I pay my respects to Al?" Sergio had the gentlemanly manner of an educated, compassionate European. When I came home from work, I found him standing in animated conversation next to my spouse's hospital bed. It was clear that he had won Al over. Al was excitedly interested in how the project had developed, and loved the feeling of being part of filmmaking again.

300

During their meeting, Sergio came up with a way to finish the film and since the documentary was conspicuously lacking an ending that only Al could provide, he agreed to be interviewed in his bed.

During the shoot, Al Lewis once more gave his all, and each day when the crew wrapped, he fell into an exhausted sleep. On the one hand, it was wonderful for Al to be needed and revered and given a chance to shine at his profession after all these miserable days incarcerated in bed. Indeed, this crew was incredibly thoughtful and caring, and treated Al like their own grandfather. On the other hand, it was physically draining, and as his energies waned, the exertions left him depleted. I was learning day by day that each of Al's actions came with a noticeable price tag attached. On the last day, celebrating the "wrap," we were all a bit tearful as this little family of crew members said goodbye, plane tickets in hand for Spain.

Ninety-six

HIS OWN MEDICINE

"I got no wheels," Al lamented, sitting up, gently rocking his head from side to side, a long soft "no." Alerted, I hurried to his bedside, this being the tabooed subject: lost feet. He needed an ear.

Somewhere or somewhen, I'd become the voice he'd shown me, rational and calm, the one he used to soothe my ruffled feathers when they stuck out, vertical and vibrating.

"I witnessed things that you couldn't, Al. You were unconscious when you lost your wheels. I know it can't make much sense to go into the hospital for an angioplasty and lose your feet. I've had time to understand what happened. Believe me, it took me days to wrap my head around it."

Al rested his eyes on me with a child's gaze that said, *you're hiding something from me*, as if he were being held captive from the truth. I wasn't hiding anything. The truth was stranger than fiction, and I didn't know how to get it across. Sometimes it felt like I was trapped in an Edgar Allan Poe tale.

"What can we do?" I said. "They're gone." I borrowed one of Al's favorite phrases: "We gotta use what we got to get what we need." That raised a smile from him, but only for a moment, and then he looked vulnerable again. This was a rare emotion for him, before the hospitalization at any rate.

"I've lost my wheels."

"Yes, my love, you've lost them." I couldn't pretend otherwise. I remembered my tears falling on his ankle the night before his foot was removed, and did not want to burden him further by asking the painful question, How does it feel?

"I've lost my wheels."

"But you have your brilliant mind, Albie, and your big heart."

He smirked, a boy's smirk that said it all: I'm sick and I missed the party. They're all there without me.

I stroked his hand. "We have to make the most of it, don't we?" He looked into the blankets piled over his lap, but didn't look up at me. I could not imagine how he felt then, about the loss of his lifelong friends and dancing partners who died while he was unconscious.

Hoping that Al would soon return to the airways at WBAI, I continued covering for him from the studio on Wall Street, and Al listened to every show.

"You were very good today, Karen," he said when I returned home after the program.

"Oh, I wasn't, Al. Did you hear how I misunderstood that caller."

"That was nothing! Infinitesimal."

"I could do much better."

"You were brilliant." And when he saw my moping face, he flicked his wrist at me. "Okay, don't believe me!" Sincerely trying to help, Al continued to praise me and give me keen pointers. Maybe he's seeing something in me that I'm not seeing. Maybe I should listen to him. After that I began to take every comment seriously.

We were holding hands at the barrier rail of his bed. Al looked into my eyes.

"You're my sweetheart," I whispered, barely audibly.

"I never had a sweetheart before," Al admitted quietly.

"No?" I asked.

"I don't know why. You're my first." His smile melted my heart into an eddy of swirling honey.

We held hands then and savored the flow of our shared love. Our hands became a new organ that sent energy up into our arms, through our chests, to soothe our aching hearts into momentary bliss. Then I said, "I never really had a sweetheart before either," and laughed at the realization. "I tried. I even used the word *sweetheart*, but I never knew what it meant to have one until you." Love welled up in my eyes making my lashes stick together, blurring Al's image, yet letting me see him more clearly than ever.

Often after supper, I climbed into the hospital bed next to Al under the covers to watch movies and documentaries. Or we listened to music, the radio or some meditation tapes. Unfortunately, the bed was narrow, and falling asleep usually meant falling into the chilly space between the mattress and the rail, a hinge or bedspring digging into my side, from which I'd extricate myself in the dark and reluctantly climb out.

"Get back in!"

"I can't. My back's all crookedy," I grumbled in defeat, looking to find a bed elsewhere. The next night I'd try again and sometimes make it through to morning snuggled next to my husband.

We did our best to preserve our happy home life. And it became clear that we were being transformed by the effects of Al's months in the hospital and outside social/political events that we could not control. It struck me as peculiar, ironic or even revolutionary that my "Fighter" of a husband was being transformed, smoothed out like a river rock, into a "Lover," whereas I, "Karen the Lover," was morphing into a "Fighter." A vigilant and edgy advocate, ready to ward off any threats to the one I loved. Perhaps it is more accurate to say that we were converting one form of energy into another, taking on the best elements of each other, even as we held to the core of who we were.

Ninety-seven

KICKIN' THE TIRES

Al's doctor felt he needed a better bed and ordered one from Medicare. The Special. Not everyone could have this model. It rippled. Air was forced through channels in the mattress to prevent, or help heal -- well, at least reduce -- the extent of bedsores. Al had too many. So this four-legged monster was delivered, carried through the door in pieces. The guys who arrived with it beamed. "Top of the line," they said. "The Rolls Royce of hospital beds," they hummed, delighted to deliver it to Grandpa.

It took only minutes for Al to figure out the new buttons to press, to raise and lower each section of the bed. He drove it with confidence and pleasure, as if it were his old Mercury. It had other options. For example, you could adjust the pressure you wanted, like tires. He could feel the difference immediately. The thickness of the mattress surged with its airflows, gently massaging and lifting his back to keep it in motion, preventing any part of his body from touching hard surfaces for too long.

"Hmm, no sharp edges or cold, protruding bars," I observed.

"All the better to snuggle with you, my dear."

Ninety-eight

GIVING THANKS

Al's foot started to bother him right where the toes had been amputated more than two years earlier. It required another operation. He underwent the surgery and was sent home the same day along with some very strong pain pills. His foot hurt.

I talked to Al about managing his pain. I was greedy to have him present and aware, so I gave him what I thought was just enough medication to kill the pain and keep him conscious and happy. But it didn't work.

"Let me decide this, goddammit! I'm the patient!" he barked. I ran out of the room, his angry words stinging my ears. I sat and thought about what had transpired and realized I'd been pushed to the limit for months and this was the last straw. My reserves were just about gone. Yes, Al's remark hurt, but he was in terrible pain. In my desire to have him close, I'd cut short his pain medication. I returned to Al a few moments later, ready to face the music. To admit my folly.

"Karen. Come here." Eyes lowered, I moved toward the side of the bed. "I don't know why I behave like that," he said softly. "Every time I do, I die inside. It eats at me for days. I'm sorry, please. Sorry, my Karen." His face bore an imploring expression.

I suddenly saw the image of Al as a young man, faced with racism and hatred, hoisting an imaginary shield over his heart. In such a world, how could he ever surrender? Yet he had just put down his shield to apologize. And I had just experienced a rare admission of guilt and remorse for all the hurts he had ever inflicted upon me in moments of frustration and anger. Tears filled his eyes. I had no words. I kissed the top of his hand, and then his brow.

"Karen, you've taken over where my mother left off."

"Listen to your new mother then. I love you." Ironically, Al had taken over where my father left off. Dad always found it difficult to say 'I love you,' but Al had me singing it freely, a love song.

Thanksgiving 2005 was a scaled-down affair. It was not a big rollicking event with food-laden tables swarming with family and friends. It was a more intimate celebration. Troy and Charlie, two of Al's amiable home health care practitioners, joined us in an effort to make that quiet New York holiday homier for Al. But he had little appetite and preferred to eat from his bed tray. Our friends stayed for a while, eating and joking, but had their own families to visit. Just after they left the phone rang.

"Karen, Happy Thanksgiving! It's Amy. Can I speak to Grandpa?" I recognized the voice immediately. "You bet!"

Amy Goodman, maverick progressive journalist and host of *Democracy Now!*, spoke to Al for about twenty minutes. I watched his energy level rise to the occasion and the twinkle return to his eyes. She reminded him about how he'd frequently called her to task when she was on the wrong track, telephoning her office and bellowing his disapproval! I could hear her grateful, cheery laughter on the other side of the room coming from Al's amplified phone. She gets him, I mused. But then, she always got him.

"Amy called me," Al stated simply, as if it was a normal everyday occurrence, but he had a very special glow. We both adored Amy, admired her pluck, and respected her Harvard brilliance, directed like a focused journalistic laser pointer on everything the mainstream media missed.

An hour later, our good friend, television producer, Kevin Burns, also called to wish us a Happy Thanksgiving. Five years earlier, Kevin had produced the one-hour A&E Biography on Al entitled, "Forever Grandpa." The two men talked for quite awhile. I breathed a sigh of relief, knowing how important it was for my sweet, exhausted husband to feel that he was still part of the fabric of life, that exhilarating social and political whirlwind in which he'd previously, and with gusto, played his part.

Ninety-nine

FINAL CURTAIN

SAVE, TOSS, GIVE AWAY

The little booklet that I didn't want to believe I needed. Give away.

When I got home from work, Troy rushed to meet me with tears in his eyes. "Dr. R. is here and he wants to speak with you. He and Al had a long talk today."

Dr. R. asked me to sit down with him on the couch away from Al. He took my hands, made eye contact, and with great difficulty told me, "I'm sorry, Karen. Al's immune system is failing. It's just a matter of time."

"How much time?" I was braving it out.

"Hard to say exactly. Possibly three months?" It was late November. Maybe we'd get through to March. When he left, I flashed back to all the times when this wonderful doctor had prepared me for Al's death and he had survived. This was different. Hope had gotten me through all those hours of waiting and struggling. It had always paid off. This time there would be no hope. I thrashed. I didn't want to give up the idea that I could see Al successfully through yet another crisis. That he would be there smiling, having "done it again."

Checking in with me week after week, my brother Jon said it was time that he sent me his little booklet left over from Mom's days in hospice care. "Alright, send it. If you think I should read it, I will." My brother had been a risks and claims manager and was a fount of information calculated to "shore up risk," and I knew I should listen to him. When it arrived I perused it in no time but instantly hated it. Nurses' graphs filled the pages, charting how much time was left ... signals and gentle warnings for those who would remain behind. With its sickly sweet prayer about crossing to the other side, the little booklet burned my fingers. In a huddle, I showed Troy and he began to cry. Together we stuck it into the dining room bookcase, glad to have it out of sight.

Our household mood shifted as more and more time was spent trying to manage Al's pain. We tried everything we could think of to make him feel at home and comfortable, moving from one painkiller to the next, seeking relief for him.

Al had his eyes on me as I flew back and forth past his bed checking things off my list: New pain medication, check. Sound

306

amplification telephone, check. Gatorade, Ensure, and Jell-o. Lots of Jell-o. Check.

"Karen. Come here." I stopped and looked at Al distractedly. "What?"

"Come here." Al held out his hand, waiting for mine.

"How much longer can you keep this up?" His sincerity bore into me.

"As long as you're here! A piece of cake." His deadpan glare made me think. I'd always felt that his presence would keep me going forever. Happiness creates energy. His spirit gave me such happiness that I mistakenly believed that I had enough energy to keep him going forever. So it was one foot in front of the other, carrying on, meeting challenges.

But Al looked weak and other worldly. He'd been surviving on Ensure and Jell-o.

"Please eat just a little."

"I can't," Al stated sweetly.

"You have to!" I pleaded. But he shook his head no and looked for all the world like a Buddha.

"Don't you see?" I begged. Al smiled such a knowing, tiny smile acknowledging my anguished frustration that I stopped speaking. He was the one dying and yet he honored my grief with his wise smile. Where had I been? Awakening to my folly and to the truth, I sobbed. Not wanting to hurt him, I tried to stifle my agonizing sounds, and sputtered like a swatted fly. Rubbery, slippery Jell-o had soothed and hydrated, but now it couldn't save him.

When he stopped asking for food, when water and ice cubes were his menu of choice, a madness struck me. I read about this phase in that damn booklet on dying, its single paragraph a violation, a red scar, a knife in my belly. It spoke of letting go. My fighting for his life would not save him. My disappointment, roaring and groaning like a rickety roller coaster, accelerating uphill and plummeting down, would not save him. His enormous will, now spent, would not save him. His soul, lost to me, clung to its own glowing thread, heading toward the other side. No companion ticket for me this time, my name printed boldly at its edge. He had to go it alone.

As if on cue, the doctor suggested it was time to call the children for a final farewell. I was jotting things in our ever-present Everything Notebook, making plans for their arrival, when Al gestured me to his bedside.

"I want to say good-bye, Karen, my love." The words were barely audible but issued with such intensity that I was pulled up short. What was Al saying? If these words had to be said, there were children and friends. Shouldn't I be the last to hear them? My mind flapped around itself like a frantic trapped bird looking for an open window, a safe haven. I looked at Al, my eyes wide with the finality of the scene he was asking me to play.

"I can't ... I just can't ..." Al looked at me tenderly. "I know what you're saying ... I know what's happening. But ... I can't say the words." My throat closed up.

"You never were very good at saying good-bye," Al whispered as he shook his head gently, sweetly taunting me, telling me the truth, the White Faced Clown wagging his finger, seeing right through me. But he was too tired to ask again and fell into sleep holding my hand.

The clock ticked and ticked until the hour arrived when all that had been previously classified as preparation was now in operation. That fact agitated like bad weather can, altering the familiar, cancelling preconceived notions of what constitutes a day. It began to dawn on me that Al was pacing himself, brilliantly managing his internal affairs. Aware that Dave, Ted and Paul would soon arrive, Al, the master of timing, had chosen to say good-bye to me first, just to be sure, and I had missed my cue.

The first son's arrival, a kind of epiphany, fed my taut nerves with narcotic relief. Soon the other two arrived and were rooted in our living room. Al spent the entire three-day visit with them, refusing any meds that dulled communication, talking, tying up loose threads, a painful dance stippled with tears and laughter. An ethereal family gathering of twisted beauty. They left on Monday.

By Friday, Al, sleeping more than waking, looked more frail and tender than ever before. I fed him ice chips. The nurse came, bearing an efficient kindness, answering my silent questions before I had to ask them, and gently tended his patient for what he surmised might be the last time. As he worked, I held Al's hand and helped the nurse with sheets and gowns. When he left, he carried cardboard boxes of supplies we'd no longer need. No longer need. Let it go.

Let it go.

I felt the manic discomfort of a failed meditation, twitching, itching, wriggling and fighting. I felt the night, its February darkness and length. Acutely agitated, I was two miserable people. One who wanted my healthy husband back, and another who wanted his pain to stop at any cost, even death.

To escape that feeling, I bolted and ran to the computer. I could lose myself in that alternate reality. It was that or jump out of my skin. I entered my password, and my emails opened with familiar comforting beeps and animation. Then, a voice as loud as a bullhorn penetrated my ear. "Get away from that damn machine! Get over here!" It was Al's distinct blast, scaring me to my feet. Where had that come from? Al was far too weak to speak, let alone shout!

I raced to Al's side. He was breathing hard. His heart pounding, trying in vain to clear his lungs. His face was as serene as spring, a softly haloed radiance. Painless peace.

Al's soul was sailing out of our harbor. Death was carrying him to another shore. My heart and mind battled against this inevitable visit. It was welcome. No, unwelcome. I know he has to go. I can't let him go. Let him go. I can't let him go. I know he has to go.

I held my husband's hand, talking and singing to him just as I had in the ICU.

May the long time sun shine upon you, all love surround, and the pure light within you, guide your way on. Guide your way on.

My face nestled next to his, I whispered into his ear about love and following the light, staying with the light. Until the light carried him away. I felt the snow begin to fall.

I looked out our window. The East River, full of February ice, was still flushing frigid hunks of winter to the sea. And the beautiful tree that charmed us when we moved in, now devoid of leaves, laden with febrile snow, still gleamed in the winter moonlight, shedding diamonds of ice. Life goes on, damn it. Life goes on.

One Hundred

AL'S LAST LAUGH

ONCE UPON A TIME there was a Magician who hated funerals. He hated them so much he swore, "I swear. I'm never going to another one." He was quite old at the time. He tried to calm this hatred by using magical powers to lessen it, but all the elixirs and spells were for naught, and the older he became the more funerals he had to attend. Even as he experimented with antidotes, the emotions of losing the people he loved, animals too, wormed their way into his soul. And then he died.

"What about your own funeral?" his widow cried. "Are you coming to that?"

"I ain't puttin' no friends of mine through no funeral," he explained in his inimitable fashion, for this sorcerer hailed from the Kingdom of Brooklyn.

"But we have so many people coming!" His beleaguered widow begged.

"That's what you think. Heh, heh, heh," gloated the magical clown as he proceeded to conjure snowflakes from the sky like downy feathers from a pillow. "How's that for openers, folks?"

Meanwhile, in another kingdom, his immediate family was informed that he had passed. The children, drawn to him by their belly buttons, their families trailing, flew between his earliest icy flakes. They wanted to commune with their Magician Elder and, missing him, wanted to experience something like the surrender of a river inexorably rolling to the sea. They arrived at the widow's, white specters bent on proving they were accurate meteorologists. They adamantly declared, "This is not a blizzard. The funeral will still take place!"

"Oh, yeah? Wait'll you see my next number, kids!"

The Magician, like the Sorcerers Apprentice, waved his arms, exhorting the snowflakes to change their form - "Ibbidy bibiddy rinkidy dink" - into shimmering veils of silver which then transformed into - "Wait for it, kids!" - opaque curtains of white. The widow could see the drifts forming like sand from a child's bucket at the beach, peaks and valleys appearing swiftly, and she recognized his handiwork. "How do you like them apples, folks??" he cackled. With that he urged the drifts to block the streets and advance with their crunching silence. He stirred up the winds, lifting the drifts almost as high as the window ledges.

"Oh, you ain't seen nothin' yet, my friends! Did I tell ya? I don't like funerals. Alakazam!"

Airport runways were slickened. Buses stopped. Cars were blighted, or blocked into their ports. The city came to a white-out halt. All those who loved the Wizard could only breathe plumes of white into the silence.

It seemed he would have his way after all. The funeral was impossible. "Ah, my spell worked like a charm!"

The family stood all in a row, peering through the fuzzy glass, as the world outside the widow's windows turned to sparkles of crystal white. Like zircons at first, then diamonds, turning the space between the house and the East River into a glittering, sugary, frozen dessert.

The little ones made snow angels and frolicked until they were too cold and had to go back into the warmth of the house. They didn't know what a funeral was, but they looked up at the snow moon and saw Grandpa smiling.

I'm in the apartment, numb. Staring at the empty boxes. Watching the memory loop of our life together play over and over. It starts where it ends: My life with Al Lewis was born in a fierce blizzard, and it died in another fierce blizzard.

Medicare forgot to pick up Al's bed. I crawled onto it and slept like a baby, wrapped in our blankets and in Al's afterglow. The snowflakes falling outside our frosty window slowly change into white cottonwood blossoms fluttering down upon a warm tree-lined Southern lane. We are driving along that lane on a clear summer day in our open car, and Al is behind the wheel. We are holding hands, as happy as two peas in a pod. I turn to look at his beautiful face. "It's been a great ride, hasn't it, Albie?"

"Yup. This old Mercury's got great shocks."

"I didn't mean that!"

"I know, Karen," he said with an impish grin. Then that ol' clown started to sing, "Take me home, country roads, to the place I belong ..." And I joined in, "Take me home, mountain mama, take me home ..."

KAREN LEWIS

ACKNOWLEDGEMENTS

Writing a memoir is an arduous process, a birthing rite of passage. There were many midwives responsible for bringing forth I Married a Munster, some on the other side, yet all of whom are in my debt. Many thanks to my brother Jon and his wife Mary Anne, for graciously offering me a writer's sanctuary when I was transitioning from grief. Likewise, endless thanks to Elisabeth McCarthy who also generously provided support. My gratitude as well to early readers Thomas Lynch, Prof. Leslie Ann Rivers, Prof. Farideh Gueramy, Tove Dalmau, John Nutt, Mimi Seton, Jonathan Morkin and Cynthia Moore for tendering their professional literary experience, especially their freely shared editorial directives. Thanks to my sister-friend, writer, Janet Galen, for her steady encouragement, and to all those courageous friends who wrote such heartening endorsements for this book: Medea Benjamin, Richard Bey, Kevin Burns, Randy Credico, Dixie Delamorto, Philip Gerson, Karen Grassle, Mr. Lobo, Fr. Lawrence E. Lucas, Cynthia Moore, Jonathan Morkin, Pat Priest, Prof. Leslie Ann Rivers, Mimi Seton, Joe Spano, John Stanley, and Howard Stern. Much gratitude to Kevin Burns for making available photos from his private collection. Joyce Keating, of JRK Literary, kept hope alive by seeking a publisher for this memoir that she believed in.

I could not have completed this work without the perseverance of my editor, book and cover designer, and partner, artist Ernie Fosselius, who encouraged me to write more visually and cinematically. My heartfelt thanks and eternal gratitude for Ernie's natural-birthing midwifery. He intuitively understood well before I did that birth pangs are inherent to personal writing, and dauntlessly coached me through the fear of remembering or forgetting the love that drives this story. Firstly and lastly, I am grateful for my late husband, clown warrior, Al Lewis, without whom this tale would never have been told.

Photo Credits

All of the photos included in my memoir, I Married a Munster! follow the chronology of our story and are part of my family archive. However, I would like to acknowledge these special contributions:

Page 192:   Al and I in our East 49th Street Apartment. Dr. Christina Kuhn-Banninger, photographer.

Page 210:   Dr. Heather Canning and me. Mary Anne Ingenthron, photographer.

Page 256:   Al at silent Vigil protesting the Rockefeller Drug Laws. Photo courtesy The William Moses Kunstler Fund for Racial Justice.

I have far too many great photographs in my private collection of Al and me to include in the text of the book, but I wanted to share more of them with you in an album. Believe me, it was very difficult job to decide which ones to choose!

In addition, Kevin Burns, who has the largest Munster collection in the world, provided some of his incredible and rare photos as vivid background images for I Married a Munster!. Thank you, Kevin.

Here are my favorites which I hope you will enjoy.

KAREN'S SCRAPBOOK

Baby Al. 1923.

Fred Gwynne and Al in the makeup studio for
The Munsters

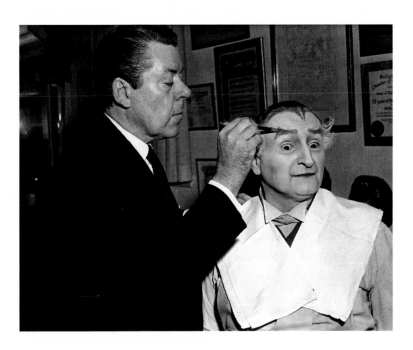

The famous makeup artist Perc Westmore
transforming Al into Grandpa Munster

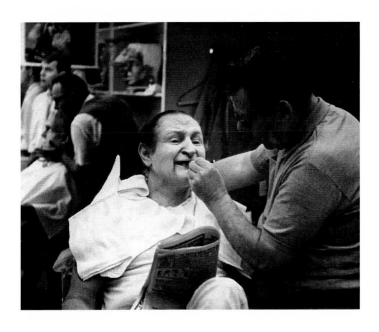

Al and Fred Gwynne riding in the famous George Barris Munster Coach for the annual Macy's Thanksgiving Day Parade. Later, Al invited his New York City friends to a feast in his hotel room at the Waldorf Astoria Hotel

Al reading to his oldest boy, David, from a book on Charlie Chaplin

Al holding his second son, Ted

Al and Gig Young on the set of
They Shoot Horses, Don't They?

*Al signing autographs for kids at his Greenwich
Village restaurant, "Grampa's"*

Al and Butch Patrick at a collectors' convention

Al on the set of Ted Turner's Super Scary Saturdays in Atlanta

Al and TV producer Kevin Burns sharing a laugh during the Famous Monsters of Filmland convention at the Universal Sheraton Hotel

Randy Credico (left) and Al protesting against the Rockefeller Drug Laws in front of Rockefeller Center.
(Photo courtesy of The Wm. Moses Kunstler Fund for Racial Justice)

Al reading for kids at WLIW's
Reading Rainbow Day

Honoring 10th Degree Black Belt Kwang J. Lee's
(seated center) California students:
Rear: Master Jim Larsen. Standing, left to right: Master Erica
Stone, 2nd Degree Black Belts Karen (me!) and Janet Galen;
Black Belt Ann Marie Grace.

*Al and I at Wrap Party for My Grandpa is a
Vampire! In Auckland, New Zealand*

*Al and I in Alameda, visiting Mom,
who snapped this photo*

Al selling his own line of pasta!

GRANDPA AL LEADS CHAMPS THROUGH CANASTOTA

Grandpa Al Lewis leads the Parade of Champions, Sunday that celebrated the boxing legends who were inducted into the International Hall of Fame in Canastota

Al marching in the Boxing Hall of Fame Parade of Champions in Canastota, New York

*Al toasting the newly married couple, our Roosevelt Island
neighbors: the famous Roumanian poet Nina Kassian and
theatrical producer Maurice Edwards. Al is also toasting you.
Thank you for reading our book.*

KAREN LEWIS holds a BA degree in Dramatic Art from UC Berkeley and an MA in Theater History from Hunter College. A teacher, writer and actor, Karen hosted, for 6 years, a radio talk show at WBAI-NY. She was married for over 20 years to Al "Grandpa Munster" Lewis and now resides in the Bay Area.

Please support Indie booksellers!

10/9/15
25.00